SIXTEEN

CANTIGAS

IN MEMORIAM

CLARE AND GERALD

...dexónos harto consuelo
su memoria.

SIXTEEN

Cantigas de Santa Maria

WITH

DOTTED RHYTHM

STUDY AND TRANSCRIPTIONS BY

Martin G. Cunningham

DUBLIN CARYSFORT PRESS MMXVII

A Carysfort Press Book
Sixteen «Cantigas de Santa Maria» with Dotted Rhythm
Study and Transcriptions by Martin G. Cunningham.

First published in Ireland as a paperback original by
Carysfort Press, 58 Woodfield, Scholarstown Road,
Dublin 16, Ireland,

ISBN 978-1-909325-45-6

Typesetting and layout by the author.
Palæographic notation font created by the author.

Cover design by Joseph Brady

Printed and bound by eprint
35 Coolmine Industrial Estate
Dublin 15
Ireland

CONTENTS

ABBREVIATIONS and CONVENTIONS

	CSM	*Cantigas de Santa Maria*
Sources:	*To*	Madrid, Biblioteca Nacional, ms 10069
	T	*Escorial, ms T.I.1
	[*F*	Florence, Biblioteca Nazionale, ms BR20]
	E	*Escorial, ms b.I.2
		See Bibliography for further details of sources.
Sub-collections:	*FSM*	*Festas de Santa Maria* (*Cantigas* 410–422)
	CJC	*Cantigas de Nostro Sennor Jesucristo* (423–427)

Numeration: *Cantigas are referred to by standard (Mettmann) numbers.*
'Toledo' numeration, where relevant, is specified as such.
Stanzas are provided with Roman numerals.
Musical phrases are given lower-case alphabetic identifiers.
Notational figures are identified by phrase-letter and a number, separated by a period (e.g., a.5*).*

Refrains: *The initial statement of the Refrain is referred to as* ℜ-0;
the statement of the Refrain following Stanza I *is* ℜ-I, *&c*

Notation:	*L*	*longa*, long
	B	*brevis*, breve
	S	*semibrevis*, semibreve
	t	*tempus*, *tempora*, beat(s)
	/ /	*used to mark off a rhythm-group*
	cum-sine	*cum proprietate sine perfectione*
	c. o. p.	*cum opposita proprietate*

N.B. Modern note-names are given according to European English and not American usage.
Thus crotchet *and not 'quarter-note'*, quaver *and not 'eighth-note'.*

Mode II *Rhythmic modes will be referred to using Roman numerals.*
Mode 2 *Melodic modes are given Arabic numerals (infrequent in this context).*
Reference will be made to musical accent *but textual* stress.

General:

vol., vols	volume(s)
p., pp.	page(s)
n.	note
l, *ll*.	line(s)

*Real Biblioteca del Monasterio de San Lorenzo de El Escorial.

PREFACE

This book is the fruit of an idea born long years ago that lay never quite dormant in my musings about notation and rhythm in the Cantigas. The germ, a fifteen-year worry that not all was quite right about how we viewed Cantiga 20, had niggled and niggled, but could not come to fruition in solitude, needing a broader patch of fertile ground to take deeper root with companions in order to grow and blossom. That cross-fertilization happened in the autumn of 2015 when, sitting with a view of the Picos de Europa in the distance, I systematically leafed through the first volume of Chris Elmes' edition — already covered in pencilled jottings, annotations, crossings-out, experimental readings and the like — to discover that the same worry applied to not one, but perhaps eight other pieces. Widening my search but at the same time limiting it to the scope of the «Toledo codex», I toyed with a draft plan that originally bore the title of «Eleven Cantigas»; then «Thirteen Cantigas». Who knows but that my fervid imagination might ultimately have pulled the whole collection into dotted readings! But no; there are limits, and they are imposed by the notation itself. The central idea is very simple; but where the notation does not wear it, it cannot be worn. And so, seventeen years after my «Loores» transcriptions appeared, here is another volume that contradicts at least two of them.

It is difficult to think oneself back seventeen years. At that moment, the forty-odd pieces I dealt with constituted the largest single group of new transcriptions since the monumental edition of Anglés published in 1943. The intervening span has seen much attention to questions of interpretation of the notation of the Cantigas, such that we now have not one complete musical edition, but three — to Anglés must be added those of Pla and Elmes —, but even more importantly we have been given research tools undreamt of in the last years of the old milennium. Most important among these, we now have workable facsimiles of two of the three musically notated sources not previously so served: the Toledo codex arrived on our desks in facsimile form in 2003; and since 2011 the magnificent Testimonio facsimile edition of the Códice rico has, for those who can afford it or find an elusive library copy, obviated the need for repeated expensive trips to the Escorial library. All this, against a background of an ever-increasing bibliography of Cantiga studies — Snow's Bibliography (2012) lists some 400 items published on various aspects of Alfonsine poetry (including the Cantigas) in the first decade of the new milennium, and the tide has not slowed.

It is surprising, then, that even with such resources the number of people actively working in the field of notational studies on the Cantigas remains but a handful. And whilst Manuel Pedro Ferreira continues to provide a steady stream of ever-authoritative contributions, the news of the death of David Wulstan, occurring as this book was in the final stages of preparation, robs the field of a colourful figure whose views, sometimes idiosyncratic, sometimes provocative, never failed to give food for thought. I wonder how he would have reacted to my driving a coach and horses through his statistics on rhythmic categories. Meanwhile, let me renew a challenge I issued in my Loores volume: that the transcriptions offered, here as there, are intended to "fuel the debate on the question of the rhythmic interpretation of the Cantigas"; for without debate and dissent there can be no honing of ideas, no productive dialectic.

The narrow focus of a volume such as this leaves no room for it also to offer entry-level treatment of essential matters. The reader is thus assumed to have some awareness both of what the Cantigas are and of the rôle of Alfonso in their creation; of the fundamental importance of Higinio Anglés in the history of their decipherment; of the rudiments of pre-Franconian notation, including such matters as alteration and perfection; and of the rhythmic modes whose dubious domination of rhythmic studies of the Cantigas is, at least in part, what this book is about.

Val de San Vicente (Cantabria)
Carraig an tSionnaigh (Dublin)
July, 2017

ACKNOWLEDGEMENTS

For allowing the priviledge of access to the primary sources of the *Cantigas*, my grateful thanks to librarians in the Biblioteca Nacional, Madrid; in the Biblioteca Nazionale Centrale, Florence; and most particularly, for his unfailing helpfulness and courtesy, to the Reverend Librarian of the Real Biblioteca del Monasterio de San Lorenzo de El Escorial. My gratitude extends also to librarians and curators in other centres in which I have had the pleasure of working: the Bodleian Library and the Library of the Taylor Institution, both in Oxford; the Biblioteca de Catalunya in Barcelona; and the Manuscript Room in the Library of Trinity College Dublin.

This volume having been put together over a relatively short period of time, I have not been priviledged to enjoy much in the way of conversations or comments — helpful or critical — from colleagues. I am nonetheless grateful for the interest expressed and encouragement given by friends and colleagues in the Music departments in both University College and Trinity College, especially those with an interest in the history of notation and in hispano-musical matters generally. My thanks too to friends in Spain, where much of the work on this book was done, for their support and enthusiasm.

For the physical existence of this book, my grateful thanks to Dr Dan Farrelly of Carysfort Press for taking on a project that will have a predictably small audience, and to all at eprint for their attention to detail. For the fact that the book has a cover, my unbounded thanks to my erstwhile colleague Dr Joe Brady — wizard that he is with Quark — not only for designing it, but (for reasons best known to an uncommunicative Patrimonio Nacional) for having to re-design it.

No book such as this comes into being without behind-the-scenes support systems. In the present case, the support has come from my wife Sheila, whom no words can thank sufficiently for her reading and re-reading, for her patient encouragement, and for her musical good sense to tell me when I am talking nonsense.

This volume is dedicated to the memory of my parents, *sine quibus non*.

ABSTRACT

This study of an aspect of the notation of the *Cantigas de Santa Maria*, together with the transcriptions embedded in it, seeks to explore dotted rhythm of the type | ♩. ♪♩ | in *cantigas* displaying ternary metre. The investigation is restricted to the first layer of notated pieces, essentially those surviving in 'Toledo notation', although the analysis of the relevant pieces covers all versions. This early corpus is characterised by the absence in all sources of any *simplex* note-shape to represent a duration of half a *tempus*; for the notation of a cell of dotted rhythm, the deficiency is overcome by writing the whole segment in double time-values, giving the appearance of a cell with characteristics of the third rhythmic mode. Such a procedure is clearly demonstrated by an examination of four pieces (here referred to as 'Rosetta' pieces) in which some sources give certain rhythmic cells with a duration of six *tempora* whilst elsewhere the same cells occupy only three *tempora*. The dotted rhythm is recoverable by reversing the notational doubling of values in the relevant cells, an operation here given the name 'selective dimidiation'.

Once the mechanism has been described, the understanding of it is applied to a further dozen pieces, expanding the number of pieces in which dotted rhythm is perceived far beyond anything previously contemplated. In the analysis given with each transcription particular emphasis is laid on features such as musical phrase-symmetry and the correspondence between musical and textual accentuation. The study is contextualized throughout by reference to the work of other investigators, particularly Wulstan, who shows awareness of the presence of dotted rhythm in some pieces, although without probing its notational mechanism; and Ferreira, who advances some cases in which note values of particular cells might be halved, although without seeing this in terms of dotted rhythm.

As an aid to performance of the transcribed pieces, full Galician-Portuguese texts and their translations into English are provided in an Appendix, with brief notes on pronunciation, syllabic division and word-stress.

NOTETUR BENE !

The transcriptions provided in this volume rely, in the first instance, on a reduction of original note-values by a factor of eight; thus the *brevis recta* in Escorial notation is here transcribed as a crotchet (▪ ⇒ ♩). The shortest note in Toledo notation is likewise transcribed as a crotchet (♦ ⇒ ♩).

When in certain contexts any notational figure — or whole rhythmic cell or longer series of cells — has been subjected to an additional halving (*i.e.*, reduced to a sixteenth of the original value) the notes so affected are here transcribed with rhombic noteheads.

RESUMEN

Este estudio de un aspecto de la notación de las *Cantigas de Santa María*, junto con las transcripciones incorporadas en él, pretende explorar el ritmo punteado del tipo | ♩. ♪♩ | en cantigas que exhiben ritmo ternario. La investigación se limita a la primera capa de piezas notadas, principalmente las que han llegado hasta nosotros en 'notación toledana', aunque el análisis de las piezas relevantes abarca todas las versiones. Este corpus temprano se caracteriza por la falta, en todas las fuentes, de cualquier figura aislada que represente una duración de medio tiempo; para la representación de una célula de ritmo punteado, se supera la deficiencia escribiendo el segmento entero en notas de doble valor, dando así la apariencia de una célula de tercer modo rítmico. Tal procedimiento queda claramente demostrado examinando cuatro piecas (aquí designadas como piezas 'Rosetta') en las que ocurren células rítmicas que en una(s) fuente(s) pueden tener una duración de seis tiempos, mientras que en otra las mismas células ocupan tan solo tres tiempos. El ritmo punteado puede ser recuperado invirtiendo el doblaje de valores en las células pertinentes, operación a la que se aplica aquí el término 'demediación selectiva'.

Una vez descrito el mecanismo, se aplica el mismo enfoque a otra docena de piezas, elevando así hasta un nivel anteriormente no concebido el número de piezas en las que se perciben ritmos punteados. En el análisis que acompaña cada pieza se hace hincapié en aspectos tales como la simetría de estructura musical, y la correspondencia entre la acentuación textual y la musical. El estudio está plenamente contextualizado con respecto al trabajo de otros investigadores, en particular Wulstan, quien muestra conciencia de la presencia de ritmos punteados en algunas piezas, aunque sin investigar a fondo el mecanismo notacional implicado; y Ferreira, que propone que en algunos casos los valores temporales de ciertas células podrían ser reducidos a la mitad, aunque sin ver este proceso en términos de ritmos punteados.

Para facilitar la ejecución de las piezas transcritas, se incluyen en un Apéndice los textos íntegros en gallego-portugués, junto con traducciones al inglés, además de breves apuntes sobre pronunciación, división silábica y acento textual.

NOTETUR BENE!

Las transcripciones ofrecidas en este volumen se basan, en primer lugar, en una reducción de los valores temporales originales a la octava parte de su valor original; así la *brevis recta* en la notación escurialense se transcribe aquí como negra (▪ ⇒ ♩). La nota más breve de la notación toledana se transcribe asimismo como negra (♦ ⇒ ♩).

Cuando en ciertos contextos una figura — o una célula entera o serie más extensa de células — ha sido sometida a una reducción adicional a la mitad (es decir, a la décimosexta parte de su valor original), las figuras afectadas se transcriben aquí con notas de cabeza romboide.

I
INTRODUCTION

In this study–*cum*–edition I propose to explore occurrences of dotted rhythm, and the manner of its notation, in pieces exhibiting ternary metre that belong to the earliest consolidated corpus of the *Cantigas de Santa Maria*.[1] It follows that what unites the pieces discussed and edited in this volume is not any shared narrative element or textual theme; in that regard, the *cantigas* dealt with here could hardly be more disparate, as a perusal of the texts or their translations (*see* Appendix) will confirm. What holds together the pieces included here, then, is rather their common dependence on particular features and mechanisms of the musical notation.

Or, more properly, one should speak of *notations*, in view of the fact that two quite distinct notational systems are employed. The first system characterizes the 'Toledo codex' (*To*), which presents the corpus as initially compiled: one hundred pieces arranged in decades, each with nine miracle narrations followed by a song of praise or *loor*, plus prologue and epilogue (the *Petiçón*); then two groups of five *cantigas* each, one dedicated to Feasts of the Virgin, the other to 'Nostro Sennor Jesucristo'; and finally an Appendix — a sort of overflow of sixteen further *cantigas*: in total, some 128 pieces, or about 30% of the eventual extent of the collection. Whether the notation of *To* is early (*i.e.*, contemporary with the assembling of the repertoire it carries) or late (showing fourteenth-century features, making *To* itself a late copy) will be touched upon later. The second notational system characterizes the other two musically-notated sources, both now held in the library of the Escorial (and so it is convenient to speak of 'Escorial notation' as opposed to 'Toledo notation'). The first of these later sources is the lavishly-illuminated *Códice rico* (*T*), containing an expanded repertoire; it begins with the *cantiga*-prologue and ends enigmatically at *Cantiga* 195; the incorporation of pieces from the earlier repertoire of *To* is not straightforward, however, and a degree of reordering, as well as the dropping of some pieces (either for later incorporation or for total banishment) means that the numeration of pieces between *To* and the Escorial sources diverges. This fact explains why some of the *cantigas* included here, although belonging to the 'earliest...corpus', bear numbers at the high end of the spectrum, as allocated according to the now standard numeration.[2] We may briefly pass over the 'second instalment' of the *Códice rico*, the 'Florence codex' (*F*), probably intended to contain the second half (pieces 201–400) of the repertoire, but left incomplete and bound jumbled; the fact that its musical notation was never inserted renders it marginal to present concerns. The second Escorial source (and

---

[1] Henceforward, on occasion, *CSM*. The name *Maria* in the title of the collection will here be thus spelled; a written accent is required — *María* — in Castilian and (since 2003) in Modern Galician. The sources of the *CSM* will be referred to by their standard *sigla*: *To*, *T*, *F* and *E*; further details are supplied in the Bibliography.

For a concise overview of the *Cantigas*, their sources, and the rôle of Alfonso X 'the Learnèd' († 1284) as instigator and possibly contributor, see the 'Introduction' to Parkinson 2015.

[2] Source *E* provides a ready numeration of pieces as far as *CSM* 402. The numeration beyond that was established by Mettmann in his textual editions, beginning with pieces present in *To* (plus two from *F*) but absent from *E*, then the enlarged set of *Festas* from *E* (410–422), and finally the pieces dedicated to 'Nostro Sennor Jesucristo' (423–427) whose only source is Codex *To*.

the last of the four surviving codices), the *Códice de los músicos* (*E*), carries the fullest expression of the corpus: the Prologue plus 402 pieces, preceded by an expanded set of Feasts of the Virgin; because of its almost completeness, *E* is familiar as the basis for most major editions to date, both textual and musical.[3] Yet whilst *E* employs a notational system broadly in line with *T*, it is regrettable that, although it contains an almost complete representation of the total repertoire, the standard of musical notation at times seems to fall short of that encountered in *T*;[4] for this reason the musical palæography of *T*, where available, will be presented in preference to that of *E* in the pieces edited here. Some of the differences between 'Toledo notation' and 'Escorial notation' will be examined in Section II below; for the present, suffice it to say that most of the pieces transcribed in this volume survive in both notations, to the advantage of the process of decipherment.[5]

The 'earliest consolidated corpus' of the *CSM*, mentioned in the opening sentence above, may now be seen quite simply as a reference to the repertoire contained in the Toledo codex, and this body of 128 pieces constitutes the pool from which *cantigas* found to exhibit dotted rhythm have been drawn and edited in this volume, whether or not they occur in other sources. There is, however, one exception: *Cantiga* 76, found in *T* and *E* but not in *To*, has also been included. The reason has to do with statistics: the inclusion of *CSM* 76 — since it displays dotted rhythm — will allow statistical observations to be made regarding the first hundred pieces (according to the 'standard numeration') even though the piece in question does not strictly fall within the defined scope of the edition.[6]

The notation of the *CSM* is slow in yielding up its secrets. Even so, much progress has been made in the last quarter-century, such that the sometimes lame or unlikely rhythms of Anglés's 1943 transcriptions may in many cases now be improved upon with insight, confidence and finesse. Among those with whose contributions it would be impossible not to engage, there are two names that deserve particular mention. The first is Manuel Pedro Ferreira, whose 1993 article provided a kick-start to the search for a more precise understanding of the nature, mechanism and dependability of the notation, and who, amongst other important contributions, has sought to rehabilitate consideration of Arabo-Andalusian elements in the rhythm of some *cantigas*.[7] The second is David Wulstan,

---

[3] Of textual editions relying in the main on *E*, *see* Valmar 1889, and the two editions by Mettmann (1959–72, 1986–89); of musical editions similarly based, *see* Anglés 1943, Pla 2001, Elmes 2004–14.

[4] 'The relatively humble production values of *E* are reflected in…the lower quality of its text and musical copy' (Parkinson 2015, p. 7); '…among the Escorial codices, the most authoritative, generally speaking…is the luxurious *códice rico*, *T*' (Ferreira 2013, p. 130). Even so, the notational differences between *T* and *E* are in the main slight, as will be appreciated below from the lists of variants given in the boxed panels that follow each transcription. A detailed and measured assessment of *T* and *E*, seen in the context of evolving notational practice, is given in Ferreira 2011, esp. pp. 198*ff*.

[5] A stemmatological account of the relationship between the sources, from a musicological perspective, is given in Ferreira 1994. On the reordering of pieces that accompanied the expansion of the collection, *see* Parkinson 1988. On the dates of the notational systems, *see* Ferreira 2013, p. 132; the dating of (the late copy of?) *To*, as it has come down to us, reveals tensions between musicological and philological opinions on the one hand, and codicological and palæographic perceptions on the other; *see* Section II below.

[6] A statistical tabulation of various rhythmic categories to which the *CSM* may be allocated is among the contributions made by Wulstan; *see* note 13 below and the corresponding main text.

[7] Discussion of such matters was effectively arrested after the trenchant dismissal by Anglés and others of Ribera's ideas on the centrality of Arabic music to the evolution of European music. Anglés (1958, p. 37) went so far as to call the eminent Arabist's ventures in musicology 'infantile'; as late as the 1980s it was possible for Llorens (1987 *bis*, p. 149) to state that 'en la música [de las Cantigas] no se vislumbra ni un solo rasgo árabe' — not a single Arabic trait is to be discerned.

who, in addition to commenting on technical aspects of the notation, has, in his 2001 book, sought to place the *Cantigas* within the much wider landscape of medieval and earlier secular song. It would be foolish to attempt any all-embracing digest of the wide-ranging contributions of these two scholars; suffice it to say that their writings are compulsory reading for all who take an interest in matters of rhythm in the *Cantigas*, and a great many other aspects besides. That this volume owes a debt to their researches will be evidenced by the many references to them that pepper the pages that follow.[8]

Implicit in what has been said so far is the view that the notation of the *Cantigas*, whatever its shortcomings and inconsistencies, is the vehicle for melodies that are themselves metrically structured and rhythmically cogent. In this context one important development in recent decades has been the shift of focus away from attempting to derive from contemporary theorists an absolute temporal value for every note-shape — away, that is, from Anglés's insistence that the notation of the *Cantigas* is fully mensural[9] — towards a realization that the notation, though falling short of that elusive ideal, is nevertheless not haphazard; whilst some would prefer to describe the notation (dismissively?) as *semi*mensural, it is rather, in the happy phrase of Ferreira (speaking of sources *T* and *E*), *para*mensural notation,[10] containing a wealth of information to define rhythmic patterns that vary greatly from one piece to another. There is thus no licence for taking refuge in easy solutions that ignore the dependable durational information that many notational figures undoubtedly convey. The rhythmic patterns that emerge from such careful consideration of what is encoded in the notation may coincide with the rhythmic modes, or with Arab rhythmic cycles; but it is difficult to reconcile the pieces with dotted rhythm, as edited in this volume, with either of these paradigms, a fact that provokes interesting questions about the sources and affinities of the rhythmic patterns concerned.

The statement of purpose at the head of this section lays down that we will be dealing here with 'dotted rhythm…in ternary metre';[11] to be more specific, this is a book about | ♩. ♪♩ | in the *Cantigas*. But it would be a misrepresentation if the impression were created that such rhythms have lain entirely unnoticed. Ferreira, in a recent article, refers to three *cantigas* in the first 100 pieces in which he finds rhythms expressed as cells of Mode III that are 'compressed'. The pieces in question are *CSM* 78, 20 and 10, for all of

[8] The reader is referred to the Bibliography to gain some idea of the scope of the writings of both Ferreira and Wulstan.

[9] Take, for example, the reference to 'la notación mensural perfectísima de las cantigas' (Anglés 1943, p. 39) and other similar expressions of certitude. Whilst Anglés appeals to numerous theorists including Franco of Cologne in arriving at his understanding of the temporal values of ligatures and *conjuncturæ* (1943, pp. 37–92), he later makes clear — in the course of drawing a distinction between 'mensural modal' and 'mensural non-modal' notation — that he considers the latter, in the case of the *CSM*, to be pre-Franconian (1958, p. 176). For a recent attempt at transcribing part of the corpus of *cantigas* by means of a strict application of rules derived from Lambertus, *see* López Elum 2005, and the highly critical review by Ferreira (2007 *bis*).

[10] *See* Ferreira 2013, p. 130. The '*semi-*' is here, of course, a moveable feast: it may refer to a notation in which (at best!) only the *simplices* have a determinable temporal value, or else, at the further extreme of the spectrum, to a system in which a high proportion of ligatures may also indicate duration. Hence the helpfulness of Ferreira's use of terminology in safeguarding the notation of the *CSM* against the risk of being dismissed as *semi*-impermeable, or, at worst, *semi*-useless.

[11] It is important that ternary metre be specified lest misunderstandings arise. In an article dealing with Arabic rhythmic traits in the *CSM*, Ferreira (2000, p. 12 and n. 30) offers a list of seventeen *cantigas* with dotted rhythms; but a look at the pieces in question shows that, with one exception, they are all in *binary* metre and so not relevant in this context. The exception, *CSM* 61, in ternary metre with dotted rhythms across phrase-breaks, will be briefly dealt with in Section VI below.

which Ferreira provides a partial transcription;[12] all will be discussed below, although the extent to which 'compressed Mode III' coincides with 'dotted rhythm in ternary metre' is a matter that will have to be teased out. Wulstan's presentation of rhythmic types is in the first instance statistical, and his conclusions are given in the form of a table with data on rhythmic categories for each group of 100 pieces, or 'cental' (a term I shall adopt);[13] he, too, finds that 3% of the pieces in the first 100 display (in his terminology) 'bagpipe rhythm',[14] although one needs to search more widely in his writings for references to specific *cantigas*. One of his dotted-rhythm pieces in the first cental is, once again, *Cantiga* 20 which is offered as exemplifying its rhythmic type;[15] a further trawl brings up a reference to *CSM* 38, also seen as displaying 'bagpipe rhythm'.[16] Finally, Wulstan provides an inconclusive hint that he considers *Cantiga* 19 to have 'bagpipe-rhythm' elements.[17]

Cantiga 20, then, with attention from both Ferreira and Wulstan, emerges as a key piece in relation to dotted rhythm, and will be the first to be subjected to examination below; beyond that, there appears to be no common ground. Meanwhile, it is my own view that the number of pieces in which dotted rhythms are present has been seriously underestimated; it is my hope that the analyses and transcriptions that follow will substantiate that view.

---

[12] *See* Ferreira 2014, pp. 50–51.

[13] Wulstan's tabulation of rhythmic types first appears in his 2000 article (which in fact derives from a conference paper delivered in 1994), and is initially confined to the first two centals. Fuller treatment is found in Chapter 2 of Wulstan 2001; the table of rhythmic categories, separated for each cental, appears in the Appendix to that chapter (p. 309), with ancillary lists and tables for certain sub-groups of pieces; the table and some of the other data are repeated, with minor adjustments, in Wulstan 2013, pp. 175–6. It must be borne in mind that Wulstan's allocation of pieces to particular rhythmic categories derives from rhythmic readings that in a majority of cases are not accessible in published form; the resultant statistics are thus insulated from systematic confirmation or rebuttal, and must to that extent be treated with caution.

[14] This term is perhaps more at home in Wulstan's broad treatment of the deep roots of European melody, and in his exploration of the short melodic and rhythmic figures that he considers characteristic of certain subcategories of the repertoire; *see again* Wulstan 2001, *passim*.

[15] *See* Wulstan 2000, p. 55, and 2001, p. 58. No transcription is offered, however, and the reader is left to work out just where the 'bagpipeyness' comes in.

[16] 'Bagpipe rhythm is the solution to problems [in *Cantiga* 38] caused by *LBB* figures' (Wulstan 2001, p. 77).

[17] *Cantiga* 19 will be briefly discussed in Section VI below. The uncertainty over whether Wulstan allocated this piece to his 'bagpipe rhythm' category in the assembling of his statistics highlights a difficulty in the statistical approach: whilst it is useful to have Wulstan's assertion that 3% of pieces in the first cental display dotted rhythm, it might have been helpful to know just *which* three pieces are involved. If *Cantiga* 19 is *not* Wulstan's third dotted-rhythm piece in the first cental, I have not succeeded in locating any more specific reference to identify such a piece.

II
TWO SYSTEMS OF NOTATION

The last quarter-century has seen the publication of significant material on the notation of the *Cantigas*, both in the form of dedicated articles and isolated comments. It is not proposed to attempt here a synthesis of widely-scattered contributions offered since Anglés — contributions that in any case do not always display complete unanimity. Some overview will nevertheless be provided, laying particular emphasis on the behaviour of the *simplex* figures in both notational codes, as a necessary basis for the case-studies that follow.[1]

THE NOTATION OF THE ESCORIAL CODICES

At first sight the notation of *T* and *E* displays many features in common with wider European practice two decades before the end of the thirteenth century. As regards *simplex* figures, it relies on a fundamental opposition between *virga* and *punctum*, ▪| and ▪ , with values of *longa* and *brevis* respectively. The former is variable as regards the duration it represents, being either imperfect or perfect (*i.e.*, representing a duration of $2t$ or $3t$ respectively) according to context; the latter normally represents a duration of $1t$, but the second of two breves is susceptible on occasion to alteration (and so has a duration of $2t$). The same fundamental opposition between *L* and *B* is also present in the plicated forms of the *simplex* figures, both ascending and descending (*see* the accompanying Chart below).[2] Any attempt, however, to apply strictly the rules of alteration and perfection, as commonly understood in the notation of polyphony, is likely to produce bizarre results, for it is an inescapable feature of *cantiga* interpretation that 'there is limited and inconsistent use of alteration rules...and it is quite unlikely that the rule "long before long is perfect" ...can be generally applied'.[3] This situation arises, not least, from the need to notate rhythm of the type | ♩ 𝅗𝅥 | 𝅗𝅥 ♩ | or its inverse, | 𝅗𝅥 ♩ | ♩ 𝅗𝅥 |; such rhythmic patterns cannot be expressed using *B* and *L* unless these figures are used with values that are absolute and not sensitive to context, or that at least do not exert influence across the boundary of the rhythmic cell.[4] In practical terms, the fact that alteration and perfection sometimes do not apply means that even a group as apparently straightforward as *LBB* is inherently ambiguous: it may represent durations of /2,1,1/ and so perhaps imply binary metre, or else with perfection and alteration it may imply /3,1,2/, characteristic of Mode III rhythm.

---

[1] On the nuts-and-bolts of the notation, particularly important are articles by Ferreira dated 1993, 2000, 2000 *ter*, 2010, 2011 (on *T*), 2013 and 2014 (*see* Bibliography); also the contributions by Wulstan: 1998, 2000, 2001 (esp. ch. 2), and 2013. My earlier publication (Cunningham 2000) contains an overview (pp. 31–52) of the notation, intended as an introduction to the subject; it further offers (pp. 26–30) a brief account of contributions by others who have engaged in the field.

[2] Wulstan (2000, pp. 39–40; 2001, pp. 43–6) refers to the plicated forms of *L* and *B* as 'double plica' and 'single plica' respectively, and goes on to discuss inconsistencies in their use; this question will be taken up below under 'plica confusion'.

[3] Ferreira 2014, p. 39.

[4] Wulstan calls these rhythms 'iambo-trochaic'; Anglés would have called them 'mixed Mode I–Mode II'. Such rhythms, whether consistent throughout a melody or employed irregularly or intermittently, are extremely important: according to Wulstan's statistics (2001, p. 309), one way or another they appear in nearly 30% of all pieces in the main sequence (nos 1–400) of the corpus.

Similarly *LBL* too is ambiguous: it may represent Mode III, but may also perhaps be indicative of quintuple rhythm of the shape /2,1,2/.[5] In a system of notation that is less than completely mensural, it might be supposed *a priori* that the ligatures would be the principal source of uncertainty. Such a view, however, is unwarranted: in the case of the *Cantigas* we ignore the vagaries of the *simplex* figures at our peril.[6]

Along with the *virga* and square *punctum*, representing *L* and *B* respectively, the Escorial codices also make use of a rhombic figure, ♦, with the value of one half of a time-unit or *tempus* — in other words, a *semibrevis*. This figure, however, does not make its appearance as an isolated note-form until *Cantiga* 150.[7] The notational system up to that point thus lacks any straightforward method of recording a half-beat note, a fact that explains why the notation of dotted rhythm, as explored in the present study, must of necessity rely on a mechanism that represents such rhythm at one remove.

Allusion has already been made to Anglés's contention that the notation of the Escorial codices, with regard to the ligatures as in other aspects, is fully mensural — a view now generally agreed to have been an overstatement. It was Ferreira who, in the 1990s, sought to establish that, on the one hand, a good number of ligatures, in the notation of *T* and *E*, can indeed be viewed with safety as representing an overall duration that is consistently either *L* or *B*;[8] on the other hand, however, there are also ligatures for which this cannot be assumed. Prominently, and perhaps surprisingly, this latter category includes the commonly-occurring binaries and , *cum proprietate sine perfectione*, to which Anglés attributed Franconian values of *BB*, but which Ferreira showed need to be treated sometimes as *BB* but elsewhere as *SS*; this important case of ambiguity has become a cornerstone of some modern *Cantiga* transcriptions.[9]

Whilst the theoretically-based Latin terminology used at the end of the previous paragraph is both familiar and convenient for identifying notational figures, it must be

[5] On the problems of *LBB* versus *LBL* and related matters, *see* Wulstan 2000, pp. 33–35. On quintuple metre, *see* Ferreira 2000, pp. 14–16, and 2013, pp. 137–8. *See also* the discussion of Mode III notation below.

[6] In the case of alteration, it is perhaps as dangerous to fail to see it as to see it where it is not. In this regard I would admit that, in my *Loores* transcriptions (Cunningham 2000), I was probably over-reliant on alteration as a solution to rhythmic problems arising from notational ambiguity.

[7] The apparent exceptions are *Cantigas* 1 and 26 in *T*, and *Cantigas* 26 and 89 in *E*, all of which make use of isolated rhombic notes. These melodies, however, are in binary metre, expressed generally as pairs of two-beat *L*s or the equivalent; the single rhomb stands either as an anacrusis, or as a single beat in relation to a three-beat *L* (written ▪‖). In such contexts the temporal value of ♦ can only be read as *B* and not *S*.

[8] *See* Ferreira 1993, p. 586 and exx. 5–6, p. 620. The list of figures to be considered as dependably mensural is summarised in Ferreira 2000 *ter*, p. 152.

[9] Ferreira 1993, p. 587 and ex. 7, p. 620. My transcriptions of the *Loores* (Cunningham 2000) were to an important degree motivated by my own understanding particularly of as an ambiguous, 'rogue' figure (*see* my Preface); the complete edition by Elmes (2004–14) also relies on seeing these figures as ambiguous. But in a recent alarming footnote, Ferreira appears to reconsider his view concerning these two *cum-sine* figures: '...contrary to what I suggested [in Ferreira 1993], I now regard the binary *cum proprietate/sine perfectione* ligatures in the Escorial codices as acknowledged mensural figures, as Anglés had proposed, with no need to attribute their *brevis-brevis* meaning to the influence of Franco' (Ferreira 2015, p. 2, n. 3). How this might affect the transcription of numerous pieces (including, but not exclusively, those listed in Ferreira 1993, p. 587) is a matter on which we must await clarification. Unless, perhaps, Professor Ferreira intended his observation to apply only to pieces in binary metre? Meanwhile, I adhere to my own conviction that the *cum-sine* binaries are mensurally ambiguous, and this view will be embodied in the transcriptions that follow.

emphasized that in the context of *Cantiga* notation it lacks any binding predictive value for establishing the duration of a ligature or its components. An illustrative example will help: ▚ and ▚ can both represent a total duration of three *tempora*, and when so, a case can be made for internal values of 1+2 and 2+1 *tempora* respectively; but both can also represent a total duration of two *tempora*, and in such a case the lack of propriety in the second figure — or indeed the attributed *perfectio* in both — is of little avail in establishing either overall or componential durations. In general it is difficult to go further than making the distinction between those ligatures whose overall value is *L* (and so perfectible) and those that are *B*, with context and rhythmic pattern playing a determining rôle in decipherment.

An aspect of Escorial notation that needs to be handled with care is the case of *opposita proprietas*, in two different regards. First, it is undeniable that *T* and *E* differ in the level of care with which the stem that connotes opposite propriety is used: whereas in *T* it generally has the expected meaning, in *E* by contrast its use is more wayward and it cannot always be taken at face value.[10] Second, in the conventional understanding based on contemporary theory, opposite propriety applies only to the first two notes after the stem, establishing their value as *SS*, with any subsequent notes before the last in an extended ligature being understood as *B*; not so in the Escorial notation of the *Cantigas*, where the effect of opposite propriety may be prolonged. Thus a quaternary figure such as ▞▘ may be understood (but only if the context requires it) as *SSSS*;[11] and a ternary ligature such as ▞ may perhaps need to be read conventionally as *SSB*, but may also stand as a triplet *SSS* within one *tempus* — a sort of melodic inverse of ▚ .[12] These and other features suggest that the notators of the *Cantigas* had to cope with notating melodic segments more intricate and perhaps more quickly executed than those required in the liturgical compositions around which contemporary theory was built.

Beyond what has been mentioned, problems occurring in this volume over the interpretation of ligatures are not of such a density as to warrant a lengthy exposition at this point, and such cases as do arise will be dealt with individually.

Finally, it is clear that that an over-reliance until recently on *E* — a situation exacerbated by the lack of adequate facsimiles of the sources until very recently (2011 in the case of *T*) — has given way to an awareness of the need to weigh the evidence of all sources. Once more it is Ferreira who has aided this process with a more detailed description and analysis of the notation of *T* than was previously available.[13] Among the inferences drawn by him is that the copyist of *T* either had access to better models than was the case with *E*, or else actively intervened to improve the accuracy of what he transcribed.[14]

---

[10] On the erratic use of *c.o.p.* binaries in *E*, *see* Ferreira 1993, p. 587; Cunningham 2000, p. 45; Wulstan 2001, p. 40; Ferreira 2011, p. 202. On Anglés's misplaced trust in the mensural reliability of ▞, *see again* Ferreira 1993, p. 587, and 2000 *ter*, p. 152.

[11] Similar observations are made in Wulstan 2000, p. 39, repeated in Wulstan 2001, p. 43.

[12] For the complete series of one-*tempus* triplets in different melodic configurations, *see* the chart in Cunningham 2000, p. 47, ex. VII.

[13] *See again* Ferreira 2011, esp. pp. 198–204; in addition to a table (p. 199) of 'formas usuais' (the most common note-shapes) found in *T*, Ferreira gives an account (p. 200) of more archaic uses of stems, and of figures showing what I shall call 'asymmetrical elongation' (for example ▚ as opposed to ▚ — the distinction is not registered by Anglés); this latter case exemplifies local, regional aspects of the notation, which by its use of intuitive visual clues can differentiate length in a way not known to 'standard' practice.

[14] *ibid.*, p. 202.

THE NOTATION OF THE 'TOLEDO' CODEX

The notation of *To* is *sui generis*, with features that stand out as odd in a wider European context. The correspondences between *To* and the Escorial codices were first synthesized by Aubry thus:

Escorial ▜ ■ ▜ ■ ▜ etc. = Tolède ■ ◆ ■ ◆ ■ etc.[15]

This may be indisputable as far as it goes, but it undoubtedly suggests a simpler state of affairs than what in fact obtains: it is simply not the case that the relationship between the two systems can be expressed in a series of one-to-one correspondences. Two essential features of Toledo notation, whose character has come into clearer focus in the years since Anglés, must be acknowledged.

The first of these concerns the shorter of the two basic note-shapes — representing a duration of one *tempus* or beat and written as a rhomb (◆) — and its behaviour in relation to the rules of alteration. Whereas in Escorial notation the corresponding figure (the *brevis*) is on occasion subject to alteration — however irregularly, sporadically or unpredictably the 'rules' are applied —, the same is not true of the shorter basic note (the rhomb) in Toledo notation, which, according to conventional wisdom, is *never* altered.[16] This fact brings an obvious consequence: if, following a note of 1*t*, a note of duration 2*t* is required, then the latter must, in *To*, be written *specifically* as a square *punctum* (■; it will be helpful to refer to the chart opposite). It follows that, in cases where there is doubt about the presence or absence of alteration in *T* or *E*, the notation of *To*, more specific in such contexts as to the duration of the second note, can clarify the duration intended.

The second important feature not dealt with in Aubry's brief encapsulation is the existence in *To*, alongside the square *punctum* (■), of a third *simplex* note-shape, the short-stemmed *virga* (▜). Whilst the former is variable — and to that extent ambiguous — in the duration it represents (being either imperfect or perfect), the short-stemmed *virga* proves to be used only when a value of 3*t* is intended;[17] it is used sparingly, but provides a specific statement of perfection in cases where the context would otherwise lack the necessary clarity. Often it makes its appearance only once in an extended passage, to provide an essential key to the rhythmic pattern, which, once established, proceeds with the use of 'ordinary' ■s, understood to be perfect, in the same position in repetitions of the pattern or of the phrase. As will be seen below, an important use occurs in cases of Mode III, where a single ▜ in *To* can provide specific information not supplied in Escorial notation.

One consequence of the foregoing cannot be stated too bluntly: that, in Toledo notation, ■ (when perfect) and ▜ are synonymous, whereas the superficially similar ■ (when *recta*) and ▜ in Escorial notation are most definitely not.

---

[15] Aubry 1907, p. 35.

[16] This statement will require qualification (a) in the context of the transitional notation that occurs at the very end of the Toledo codex — *see* below, 'Transitional Notation' —, and (b) possibly in specific circumstances in some instances of dotted rhythm, as will be analysed in due season. The case of *CSM* 162 — over which Ferreira (2010, pp. 292–3) raises doubts concerning inconsistency in the use of ◆ and a possible case of its alteration — will be analysed in Section IV.

[17] As early as 1993 Ferreira (pp. 592–3) gave a reasoned defence of the reading of ▜ = 3*t*, against the earlier views of Anglés (who saw it as a frequent copyist's error) and Ribera (who saw it as a plicated figure). Whilst the understanding of ▜ as invariably perfect may be allowed to stand for the present, it will become necessary to make an adjustment to how we view it, most particularly in some contexts occurring at the *point of exit from a cell of dotted rhythm*.

'TOLEDO' NOTATION 'ESCORIAL' NOTATION

NOTÆ SIMPLICES

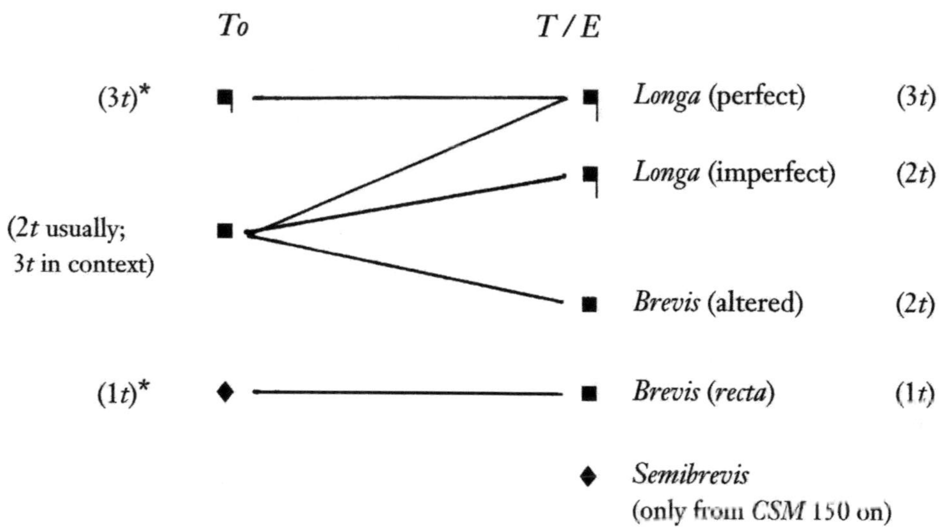

NOTÆ SIMPLICES PLICATÆ

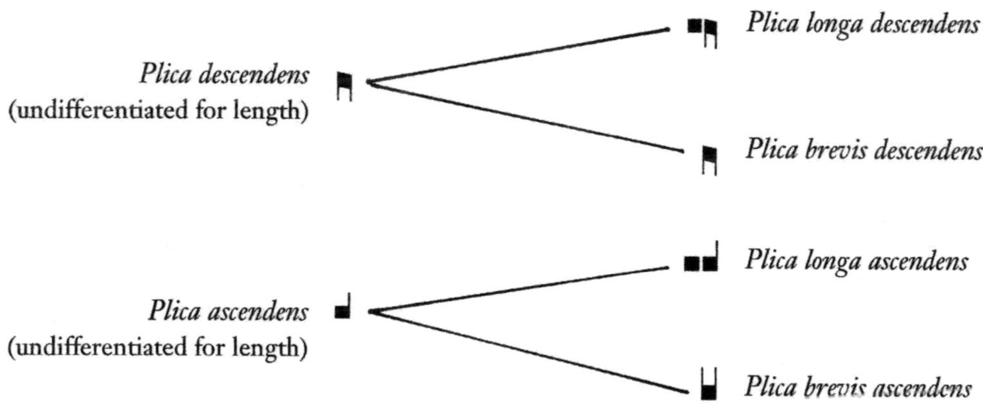

CHART
of equivalences between the notation of *To*
and that of *T* and *E*

* Some refinement of the attribution of immutable durational values to ▪ and ♦ will be required in due course; for the present the absolute statement given here will be found to cover the overwhelming majority of cases.

The trinal sophistication present in the *simplex* system in *To* disappears, however, when we turn to the plicated forms. Here, for all temporal values there is only a single figure available in each direction; thus ▜ , for example, must stand as the descending plica of both ♦ and ■ (reference to the chart will again be helpful), with consequent loss of mensural information. The same durational non-specificity characterizes the ligatures, among which Ferreira finds only two figures, or at most three, that can dependably be interpreted as having a value that is always *L*.[18] For all others, including the ubiquitous *clivis* (▜▄), the duration must be determined by the context and/or the prevailing rhythmic pattern. The notation of *To* is thus accurately described as semi-mensural, and not very mensural at that. Whilst some rhythmic patterns can be read straight off the page with surprising ease, others are more difficult, especially where there is heavier dependence on the use of ligatures; hence it is no exaggeration to say that if *To* were the only source, decipherment would have proceeded a good deal more tentatively.

The immense value of *To* thus lies in the complementarity of its *simplex* system to that of *T* and *E*: *To* is the arbiter of the presence of alteration by its specific statement of a two-beat note; and *To* has the capacity to clarify the presence or absence of perfection by its use of a specifically three-beat note. Although *To* was all but dismissed by Anglés as late and poorly notated, it has in recent decades undergone reappraisal as a musically indispensable source in large part because of this complementarity.

Chronology of the Sources

The first and most important point that must be made is that the relative chronology of the two systems of notation is not of any fundamental consequence in the present context. Each notation has its own internal logic — however incomplete or imperfect —, and the confrontation of the notations of a particular piece in the two systems permits clarification or reinforcement of interpretation without reference to questions of precedence.

Even so, relative chronology, and absolute dating of the sources, are questions on which differing opinions have been expressed. No one now doubts that the two Escorial codices date from the last years of Alfonso's reign: Source *T*, the *Códice rico*, was probably begun in the early 1280s, to be followed by its planned continuation *F*; it is probable that, as this extremely luxurious project seemed less and less achievable, a more modest version (Parkinson refers to it as an 'insurance policy'[19]) was commenced in the form of *E*; this was in all likelihood completed by or around the time of Alfonso's death in 1284, while the parallel 'luxury' project — *T* plus *F* — stumbled on and fizzled out.[20]

It is against this background that the Toledo codex must be situated. With 100 pieces in its main sequence, *To* represents the first consolidated manifestation of the anthological project.[21] The texts themselves confirm as much: the opening 'Proclamation' (also called 'Prologue A'), though later amended, originally referred to how Alfonso *fez cen*

[18] *See* Ferreira 1993, pp. 589–90, summarised in Ferreira 2000 *ter*, p. 152, ex. 9.4a.

[19] Parkinson 2015, p. 6; Wulstan (2013, p. 176) refers to *E* as a 'compromise…edition'.

[20] Questions of the dating of sources may be approached through Ferreira 1994; for a more recent formulation, putting the compilation of *To* between 1270 and 1275, *see* Ferreira 2013, p. 132. The sequence given here for the creation of the sources is that now generally accepted; the precise dates are broadly consensual, that for *To* possibly marking the end of a long period of assemblage. The chief question at issue is whether the *To* that has come down to us is a late copy of a lost original.

[21] Parkinson (2015, p. 6) insists on seeing each of the sources as a separate 'compilation', thus laying emphasis on the complexity and non-linear nature of their interrelationship, while Schaffer (2000) similarly considers the three manuscript collections (*To*, *T/F*, *E*) as essentially distinct works.

cantares e sões, 'composed a hundred songs and [their] melodies'; and the closing *Petiçón*, as it appears in *To*, begins *Pois cen cantares feitos / acabei*, 'Since I have completed a hundred finished songs'.[22] It is an inescapable conclusion that these two texts were first designed to frame a collection of 100 pieces seen as a single, rounded and coherent entity. Yet whilst it may be agreed that the process of *compilation* was completed no later than 1275, the act of *copying* need not be contemporaneous.[23] And whether we can date the Toledo codex itself to around 1275 (either as the *Urtext* or as an early copy of a lost original[24]), or must see it as a much later copy, depends at least in part on what view is taken of its musical notation.

The problem arises because the rhomb and the square *punctum*, functioning in *To* as the shorter and the longer of the two basic notes, are forms that, at first sight, are out of place two or three decades before 1300. Aubry — quoted above on the correspondence between Toledo and Escorial *simplex* notes — seems baffled; he is willing to concede an early date to *To*, but cannot conceive how the rhomb, which he perceives as a *semibrevis*, can appear so early: 'The Toledo ms is known to be the oldest collection of *Cantigas*. It is earlier than 1275, and so it is all the odder to see this isolated use of the semibreve'.[25] Conviction that ▪ and ♦ are breve and semibreve respectively fuels subsequent disbelief in the early date of the Toledo codex itself; it is left to Anglés to consolidate the view that what we see in *To* is a poor late copy — possibly even from the following century — in which the values of the *simplex* notes have been halved, the plicas have lost distinction of length, and ligatures are transcribed in a way that betrays scribal ignorance or incompetence.[26] The idea of the Toledo codex being late, or notationally unreliable, or both, reverberates through the ensuing literature. Wulstan, for example, speaks in regard to *To* of 'a later [notation] which often replaces the breve with the semibreve';[27] this view has knock-on effects for his interpretation particularly of the notation of Mode III. And from a codicological standpoint, L. Fernández has argued — taking Anglés's view as her point of departure — for a fourteenth-century date for *To*.[28]

---

[22] The first of these texts is amended by a later hand to read *fezo cantares con sões*, 'composed songs with [their] melodies', while the *Pitiçón* is rewritten in *E* in a form that likewise eliminates the numeral 100. *See* Parkinson 2010 on the rewriting of these two framing texts.

[23] Shaffer (2000) is careful to draw a distinction between the date of assemblage of a particular collection, and the date at which a surviving source was copied.

[24] Whether *To*, assuming it to be early, is nevertheless an early copy of a lost original (*see* Ferreira 1994) or is the royal codex itself (*see* Parkinson 2000) need not concern us here.

[25] 'On sait déjà que le manuscrit de Tolède est le plus ancien recueil des *Cantigas*. Il est antérieur à 1275. Il n'en est donc que plus étrange de voir cet emploi isolé de la semi-brève', Aubry 1907, p. 35.

[26] *See* Anglés 1943, pp. 23–5, where we find a nine-point dismissal of the musical usefulness of the Toledo ms; it must be acknowledged, however, that later in the same section Anglés is careful not to present his view as definitive, merely as an expression of doubt over the antiquity of *To*. From a historical perspective, it is relevant to note that Anglés's treatment of the subject follows closely on his harsh criticism (p. 23) of Ribera's 1922 transcriptions which had been based on *To*. The supposed 'late and decadent' character of the notation of *To* thus becomes a convenient rod with which to belabour Ribera.

[27] Wulstan 2000, p. 33, repeated in Wulstan 2001, p. 38. General stemmatic arguments, including those for a late date for *To*, are given in Wulstan 2000 *bis* (*see* pp. 165, 177–80); *see also* isolated comments ('late copy...') such as that in Wulstan 2013, p. 176.

[28] *See* L. Fernández Fernández 2009, p. 325 and n. 5. Fernández takes as the starting point for her reasoning Anglés's contention of late date, a view she presents as established fact; her argument thus risks collapse under the weight of its own circularity; meanwhile her conclusions, regrettably, are presented as definitive in comments provided in as influential a reference-work as Snow's *Bibliography* (Snow 2012, entry no. 1936, p. 396). The fourteenth-century view is reiterated in Fernández 2011, p. 48.

In spite of such broad advocacy, however, there are aspects of the 'late' theory for the date of *To* that make it hard to accept, especially from a notational viewpoint.[29] Most obviously, it is difficult to explain, if the *simplices* are being 'updated' and (as perceived within the theory) halved in value, why the ligatures appear to become more primitive; as to the third *simplex* figure in *To*, advocates of a late date do not broach the question of how the short-stemmed *virga* can be contextually interchangeable with the square *punctum*, rather than be a multiple of it. More technically, if we view the creation of *To* as involving a sort of 'notational translation' from some earlier model now lost (presumably written in a notation similar to that of *T* or *E*), we must ask how the translator could have the necessary in-depth skill to iron out all cases of alteration found in his model, yet fail to maintain distinctions of length in the *plica* system. We might also muse on the difficulty of imagining a possible scenario in which a manuscript of the *Cantigas* could be brought into being outside the royal scriptorium, years after Alfonso's death and the abandonment of the wider project[30] — a manuscript, moreover, which although based on the collection in its earliest form nevertheless bears marginal corrections which suggest it served as a working copy.[31]

It will be clear from the above that, if the supposed late character of the *simplex* figures is allowed to oblige a late date for *To* and its notation, problems arise in explaining almost every other feature of the notation; but if we assume an early date, most aspects of the notation fall into place — durationally undifferentiated *plicas*, ligatures that in the main are non-mensural —, leaving only the question of the use at this date of ▪ and ♦ as the longer and shorter basic notes to be explained, and the additional complication of ▪ . It is once more Ferreira who has provided the necessary framework, in three instalments. First is a stemma within which to see *To* as antedating both *T* and *E*.[32] Second comes the provision of a plausible explanation of how the forms ▪ and ♦ came to be differentiated for use as the longer and shorter basic figures in a tradition of notation that developed in the Peninsula.[33] Third and more recently, Ferreira has persuasively pointed to a chain of historical events which serve as a backdrop against which to see the shift in notational practice: crucial was Alfonso's lengthy stay in Southern France in 1275, which would have provided the opportunity for musicians in his entourage to gain exposure to wider European (and, more specifically, French) notational practice, which thereafter supplants a locally-developed (*i.e.*, Peninsular) notation such as that found in *To*.[34]

[29] The arguments are persuasively assembled in Ferreira 1994, pp. 87–88.
[30] Take, for example, the elaborate scenario constructed by Wulstan (2000 *bis*, p. 177), involving a 'well-placed patron', possibly Alfonso's grandson or 'maybe an old retainer', whose copyists 'were unaware of the existence of the larger collections' of *cantigas*.
[31] On the marginalia of *To*, *see* Schaffer 1995, 2010.
[32] *See* Ferreira 1994. The view of *To* and its notation as earlier than the Escorial sources is present whether explicitly or implicitly in Ferreira's subsequent contributions; it is for example stated again in Ferreira 1997, p. 245; *see also* scattered comments such as the observation that some of the ligatures found in *T* are vestiges ('resquícios') of the notation of *To* (2011, p. 200). As noted earlier, Wulstan sees *To* as late, based on ▪ and ♦ as fourteenth-century forms; *see again* Wulstan 2000 *bis*.
[33] *See* Ferreira 1994, p. 88; the arguments are summarised in Ferreira 2013, p. 132 (*see also* next note), and a date of between 1270 and 1275 is offered for the copying of *To* as we have it.
[34] *See again* Ferreira 2013, pp. 131–3. In pursuit of his ambition to be declared Holy Roman Emperor, Alfonso travelled for an encounter with Pope Gregory X, passing in early Spring 1275 via Perpignan and Montpellier to Beaucaire (between Arles and Avignon), where he remained until late Summer. On the return journey he was gravely ill in Montpellier, as recounted in *Cantiga* 235.

If the early date for *To* is accepted (and it is my view that such acceptance is inescapable[35]), it follows that the incorporation into *T* and *E* of pieces already anthologised in *To* involved a 'translation' *from* Toledo notation *into* Escorial notation, thus reversing the view of *To* as itself a (bad) translation. An important aspect of such a process is its unidirectionality — that is, features of the earlier notation may condition or even determine features of later practice, but not *vice versa*. A valuable tool is thus provided to help explain certain aspects of the notation of *T* and *E* that would otherwise remain puzzling;[36] some features of Escorial notation that fail to conform fully with notational practice as described in contemporary theory may also be ascribed to lingering substratum influence.[37]

Even so, the observation made at the head of this subsection may now be repeated: an acceptance of an early date for the Toledo codex and its notation — however much such a view contributes to explaining notational practice — is not a prerequisite for understanding the notation of dotted rhythms as presented below.

Nomenclature

In a context in which opinions differ fundamentally even as to the very identity and nature of certain symbols — is ▪ *L* or *B* in *To*? —conflict inevitably arises over the nomenclature to be applied. In a nutshell, the third-mode string ╕ ♦ ▪ in *To* is *LSB* for Wulstan,[38] but *LBL* for Ferreira.[39] Whilst my own preference lies firmly with the latter, I recognize that in naming the same thing differently there is a real danger of sowing confusion. Accordingly a decision has been taken to attempt, in this study, to circumvent such questions of nomenclature in *To* either by referring to figures descriptively ('short-stemmed *virga*', 'square *punctum*', 'rhomb') or by using notational symbols (╕ , ▪ , ♦) in running text.[40]

Third Mode Notation

Since in much of what follows we shall be dealing with the treatment of (often isolated) rhythm-groups or 'rhythmic cells'[41] notated as third mode, it will be helpful to take a look at the basic notation of Mode III in the two notational systems.

In the Escorial sources, two variant notations of a Mode III cell arise depending on whether or not the third member of the group is notated in a way that relies on alteration. This third element of the cell may therefore sometimes be written as *B* (thus ╕ ▪ ▪ , *i.e.*,

---

[35] It has long been my conviction that Toledo notation antedates that of *T* and *E*; *see* my comments in Cunningham 2000, p. 32. I also consider that Ferreira's linking of the change in notational code with Alfonso's French sojourn, mentioned in the preceding paragraph, goes a long way to clinching the argument. I further believe that an early date for *To* and its notation — *pace* Wulstan — provides the only firm basis for a fuller understanding of both notational systems.

[36] Some of the import of this comment will become apparent below, in the subsections on 'Plica Confusion' and 'Transitional Notation'.

[37] A case in point is the apparent reluctance in Escorial notation to engage fully with the practice of breve-alteration, a feature surely not divorced from the absence of alteration in Toledo notation.

[38] For example, speaking of the strings ╕ ♦ ▪ and ▪ ♦ ▪ as they appear in the Toledo version of *CSM* 25 (*To* 38), Wulstan (2000, p. 36) comments that *To* '...has *LSB* or *BSB*, neither of which makes sense in the context.' (On the specific point, *see* the discussion of *To* 38 in Section VII below.)

[39] The question of nomenclature is discussed in Ferreira 1994, p. 86.

[40] The reader will already have noticed that in the foregoing Chart of Equivalences, no note-names have been attached to the *simplex* figures that occur in the Toledo source.

[41] The importance from an editorial standpoint of the correct isolation of rhythmic cells will be further explored under the penultimate heading ('Editorial Perspectives') of this Section.

LBB) with the expectation that the second of the *B*s will be altered; but if alteration is not invoked, then the third element must be spelled out literally as *L* (and thus ▜ ■ ▜ , or *LBL*). In either case the durations are of /3,1,2/ *tempora*. The two methods of notating are often found mixed in the same piece, and a not infrequent sequence, in the case of phrases with several successive cells of this pattern, takes the form

▜■▜ ▜■▜ ▜■■ ▜

where only the last cell before the final *L* of the phrase has a *brevis altera*. An accurate statement of what rules, if any, govern the seemingly wayward variation in notating this rhythm — whether it depends on position in the phrase, on the precise identity of the figure that follows, on scribal whim — is a question that would benefit from a dedicated study; for the present, it may merely be observed that if the note following is *not* a *simplex* *L*, it is unlikely that the Mode III cell will be notated *LBB*.

The Toledo source also presents two ways for cells of this mode to be notated, but in this case the variability affects not the third component but the first. The normal and by far the most frequent notation of this rhythmic pattern is ■ ◆ ■ , relying on the variable value of ■ to give the /3,1,2/ durations. The first component, however, may be given more specific triple length by use of the short-stemmed *virga*, ▜ , and so the cell may be given as ▜ ◆ ■ . In practice this happens infrequently, often only once in a piece, in order to resolve any possible problems of ambiguity. So it is that, if we wish to replicate in Toledo notation the whole phrase given above in Escorial notation, we find

■◆■ ■◆■ ■◆■ ■

which, perhaps once only in a given piece (maybe in the first phrase, though not always), will be made more specific with

▜◆■ ■◆■ ■◆■ ■

where the first figure in the line gives specific duration of 3*t* to the note it represents.

It will be noticed from the above examples that each notational system functions within its own conventions, and any one-to-one cross-system correspondence of note-shapes, or any transferability of which elements are variable, is illusory.

The notation of Mode III has been presented here entirely in terms of *simplex* notes. It should hardly be necessary to point out that any of the components may be substituted by a plica, or by a ligature with the same overall duration. Such ligatures will, as may be expected, tend to be more specific as to length in *T* and *E* than in *To*.

Plica Confusion

In *To* the usual plica forms, ▜ and ▟ , are undifferentiated for length and either may be used with a value that is either *B* or *L*. The same is not true in Escorial notation, where distinct forms are available according to the duration required. It sometimes happens, however, — both in *T* and in *E* — that a *plica brevis* (▜ or ▟) is found where the rhythmic pattern would lead to an expectation of a *plica longa* (■▜ or ■▟). There are even cases in which the rhythmic interpretation of a particular piece seems intractable until this phenomenon is invoked, and an apparently short plica is read as *L*.[42]

[42] A case in point is *Cantiga* 97 (*see* below, Section VII), where the rhythmic cogency of the whole refrain section depends on the first figure in the opening phrase being read in this way.

In seeking to understand why this happens, it is possible to take the view that it is simply a fact of life that in *T* and *E* the plicated forms of the *simplex* figures are used with a degree of inconsistency.[43] If, however, we are willing to see this facet of the notation in the context of the chronological precedence of *To* as discussed above, then it is explicable as a retention in *T* or *E* of the undifferentiated figure present in *To*. Thus for example a plica occurring in *To* might be carried over unchanged, without too much care being lavished on what duration it represented. Ferreira has referred to this unthinking replication (of form rather than of content) as 'notational inertia'.[44] It will be clear that this explanation is applicable only to cases of the erroneous use in *T* or *E* of the *plica brevis*; by extension comes the implication that the *plica longa*, when it occurs in a 'translated' piece, is more reliable — an expectation that seems to be matched by the evidence.[45]

Cadential Lengthening

It happens on occasion that even when a strongly characterized rhythmic pattern has been established within a phrase — as might be, for example, simple repetitions of the type *BL BL*... or *LB LB*..., but also with more complex patterns – , the last rhythmic group of the phrase is given as undifferentiated *LL*. An editorial difficulty arises over whether this should be taken literally, or, as often appears to be the case, it is merely a notational habit, perhaps a throwback to an earlier stage in the evolution of the notation, and that the appropriate *L* should be read as *B*.[46] The possibility that such notational lengthening may represent an actual *ritardando* or *rallentando* at phrase-ends in performance must remain in the realms of speculation.

The '*Tractulus*'

An important element in the notation of all sources is the small vertical stroke inserted after some figures, for which the name *tractulus* will here be used.[47] It is to be distinguished from the longer line that cuts through several lines of the stave if not the whole of it, generally to mark phrase-endings, for which I propose to use the modern term 'bar'.[48]

---

[43] In the words of Wulstan (2001, p. 44), 'On the whole, **E** and [**T**] attempt to differentiate between these two types of plica [*i.e.*, the *B* and the *L*] more or less unequivocally, though there are many instances of infirmity of purpose.'

[44] *See* Ferreira 2000, pp. 13–14.

[45] Without recourse to arguments based on the chronological precedence of *To*, Wulstan (2000, p. 40) nevertheless acknowledges the reliability of the *plica longa*: 'Where the double plica is used in **E** and **T**, it should normally be treated at face value.'

[46] This phenomenon is mentioned briefly, in relation to *CSM* 49 and 3, in Wulstan 2000, p. 36; further brief mention, and exemplification from *CSM* 70, is given in Wulstan 2001, p. 41 and ex. 2.18, p. 74. The case of *CSM* 25, also mentioned by Wulstan, is dealt with below.

[47] From Latin *trahere*, 'to drag', 'to pull'; the ending *-ulus* has diminutive force, and so literally 'a little pull [of the pen]', 'a short pen-stroke'. Wulstan (2000, p. 40; 2001, p. 46) prefers the invented term *lineola*, 'a little line'. The word *tractulus*, however, is used — in a general sense which is then glossed using a more specific term — by no less an authority than Franco of Cologne: «*Nisi... ponatur tractulus...qui etiam alio nomine divisio modi appellatur*», 'Unless...a short stroke be inserted ...which by another name is also called *divisio modi*' (ed. Reaney & Gilles, p. 32; my translation).

[48] Ferreira (2013, p. 143) insists on the need, in palæographic transcription, to distinguish more differences in length of such strokes. In my own experience, however, I have not found it profitable to distinguish more that the two mentioned; and whilst there may be contexts in which scribal intention is unclear, in general I have found the maxim 'if it isn't a bar, it's a *tractulus*' adequate.

The functions for which the *tractulus* is inserted fall broadly into two categories.[49] The first has to do with prolongation, perhaps better understood as implying extension to maximum possible duration of the figure after which it is placed. In ternary metre when it follows a figure with the value of *L* it thus implies a duration of 3*t*; but it may also be found in other situations, most particularly in Escorial notation after the ambiguous *conjunctura* ⬥⬥, often of duration 1*t*, but where a following *tractulus* generally implies a duration of 2*t*. The use in binary metre of a double *tractulus* after a *L*, implying extension of the note to three beats, will not be found in the pieces dealt with in this volume.

The second usage may be termed 'divisory', with the *tractulus* placed after a note to be considered as last in its rhythmic group or cell. This usage comes close to that referred to as *divisio modi* in contemporary theory. When used thus the *tractulus* can be of immense help in determining the rhythmic pattern of a musical phrase. It is, of course, possible for the two uses to coexist, as when in mid-phrase a *L* with *tractulus* is thereby flagged both as perfect and as being in a separate rhythmic compartment from what follows.

As will be seen, in the cases of dotted rhythm to be discussed later there will be contexts in which possible confusion may arise over what meaning should be attached to a *tractulus*, with the danger that a cell-boundary may be perceived where none exists. Some cases of dotted rhythm will also throw up interesting instances of the presence of a *tractulus*, used in ways that I believe have not previously been described; these will be analysed at the appropriate time.

Transitional Notation in *To*

In relation to the short-stemmed *virga* (▪), the notation of *To* maintains a high level of consistency throughout almost all of the codex both as regards the shape of the figure and — except as will be explored in the context of cells of dotted rhythm — in its use to represent a note of 3*t*. There comes a point, however, where we begin to see the use of a normal 'long-tailed' *virga* (▪) much as we would find it in the Escorial codices. This phenomenon appears to arise late in the compilation of *To*, and may best be explained as a transitional feature as the conventions of *Escorial* notation are adopted; it affects some of the pieces edited here, as will be pointed out at the appropriate time.

The matter of the rhombic figure ⬥ (= 1*t*) and its possible alteration (= 2*t*) is, however, a different kettle of fish. The conventional wisdom is that in *To*, this figure has a constant value of 1*t*, and is not subject to alteration. This appears to work in the vast majority of cases, and it is a valuable principle that underpins the usefulness of *To* in clarifying contexts that in Escorial notation are potentially ambiguous. Even so, there appears to be a number of cases in which doubts arise and alteration may be suspected. One problem is that not all of these cases belong to the later stages of the copying of *To*, and so it is difficult to dismiss them as a phenomenon belonging to a transitional phase in the adoption of 'Escorial conventions'; another aspect, however, is that in those cases that occur in this volume, explanations other than alteration are possible — in particular, the context of dotted rhythm and its notational peculiarities suggests that alteration is not what is being seen. Whilst cases occurring in this volume will be pointed out, this does not constitute an exhaustive treatment of an area that would benefit from a dedicated study.

[49] On the workings of the *tractulus* or *lineola*, *see* Wulstan 2000, pp. 40–1 and 2001, pp. 46–7.

EDITORIAL PERSPECTIVES

The task of rhythmic decipherment of the notation(s) of the *Cantigas de Santa Maria* is not a simple one. Rather, it depends (at least in the experience of the present transcriber) on simultaneous attention to three separate tiers of rhythmic organization, requiring focus now on individual notes or figures, now on the rhythmic profile of whole phrases; and, intermediate between these two, on the presence of 'local' groups of figures — rhythmic cells — that draw on the one and, exhibiting internal coherence, contribute to the other.

The first and narrowest focus involved in the task is the need to be aware of the range of possible durations attributable to each individual notational figure. On this level, as the foregoing paragraphs have been at pains to emphasize, rhythmic interpretation cannot be reduced to a list of figures and their supposed durations. Both systems of notation (the *toletana* and the *escurialensis*) are founded on a basic opposition of figures that are either *brevis* or *longa*. But, as must be evident, variabilities built into the systems mean that even the *simplex* figures, with alteration and perfection, are elastic; and at the same time the composite figures (ligatures and *conjuncturæ*) may offer similar variability if long, or even be totally ambiguous in relation to the question '*B* or *L*?'. An awareness of the *range of possibilities* for each individual figure is thus an essential first step in rhythmic decipherment; and yet, decisions about what duration to allocate to a particular figure cannot be arrived at without taking a wider view and looking at some larger unit. Whereas it might be supposed that this involves moving directly to consider what can be discerned of the rhythmic *pattern* of the piece, there is I believe an intermediate level of focus which involves the grouping of notational figures into meaningful groups within which elasticities subside, and pairs or tercets of figures lock into internally well-formed entities[50] — rhythmic compartments, so to speak, that are the components of phrases and of whole melodies that are rhythmically well structured.

This second level of focus, then, concerns what may be referred to as 'rhythmic cells', an idea that provides a helpful intermediate unit between the single notational figure on the one hand and the complete phrase on the other. The term is used here in relation to ternary metre to refer to a single occurrence of a short rhythmic germ or idea, usually corresponding to the briefest possible segment of one of the rhythmic modes, used as a building-block, either by repetition or by mixture with cells of different composition, to create longer rhythmic patterns. Modal terminology provides a useful means of reference; thus a segment with the rhythm | 𝅗𝅥 ♩ | may be spoken of as a 'cell of Mode I', *et cetera* (though without any necessary implication that the piece to which it belongs was conceived with modal rhythm in mind). A cell of dotted rhythm of the form | ♩. ♪♩ | is an exception, falling outside the modal ambit and not covered by its terminology. Such rhythmic cells generally translate into three-beat segments in the process of transcription, although cells of Mode III, if left unmodified, occupy six modern beats.[51]

[50] Examples of such a 'locking' would include the relationship between an adjacent *L* and *B* figures, where the latter binds to the former ensuring its non-perfection; or the group *LBL* which bind into a Mode III cell in which the first figure is perfected. The concept is not dissimilar to that of syntactic binding in a linguistic context.

[51] As an alternative to modal terminology, metrical terms may be brought into service, and are preferred by some commentators — notably by Wulstan, a fact commented on in Ferreira 2013, p. 138. So for example, the cell | ♩♩♩ | may be referred to as a 'tribrach'.

The correct sectioning of whole phrases into ‘meaningful groups each displaying internal coherence’ — rhythmic cells — , is perhaps the single most important procedure undertaken by the transcriber, for without it larger rhythmic patterns, common perhaps to more than one musical phrase, cannot emerge. It is the part of the procedure in which the real character of the rhythmic profile of a piece becomes revealed, and during which there is an opportunity to iron out larger ambiguities.[52] By way of exemplification, a brief string of four figures will suffice: how should 𝆷 ▪ ▪ 𝆷 be read? It might be | 𝆷 ▪ | ▪ 𝆷 | (a cell of Mode I followed by one of Mode II), but in another context perhaps | 𝆷 ▪ ▪ | 𝆷 | (a cell of Mode III followed by a perfect *L*). The decision taken will depend on numerous factors — the rhythmic character of the wider environment, the cogency of the phrase-structure to which the segment contributes, or perhaps (dare one suggest?!) the textual stresses present in the underlay. All of which goes to illustrate how crucial it is, in the process of decipherment, to ensure a correct reading of the position of cell-boundaries.

The third and broadest level of focus is that which involves an awareness of the larger *patterns* of rhythm within a piece, since the same pattern may well be repeated in successive phrases. This becomes doubly important when the patterns in question stray beyond rhythmic types known to contemporary theory. It is by no means unknown for a seemingly intractable passage — either through notational ambiguity, or perhaps a scribal error — to make sense only after comparison with a different phrase with which it can ultimately be shown to be rhythmically cognate. The hardest *cantigas* to understand rhythmically are those in which successive phrases do not conform to a discernable common pattern.

Envoi

It is undoubtedly confusing to have to be continually aware of two different notational practices, particularly when some basic figures are used in both but with differing import. The most helpful comment that can be offered to the reader, to be borne constantly in mind, is this: that in the notation of the Escorial codices (*T* and *E*), the group ▪ ▪ ▪ represents values totalling three *tempora* (in modern terms, ‘beats’), whilst in *To* the same total duration is represented by ♦ ♦ ♦ . On this equivalence depends much of what follows.

[52] A striking example of this process at work will be found at the very outset of the next section on *Cantiga* 20, where decisions involving which *L* to perfect ultimately allow a larger component — a cell of Mode III — to emerge.

III
THE CASE OF *CANTIGA* 20

A useful starting point for considering dotted rhythms in the *Cantigas de Santa Maria* is the case of *Cantiga* 20; insofar as there has been any previous discussion of the question, it has centred largely on this piece, and more specifically on its outer sections (the refrain and the *vuelta*), since the middle section or *mudanza* — that is, the start of the stanza — is distinct in metrical syllable-count and, by common consent, in musical rhythm.

CANTIGA 20: FIRST APPROACHES

A single melodic phrase, heard twice, constitutes both the refrain and *vuelta* sections of this piece. The phrase may be broken into three segments, carrying 5+5+7 (real) syllables, reflecting the metrical pattern of the text.[1] The first two of these segments display a rhythm notated *LBLBL* (with the last *L* being either plicated or, depending on the source, represented by a binary ligature). If this repeated notational pattern is to be understood in

EXAMPLE 1
Cantiga 20: Refrain and opening of stanza
(Anglés, 1943)

[1] Syllable-counts, here as elsewhere in this volume, refer to real syllables, sidestepping the metrical convention — irrelevant in the context — whereby any syllable following the last textually stressed syllable in the line is discounted.

It is a matter of debate whether a textual edition of *CSM* 20 should be laid out in long lines with internal rhyme, the better to match the musical structure, or (as here — *see* Appendix) in short lines, enhancing the prominence of rhyme-words. Either way, subdivisions of the musical phrase in this piece perfectly match natural breaks in the text. On the general question, *see* Huseby 1983 *bis*.

ternary metre, clearly one *L* must be perfected (not least because the third segment of the phrase also begins with *L* and not *B*).

The response offered by Anglés (1943; *see* Ex. 1) is to perfect the second of the occurrences of *L* in each sub-phrase, giving durations of /2,1/3/1,2/. This interpretation may be seen as cogent, and certainly not objectionable from a notational point of view. It is, however, open to the charge of arbitrariness in the choice of which *L* is to be perfected, with two further consequences: first, whilst not doing outright violence to textual stress, it nevertheless enhances syllables that are relatively unimportant (such as the prepositions *de* in the first phrase and *por* in the following); and second, it brings to prominence notes, in particular B flat and E, that are at odds with the tower of thirds (F, A, C) on which the melody otherwise seems to be built — and this is true whether or not one takes a modal view of this melody as transposed *deuterus*. For these reasons Anglés's transcription appears as possible rather than entirely satisfactory or compelling.

Leaving aside for a moment Huseby's 1983 transcription of *Cantiga* 20, it was not until over half a century had elapsed after Anglés's publication that a cluster of new editions became available. The first to appear was my own transcription which appeared in 2000 (partially reproduced[2] in Ex. 2; the musical palæography is from *E* — Anglés's E_1).

EXAMPLE 2
Cantiga 20: Refrain and opening of stanza
(after Cunningham, 2000)

[2] I have permitted myself the liberty of doubling the note-values of my original publication, not only as an aid to comparison with a majority of other transcriptions, but more particularly to make more transparent the transformations that will subsequently be performed on it.

Focusing once again on the opening *LBLBL*, it will be seen that I have perfected not the second *L* but the first; the same procedure has been applied to the second and third sub-phrases (at a.6 and a.11), such that the rhythmic unity of the whole phrase is maintained. (Let it be noted in passing that this relies on alteration of the *B* at a.13 and b.13 — *i.e.*, the thirteenth figure in each occurrence of the phrase —, and allows the elimination of Anglés's exclamation point by which he draws attention to a figure whose apparent import he wishes to override.) The change brings with it, I believe, a number of benefits. First, it will be seen that non-structural notes (the B flat and E alluded to above) have receded in prominence; second, the unwanted accentuation of some weak syllables has also been ameliorated. More important than either of these observations, however, is that the perfected *L* may now be perceived as belonging to a greater rhythmic unit — as reflected in the barring —, namely, a cell of Mode III-type rhythm, written *LBL* (or *LBB* in the third segment of the phrase) and interpreted with values of /3,1,2/ *tempora*. This way of viewing the notation as meaningful *groups* of figures, or 'rhythmic cells', helps to remove any arbitrariness in the choice of which *L* to perfect, and legitimises the incorporation of an 'extra' beat to make up the nine. I view this solution, then, as an advance on Anglés's, although — in view of what is to follow here — not the final word.

A further group of transcriptions appearing in the early years of the new millennium offers a variety of responses that nevertheless concur in rejecting Anglés's perfection of the second *L* (see Exx. 3, 4, 5). The first of these, from Roberto Pla (Ex. 3), eschews the opportunity to perfect *any* of the *L*s (except, that is, the very last in the whole phrase), effectively interpreting the first two segments of the phrase as being of eight *tempora* (quavers in this transcription) as opposed to Anglés's nine. The remainder of the phrase exhibits a repeated insistence on non-perfection of *L*, whilst at the same time allowing the alteration of *B* (on the syllable '*co-*'). Pla's characterization of the metre of the refrain as 'hypodochmiac tetrameter' may be an accurate description of what he has produced, but in my view does not constitute a justification of it.

Vir-ga de Jes-se, ¡quen te sou - bes-se lo - ar co - mo me-re-ces,
1)
2)

EXAMPLE 3
Cantiga 20: First phrase of refrain
(Pla, 2001)

The other two transcriptions, that of Chris Elmes (Ex. 4) and Pedro López Elum (Ex. 5) have in common that they take the opening *LBLB*, in each of the first two segments of the phrase, in the rhythm /2,1/2,1/ (*i.e.*, as two cells of Mode I-type rhythm), leaving the fifth note of the segment to be perfected — in one way or another (Elmes's insertion of a rest amounts to the same thing) — in order to maintain the ternary metre.

EXAMPLE 4
Cantiga 20: First phrase of refrain
(Elmes, Vol. 1, First edition, 2004)

The chief disadvantage of such a procedure is the violence done to textual stress in words like *soubesse*, *ouvesse* (stressed syllables underscored); it may be that this outcome is what led Elmes to a thorough reconsideration, and in his revised edition (2014) he reaches conclusions similar to my own of 2000. López Elum's transcription offers what is effectively a cell of Mode III (bars 7–8 and 18–19); the idea might have proved more fruitful if it had been applied consistently, in other contexts earlier in the phrase where the opportunity is also present. Moreover, in a rigid adherence to a notational distinction present only in source *E* (*see* Anglés's palæography, Ex. 1), López Elum treats the first phrase differently from the second (compare bar 9 with bars 20–21); such literalism is, regrettably, a feature of this edition.[3]

EXAMPLE 5
Cantiga 20: Refrain and opening of stanza
(López Elum, 2005)

[3] For an extremely critical review of López Elum's transcriptions, *see* Ferreira 2007 *ter*.

It is striking that the available published transcriptions of *Cantiga* 20 discussed above cover all possible permutations of choice as to which component to perfect: in my own edition and in the revised edition of Elmes, the first *L* is perfected; the second *L* is perfected by Anglés; the third (generally written as a plica) is allocated three beats by Elmes (first edition — including the inserted rest) and by López Elum; and no perfection is offered by Pla. These transcriptions thus differ from one another within a very strictly limited availability of options: the temporal values of *B* (*recta*) and *L* (imperfect) are fixed in relation to each other, and the only variables arise from whether, or where, to apply alteration of the *B* and/or perfection of the *L*. The fact that the melody is written overwhelmingly in *simplex* figures (if we may include plicated forms) serves to highlight the tightness of the system.[4]

CANTIGA 20: ANOTHER VIEW[5]

A different approach, characterised by a rather freer view and — at least at first sight — a more intuitive approach to the rhythm, is embodied in a transcription that is provided as a musical example in the 1983 thesis of the Argentinian musicologist Gerardo V. Huseby (*see* Ex. 6 below).[6] Given that the thesis itself deals with the analysis of *cantiga* melodies within the octomodal system of classification, it is not surprising that there is no discussion of the

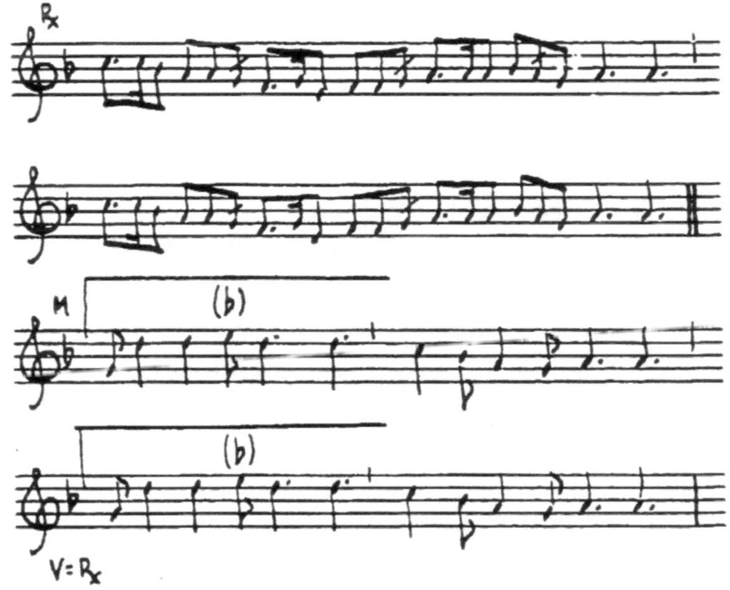

EXAMPLE 6
Cantiga 20: Refrain and *mudanza*
(Huseby, 1983, p. 216, repeated p. 251)

[4] Transcriptions that fail to observe the limits of what is explicable are for that very reason to be rejected. Such is the case with Ribera's 1922 edition, which, in the case of this piece, transcribes the opening ■ ◆ ■ ◆ of *To* as four even quavers, &c., &c.

[5] The content of this subsection necessarily relies on the same material as Ferreira 2014, esp. 49–51.

[6] It should hardly be necessary to point out that Huseby's choice of a different reduction in note-values (■ → ♪ as opposed to ■ → ♩) is *not* relevant here, nor does any supposed implication of *speed* have any bearing whatsoever. What is at issue is the *relative duration* of all notational figures used.

rhythmic aspect of the transcription, and the melody of this piece is presented without text or musical palæography — indeed, in the absence of the latter, and amid a general focus on *melodic* analysis, it would be quite possible for the *rhythmic* significance of Huseby's version to remain unnoticed.[7]

What is different in Huseby's transcription is the introduction of a new variable, one that allows the basic temporal values of the notational components in *some* segments of the melody to be halved with respect to others. The additional halving is not applied haphazardly, however, but rather *selectively*, to affect *whole rhythmic cells*, more specifically those that are written with an apparent Mode III rhythm. In consequence, what previously appeared up to the cadential zone as alternate cells of Mode III and Mode II (as in Ex. 2) now takes the form of alternations with a cell of dotted rhythm[8] as one of the alternants. As will be argued below, admitting this new variable brings with it such advantages that Huseby's version invites adoption.[9] In the meantime, since the graphic aspect of Huseby's presentation and the absence of original notational symbols in it (Ex. 6) do not readily facilitate discussion, it seems necessary to anticipate conclusions by providing a full transcription at this point (*see* facing page), to which reference may be made from now on.[10]

Terminology and Typography

The additional variable embodied in Huseby's transcription is of course a halving; but it is a halving in such specific circumstances that a specific term seems required. I propose, therefore, to adopt the word 'dimidiation' — *selective* dimidiation — to apply to cases of the halving of temporal values in cells notated as (apparently) Mode III but intended, as will be argued, to be read with halved values. As will be emphasized again below, dimidiation is part of the *editorial* process, reversing a mechanism employed in the course of the *notational* process for the encryption of dotted rhythm.

In the full transcription on the facing page, an important typographic convention is established that will characterize the presentation of all pieces edited in this volume. Whereas the basic process of transcription relies on a standard reduction of note-values by a factor of eight (Escorial ▪ → modern ♩), attention is drawn visually to those groups or cells of notes that have been subjected to an additional halving or dimidiation by the use of rhombic noteheads for the notes so affected.

A comparison of the full transcription with that provided in Ex. 2 will allow ready appreciation of the transformation that has been applied, whilst at the same time highlighting the importance of Ex. 2, with its Mode III cells, as a necessary provisional reading.

---

[7] Certainly at the time of preparing my 2000 edition, although I had read Huseby's thesis, his novel approach to the rhythm of this piece had passed me by. I note, too, from around the same time, the view that the notation of this *cantiga* indicates 'o terceiro modo rítmico…misturado com o segundo modo' (Ferreira 2001, p. 202) — a comment that brings us back to Example 2 above.

[8] Or, perhaps, a decorated form of Mode VI (♩. ♪♩ for ♩ ♩ ♩), should we wish so to conceive of it.

[9] In a recent comment, Ferreira (2013, p. 144) speaks of the rhythmic solution 'first proposed by Huseby…and recently adopted by Cunningham'. This perhaps requires some clarification. My 2000 transcription (*see* Ex. 2) agrees with that of Huseby only to the extent of reading the rhythm as 'third rhythmic mode mixed with the second' (Ferreira, *ibid.*; *see again also* n. 7 above).

[10] In spite of a history of discussion of this piece (Huseby, Wulstan, Ferreira), this is (I believe) the first time the complete melody of *Cantiga* 20 and its original notational figures have been presented together, with text, transcribed in this way with dotted rhythms.

CANTIGA 20

DE LOOR DE SANTA MARIA
POR QUANTAS MERCEES NOS FAZ

IN PRAISE OF HOLY MARY
FOR ALL THE MERCIES SHE PERFORMS FOR US

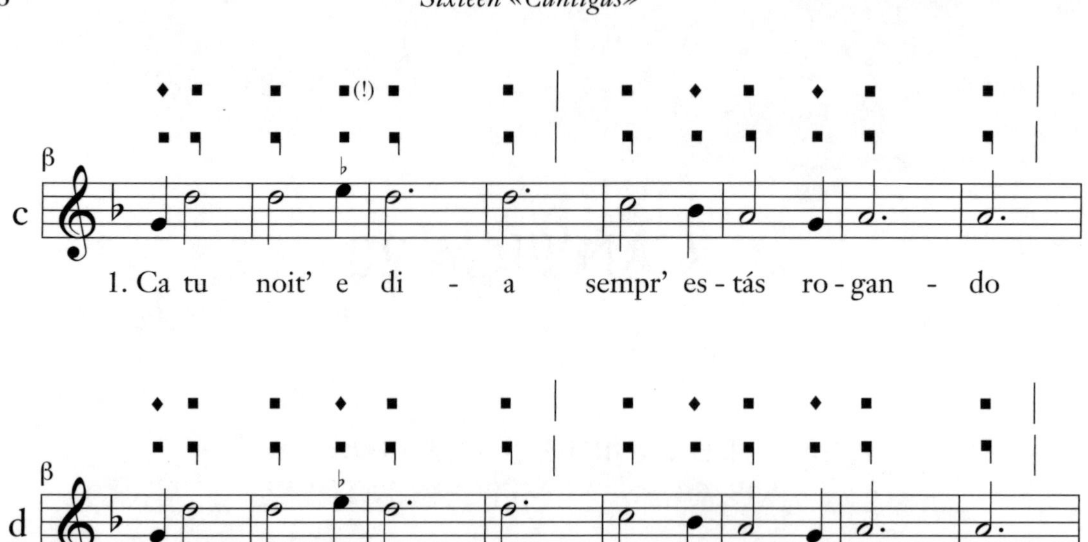
(!)
β
c
1. Ca tu noit' e di - a sempr' es - tás ro - gan - do
β
d
teu Fill', ai Ma - ri - a!, por nós, que (an - dan - do

(!)
α
e
a - qui pe - can - do, e mal o - bran - do

que tu muit' a - vo - rre - ces)

(!)
α
f
non que - ra, quan - do se - ver jul - gan - do,

ca - tar no - ssas san - de - ces.

CSM 20: Musical palæography		
To 20, f. 30r–v Notated: 𝔑-0; I *only*. Flat signature throughout. a.13: Anglés perceives a *tractulus* here (*see* Ex. 1).	*T* 20, f. 32r Notated: 𝔑-0; I, incipit of 𝔑-I; II, incipit of 𝔑-II. Flat signature throughout. Variants: II: e.10: without *tractulus* f.17: with bar 𝔑-II: a.10: ▪▪▪	*E* 20, f. 46v–47r Notated: 𝔑-0; I *only*. Flat signature throughout. Variants with respect to *T*: a.10, b.10, e.10: ▪▪▪ with *tractulus* a.13, b.13, f.13: ▪ b.14, e.14, f.14: ▪▪ f.10: without *tractulus*; f.17: with bar.

HUSEBY AND *CANTIGA* 20

Huseby, as has been observed, offered no discussion of, or justification for, the rhythm of his transcription, and so we shall never know whether his halving of durational values in *some* cells was the product of intuition, or whether some rational process lay behind his decision to transcribe in this way. In particular it would have been interesting to know whether his approach to the notational groups in question viewed them as strings of symbols that simply 'said what they said', to be read by nothing more complex than a 'look-say' process,[11] or whether he saw them as the output of some mechanism of encryption susceptible of further analysis. The search for any deeper understanding must therefore begin with an examination of the views of Wulstan and Ferreira on how the notation of this *cantiga* functions.

WULSTAN AND DOTTED RHYTHM

As already commented on, Wulstan on more than one occasion uses *Cantiga* 20 as his exemplar of dotted or 'bagpipe' rhythm.[12] The absence of a transcription, however, makes any direct reaction to Wulstan's reading of this piece difficult, and any response must be directed at his broader overview of the notation of dotted rhythm in the *CSM* as a whole.[13] The groups ▪ ▪ ▪ and ▪ ▪ ▪ , occurring in *Cantiga* 20 and interpreted in the foregoing transcription as representing dotted rhythm, are included by Wulstan in his general treatment as the sixth and seventh in a list of seven ways in which dotted rhythm may be found notated in the *CSM*.[14] (Since perception of dotted rhythm here depends on the interpretation of these groups, it may be deduced that the solutions offered by Huseby and Wulstan for this piece cannot be fundamentally at odds.[15]) But Wulstan also warns that both groups are ambiguous: the former 'might be confused' with Mode III notation,[16] while the latter is also the way dactylic binary (♩ ♪♪) and 'various other rhythms' may be written.

---

[11] The term 'look-say' is borrowed from a methodology of teaching reading — the reading of English — to primary-school children, made popular in the late 1950s; under this régime, a child was expected to learn the pronunciation of each word as a complete entity, without reference to any separable phonic elements or orthographic processses present in the spelling. In the present context, for 'phonic' and 'orthographic' read 'durational' and 'notational'.

[12] *See again* n. 15 to Section I above, and corresponding main text.

[13] This broad presentation is to be found in Wulstan 1998, esp. pp. 103–6.

[14] *See* Wulstan, *ibid.*; the actual list is given in longhand (*i.e.*, without notational symbols) on p. 106. Illustrative reproductions of small sections of the original mss are provided on pp. 104–5; these are repeated in Wulstan 2001, pp. 305–6, although without discussion.

[15] I have found no point at which Wulstan alludes to Huseby's transcription.

[16] Let it be observed in passing that, if the context allows alteration, ▪ ▪ ▪ may represent Mode III as readily as ▪ ▪ ▪ does.

Wulstan's presentation, thus briefly summarised, provides a helpful platform on which I nevertheless believe it is necessary to build further, in two respects. The first of these concerns a differentiation that is surely necessary in respect of the seven notational groups advanced by Wulstan as representing dotted rhythm. Of these groups, the first five[17] use a rhombic note (presumably to be read as *S*, since Wulstan's exemplification relies on Escorial sources from *CSM* 150 onwards) as the middle (half-beat) note in the group of three; the two groups with which we are dealing here, however, employ a square *punctum* in that position in the Escorial sources. I would argue that there is a substantive difference, demanding a separate explanation, between methods of notating dotted rhythm that employ as the middle note a *semibrevis*, which speaks for itself, and those that employ a *brevis*, which requires to be read with halved temporal value in that context. All this, without the further complication of any reference to Toledo notation, which Wulstan's general treatment of dotted notation appears not to cover.[18] Stepping back from the details of the discussion, one may take the view that Wulstan's assertions (namely, that the groups ┓ ▪ ┓ and ┓ ▪ ▪ are among those that may express dotted rhythm), although we might not dispute them, would still benefit from further inquiry into the underlying workings.

The second point at issue is that Wulstan's presentation appears to drive a wedge between Mode III notation on the one hand and dotted rhythm on the other, warning that one can be 'confused' with the other. A contrary case might, however, be made: that the notational groups in question represent dotted rhythm precisely *because* they are basically notations of Mode III, at least insofar as the relative durations of the three components of both rhythmic groups coincide; this view will be further developed below.

Ferreira and Mode III Compression

For Ferreira, examination of Huseby's rhythmic interpretation of *Cantiga* 20 does not arise from direct consideration of dotted rhythm; rather, Ferreira focuses on the often complex relationship between speed of execution and notational convention, and the possibility of variation in the speed at which different components might be taken, even within the same melody, as implied by and argued from the notation. Whilst the idea is presented as being of broader applicability, three cases are examined in which cells of Mode III are 'compressed' (Ferreira's term) to occupy the same overall duration as the surrounding cells; one of these three pieces, briefly dealt with, is *Cantiga* 20.[19] This approach does not amount to an acknowledgment of dotted rhythm as such — indeed, it may even be possible to contemplate such durational equivalence without any direct dependence on the concept of halving, and without reference to dotted rhythm at all. The approach does, however, provide a mechanism by which (if I may so encapsulate it) the constraint of

[17] These are (i) ▪ ◆ ▪ ; (ii) ▪| ◆ ◆ ; (iii) ▪ ◆ ◆ ; (iv) ┓ ◆ ◆ ; and (v) ┓ ◆ ▪ . For his examples Wulstan relies heavily on *Cantigas* 150 and 367, both fecund in dotted rhythm and ways of representing it, and to a lesser extent on 262 and 384. *See again* Wulstan 1998, p. 106. For comments on *Cantiga* 150, in which Escorial notation employs both 'old' (*i.e.*, *punctum*-based) and 'new' (*i.e.*, *semibrevis*-based) methods of notating dotted rhythm, *see* Section IV below.

[18] I say 'appears', because some of Wulstan's seven groups (*e.g.*, the first of them) might be visually congruent with — though semantically distinct from — groups also possible in Toledo notation.

[19] *See* Ferreira 2014 (*CSM* 20 is dealt with on p. 50, including the transcription of the *incipit* reproduced here as Ex. 7); this analysis follows on from Ferreira's discussion of word-stress in relation to musical accent in this piece in Ferreira 2013, pp. 143–4.

constant breve-duration is removed, to be replaced, in this case, with that of *constant cell-duration*. With this perspective it is possible to approach Huseby's treatment of *Cantiga* 20 with a degree of understanding of how the cells of apparent Mode III rhythm may equate in duration to the adjacent Mode II cells.

A detailed examination of Ferreira's presentation, however, throws up a problem that cannot be brushed aside: his retention of *internal* rhythmic features of cells that have been 'compressed'. In the case of the alternations of cells of Mode III with those of Mode II in this piece, Ferreira is insistent on transcribing them in '6/8 for compressed third mode, and 3/4 for second mode'[20] (*see* Ex. 7) — retaining in the Mode III cells (to use the phraseology of the abstract to his article) a binary subdivision within a ternary framework —, even though, as may be seen from Ex. 7, his application of particular metres to specific bars of the transcription is not made explicit.[21] For the distinction to work we must

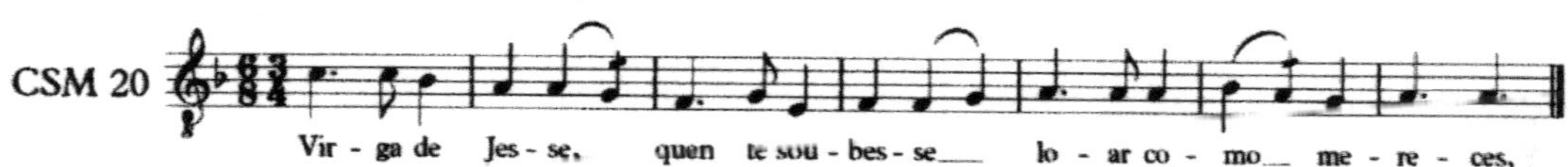

EXAMPLE 7
Cantiga 20: Opening of Refrain
(Ferreira, 2014, p. 50)

presuppose a secondary accent on the middle note of the dotted group. A first difficulty with this is that any such musical accent, in the vast majority of cases, is not matched by any textual stress.[22] Second, I have serious doubts about whether the contrast between 6/8 and 3/4 could be sustained in performance; there are simply not enough notes 'struck' in the supposedly 6/8 bars to define a compound duple rhythm sufficiently clearly.[23] It seems we are being asked to hemiolicate the unhemiolicable. Third, attention may be drawn to the final bar of Ex. 7, which halves note-values in relation to Huseby's version; this may be yet more 'compression', but although it retains a binary internal subdivision it is surely *not* a compression of Mode III in any recognizable sense. And fourth, if the perceived need to retain a secondary accent at the mid-point of a compressed Mode III cell derives from a conviction that Mode III itself necessarily had an accent at this point, then the matter is surely debatable; even supposing that such an accent could be justified from theoretical sources — surely a doubtful proposition —, it might still be asked why, if theory is not binding on the interpretation of *Cantiga* notation in other respects, it should hold sway in this.

[20] Ferreira 2014, p. 50.

[21] A question that might be raised is whether keeping such Mode III features was part of Huseby's intention; for my own part, I do not find any alternation of metres suggested in his transcription (*see again* Ex. 6).

[22] Here and in what follows I shall speak of musical *accent* and textual *stress*. General questions concerning the relationship between the two will be further discussed below, as will more particular aspects of how they relate in *Cantiga* 20 as transcribed here.

[23] The problem is exacerbated by the fact that, in two of the three cases occurring in the phrase (the first and third, bars 1 and 5 of Ex. 7), the middle (half-) note repeats the pitch of the one before, a fact that makes it all the more difficult to see this note as the start of a new rhythmic subgroup.

Understanding the Mechanism

There is in any case a different way of engaging with the question of notating dotted rhythm that may help to give an understanding of the basic mechanisms at work whilst avoiding any question of medial accentuation. It arises from inverting the order in which rhythm and notation are seen to occur — that is, the idea that 'the notation determines the rhythm' is replaced by that of 'the rhythm provokes a notation'.[24] If we put ourselves in the position of a thirteenth-century notator who has a need to commit to parchment a rhythm ♩. ♪♩ using the resources available to him, how is he to do it? He needs notes with relative duration 1½, ½, 1. He might most obviously use ▪ ♦ ▪ (Wulstan's fifth way dotted rhythm can be notated, one he describes as 'pellucid'); or perhaps ▪| ♦ ▪ or even ▪♦ ♦ ▪ (even if neither of these, according to Wulstan's list, seems to occur in practice); but all of these, and others we might invent, rely on the semibreve — the isolated semibreve —, a figure that (as has been repeatedly observed) was simply not available in the early period of the compilation of the *Cantigas*: in the Escorial sources (*T*, *E*) it does not make its appearance until *Cantiga* 150, while in the Toledo source (*To*) the rhomb-shaped note is already in use as the shorter of the two basic notes, and the shortest duration available with a value of one *tempus*. The notator does, however, have another option, provided his focus is on the *relative duration* rather than the *absolute*, for 1½,½,1 stand in the same relationship as 3,1,2, which is none other than the set of values present in a cell of Mode III. By doubling the note lengths, then, the ratios can be preserved; all that is necessary for the melody to flow properly is to reverse the process applied by the notator: if in order to preserve ratios the notes were written with double time-lengths, they must be read halved. In doing so, the performer's response will also be conditioned by the basic rhythmic pulse of the piece, and so the principle of *constant cell-duration* would seem to have a role to play here too. In sum, the process may be reduced to a simple formula: 'write double, read halved'; it follows from this that if the doubling of time-values is part of the process of *encoding*, then *decoding* requires halving. 'Dimidiation' is an essential component of the *editorial* process.

By way of conclusion three views of how the notation works in this context may be summarized. First, in what may be termed a 'look-say' method, the notation is regarded as saying what it says — a dotted rhythm —, with no mention of Mode III or of halving of values. In their different ways, Huseby and Wulstan represent this strand of interpretation. Second, Ferreira, whilst carefully avoiding direct reference to dotted rhythm, proposes that the duration of a Mode III cell may be 'compressed' to match that of surrounding components. The concept is helpful, and of wider applicability than the present discussion; the principal difficulty arises from the perceived persistence of rhythmic characteristics proper to Mode III; one is left with an abiding impression that Ferreira is answering questions other than those provoked by the possible presence of dotted rhythms. Finally the question may be brought into focus as a response to a particular notational need; this view rests on the conviction that the rhythm was there before it came to be notated, and that some level of tolerance towards the stretching of notational resources must be exercised so that the rhythm may again be extracted.

[24] This argument is of course open to the charge that it presupposes that the rhythm to be notated was dotted in the first place. Whilst this is a difficulty in the case of *Cantiga* 20, the reader is asked to suspend judgment until the next Section below; there, cases of the undeniable equivalence between a cell of Mode VI in one source and a cell of [compressed] Mode III in another will be analysed, making any expectation of medial accent in the latter unwarranted.

CANTIGA 20: PHRASE SYMMETRY

A striking feature of the transcription offered above is that the dimidiation of the Mode III cells has brought about an equalizing of musical phrase lengths throughout the whole piece.[25] Indeed, with all phrases exhibiting eight bars, and mid-phrase articulation in full alignment throughout, the piece now looks very foursquare in overall structure. It was in no way an *aim* to bring about such symmetry by halving time-values in the rhythmic cells concerned, but as an *effect* the equalization of phrase-lengths might be seen as bringing its own contributory measure of justification to the procedure.

When seen from the point of view of the metre of the text, this musical phrase-symmetry is all the more remarkable, for while the outer sections (refrain and *vuelta*) carry seventeen (real) syllables per musical phrase, this figure is reduced to a mere twelve in the middle section (*mudanza*). The mechanism whereby this imbalance is overcome depends entirely on the availability of dotted rhythms, which provide the means for three syllables to be accommodated in certain cells in the phrases with the greater number. A comparison

Lines 1–3 (Phrase α)

Vir- ga de	Je-sse	quen te sou-	be-sse	lo- ar co-	mo me-	re-	ces

Lines 7–8 (Phrase β)

Ca tu	noit' e	di-	a	sempr' es-	tás ro-	gan-	do

EXAMPLE 8

Cantiga 20: Comparison of musical phrases showing accommodation of additional syllables in Phrase α whilst maintaining constant phrase length

of how the two musical phrases carry such a differing number of syllables may be apprecia-ted from Ex. 8 (*see* above), in which the vertical comparison of progressive rhythmic cells (bars in the transcription) shows the way in which the dotted rhythms 'mop up' extra syllables. The greatest discrepancy between the two phrases occurs in their respective third bars, in which the α-phrase bears three syllables and the β-phrase only one. Viewed in this way, dotted rhythms may be seen as an essential tool in providing musical symmetry in a case in which textual metre presents a considerable challenge.

Example 8 also shows in diagrammatic form how, in the two musical phrases that comprise this *cantiga*, the rhythmic patterns (as they turn out in this transcription) con-verge, such that for the last 40% of the way they are identical — a perhaps unexpected conferring of rhythmic coherence on the piece as a whole.

A second important feature of the dotted-rhythm transcription of *Cantiga* 20 is the rela-tionship between musical accent and textual stress, a slippery topic that first requires some general words to explore the limits of how it may be approached.

[25] The eight bar phrase, as already observed, is *not* a feature of the transcription offered by Ferreira (*see again* Ex. 7), who 'compresses' the last two cells of the α-phrase.

A Brief Excursus on Accentuation

Seen in general terms, musical accentuation of a textual syllable is the imparting to it of greater prominence.[26] This happens most obviously when a syllable coincides with the first note in a rhythm-group; in modern terms this could be termed a 'downbeat' accent, or a 'first in the bar' accent. Whilst this might be considered the most obvious form of accentuation (being, in measured music, regular and predictable), other forms of emphasis also occur. In particular a note that is higher than the surrounding notes gives prominence (tonic accent) to the syllable it bears, as does a note that is longer than its neighbours (agogic accent). The distribution of the various types of accentuation throughout a melody may sometimes mean that surprisingly few syllables are disadvantaged; a rhythmic pattern such as Mode II, for example, might be viewed as a perfect vehicle for irregularly stressed texts, since every note is either a downbeat or long.

From a textual perspective, the most fundamental point to be borne in mind is that versification in Medieval Galician works by syllable-count and not by any regular pattern of stressed and unstressed syllables. Poetic convention thus allows variability in the position of stressed syllables from line to line (with the exception of the last stressed syllable in the line — generally a rhyming syllable — whose position is always fixed) and from stanza to stanza. As a result, two lines of verse sung to the same musical phrase will frequently display differing textual stress-patterns. Given these facts, it is simply not feasible to demand that textual stress and musical accent display a perfect correspondence.[27]

Categorical statements about where textual stress is 'expected' are by no means straightforward to devise. On the one hand there is a clear expectation that nouns, verbs and adjectives will have one syllable that is prominent; conversely articles, conjunctions and (monosyllabic) prepositions are words that are not stressed. But then in the middle there is an ill-defined group of word-types, including some kinds of pronouns, adverbs of degree and other common (monosyllabic) adverbs, polysyllabic prepositions and functional particles such as *end(e)*. The best way to regard these, perhaps, is as words that do not *require* enhancement by musical accentuation, but when they receive it, it is 'not irksome'.

The difficulty in pinning down just which syllables naturally bear a stress is matched by the difficulty in reaching a judgment over whether a musical accent is well placed. It is sometimes possible to say that a syllable is 'wrongly' accented, but in general verdicts tend to be less absolute, for a variety of reasons. It is possible, for example, to say that the incorrect accentuation of an unstressed syllable is more 'grievous' than the

[26] On the use of the terms 'accent' and 'stress' the reader is referred to n. 22 above. The question of musical accentuation of text is briefly discussed in Wulstan 2000, pp. 56–8, in ch. 1 and ch. 2 of Wulstan 2001, and there are comments on specific pieces in Wulstan 1998, pp. 97–100. *See also* the general treatment of text and music in Campbell 2011, esp. p. 91 and p. 120.

[27] Such a requirement is sometimes forced on Iberian and adjacent Romance languages, most typically by commentators whose native language is of Germanic stock, and when the correspondence is found wanting, used as an excuse to impose a non-metrical interpretation on the musical notation — on the pretext that a metrical rendering 'violates' textual stress whereas a more declamatory performance 'respects' it. Such an approach, which in the case of the *Cantigas* generally goes hand-in-hand with a denial of any mensural component in the notation, represents, in the present writer's view, a fundamental misunderstanding of the fluid patterns of textual stress and of the subtle interplay between it and musical accent. For a contrary though influential view *see* van der Werf (1987) — who, it must be observed, only ever commentated on one *cantiga* (*CSM* 340, which is in any case an entirely uncharacteristic piece and a contrafact).

absence of a musical accent where the text is stressed; and that a missed accentuation of a stressed monosyllable is less 'grievous' than the incorrect accentuation of a disyllable. Certain common expressions in the *Cantigas* appear to float free of any expectation of regular or consistent accentuation;[28] and strange things can happen — as to this day in connected speech — when two stressed syllables come together.

Suffice it to say, then, that 'correct musical accentuation of a textually stressed syllable' is a matter of spectrum, not of right or wrong. And in comparing two versions of a transcription, it may not be possible to say that one is 'wrong' as regards accentuation of the text, but it *may* be possible to say that the other is *better*. Finally, the whole question may be inverted, putting the spotlight on how good the correspondence is between notes inherently unaccented and syllables that are unstressed; this approach is particularly instructive in relation to the middle note in dotted groups, and frequent recourse will be had to this approach in what follows.

MUSICAL ACCENT AND TEXTUAL STRESS IN *CANTIGA* 20

Ferreira has shown how, in the quest for a solution to what rhythm is represented by the notation, the level of musical support for textual stress has, from Anglés to Huseby, been progressively improved.[29] The analysis may now be pressed further by focusing on the short notes (quavers in the transcription) in the middle of the dotted groups, which, as discussed above, it will here be insisted are musically unaccented.

For the notated rhythm to be an adequate vehicle for the stress-patterns of the text, the syllables carried by these short notes (a.2, a.7, a.12 in the first phrase, *etc.*) would need to be in large degree unstressed; indeed, an impression may be created in the opening phrase that the dotted rhythms and the patterns of textual stress go hand-in-glove, given the weak syllable *-ga* of *Virga* and the weak pronoun *te*, both occurring on the unaccented short note. A broader survey of the whole text shows prepositions, articles, weak pronouns, conjunctions, and unstressed syllables in longer words occupying these positions in a majority of cases — perhaps 65% of the time.[30] This does not mean, however, that all remaining cases amount to gross musical misaccentuation of the text. Of cases of textually stressed syllables that fall on the short note (*i.e.*, omission of an expected stress) four are monosyllables, which may perhaps be an extenuating factor;[31] two, curiously, are infinitives;[32] If these cases are treated with leniency, there remain remarkably few clear cases of words that must be viewed as misaccented — indeed, they occur at the rate of one per stanza: *quera* (*l.* 14), *sabores* (*l.* 23), *demo* (*l.* 36) and *santus* (*l.* 43), and even here, it would not be possible to rectify the case of of *sabores* even by accenting the short note of the dotted

[28] On this question *see* Wulstan 2000, p. 58.

[29] *See* Ferreira 2001, pp. 201–2 (in Portuguese), repeated in essence (in English) in Ferreira 2013, p. 144, and referred to in passing in Ferreira 2014, p. 50.

[30] These statistics are of necessity approximate, as will be clear from the foregoing Excursus. By way of illustration of the difficulties, it might be asked just how stressed is a supposedly strong pronoun, when it is superfluous both to sense and syntax (*cf.* '*tu*' in both *l.* 13 and *l.* 24).

[31] These are *sén* (*l.* 4 of the refrain), *mal* (*l.* 12 of Stanza I), *vai* and *vas* (Stanza II, *ll.* 23, 26). As was suggested in the Excursus, the 'offence' (if such it be) is not as 'grave' as would be the 'wrong' accentuation of a disyllable.

[32] Namely *loar* (*l.* 3 of the refrain) and *catar* (*l.* 16 of Stanza I); alongside them we might also include the subjunctive form *sever* (*l.* 15). I have an impression (but it is a question that would merit further research) that musically unaccented infinitive endings are not infrequent.

group.[33] All this leaves us with only one possible conclusion: that although the match is not 100% perfect, a correspondence between textual stress and musical accent is achieved to a remarkably high degree in these dotted groups. In this respect the transcription is more successful with dimidiation of the Mode III cells than without.

CANTIGA 20: A NOTATIONAL BLIP

Attention must be drawn to the notation of *To* at e.3, where a rhomb is found instead of the expected *punctum*. Before jumping to conclusions about the presence of alteration in Toledo notation, other possible explanations must be explored. One such would be that we are dealing with a case of 'early exit from dimidiation' — a phenomenon that will be examined more closely later on —, and that the rhomb is written to represent a duration of 1*t* in anticipation of the following figure at e.4, also a rhomb (undimidiated) and also representing 1*t*. But a much more likely explanation in the present case is that it is merely an instance of scribal carelessness, to be taken in the context of similar manifestations at c.4 and f.1. In the presence of competing explanations, this instance provides too weak a basis on which to build a case for alteration.

CANTIGA 20: SOME FINAL CONSIDERATIONS

It is well to point out that the musical palæography of this *cantiga* offers no clue, no prompt to the transcriber, that certain rhythmic cells are to be taken at double the speed of what is written. Given that this is so, there are three possible responses to the transcription given above, if this piece is to be considered in isolation: (i) that the transcription is insufficiently founded and cannot be justified; (ii) that the 'dimidiation' of Mode III cells (my term), or 'compression' (Ferreira's term), though plausible, is based only on intuition, as may have been Huseby's version; or (iii) that the advantages of the transcription, in terms of both the musical enhancement of textual stress and the structural regularisation of the piece, as outlined above, weigh sufficiently in favour of the dotted rhythms proposed. There might the matter rest if this were the only *cantiga* susceptible of such treatment. What is missing is some more concrete demonstration that six *tempora* must be executed as three in certain cells. It is perhaps unfortunate, then, that *Cantiga* 20 has attracted relatively wide attention when there are, as I believe, at least four other pieces whose musical palæography, when all sources are brought together, goes much further towards showing that 'dimidiation' was part-and-parcel of the expected response to what the notator had written as cells of Mode III. Whilst the notation of one of these four pieces — *Cantiga* 87 — is so remarkable (and so fraught) that it may with benefit be held over until the very end, I propose to dedicate the next section to the remaining three. Thereafter, the fruits of what emerges may be applied to more pieces — as well as (if the reader will allow retrospection) to *Cantiga* 20.

---

[33] Among the detail that lies behind this abbreviated analysis is the curious fact that Stanza I contains a rather high number of marginal cases: in addition to *quera*, *sever* and *catar* already mentioned there occur *aqui* (*l.* 11), a common adverb — how strong is the expectation of stress on its second syllable? — and *mal* (*l.* 12), another monosyllable, probably to be read as a noun though perhaps as an adverb. Whether or not this constitutes a case for establishing a stylistic distinction between Stanza I and the rest of the text is a question that falls beyond the scope of this study. Questions of stress in the hypermetric *l.* 44 are not dealt with here; for a performing solution to the difficulties posed by the extra syllable, *see* the notes to the edition in the Appendix.

IV
THREE 'ROSETTA' PIECES

In this section I propose to examine three *cantigas* in which notational clarity in one codex allows clearer interpretation of a particular rhythmic cell, phrase or passage in another source.[1] To be more specific, these are cases in which a particular rhythmic cell has an unequivocal duration of three *tempora* in one source, whilst apparently occupying six *tempora* — a cell of Mode III — elsewhere. Of the three pieces in question, *Cantiga* 162 will be taken first, followed by nos. 38 and 97.

CANTIGA 162

This *cantiga* appears in the Appendix to *To*, yet its inclusion in the expanded repertoire of the Escorial codices *T* and *E* did not occur until compilation of the second cental was well advanced; it is tempting to think that the implied hesitancy in its incorporation may have had to do with some perplexity at the way it is notated. Anglés's 1943 transcription was subject to revision in his 1958 volume; more recently the notation and rhythm of *CSM* 162 has been the object of a detailed study by Ferreira, who concludes that notational differences between the sources represent rhythmic divergence.[2]

CANTIGA 162: PRELIMINARY READINGS

Much depends on what view is taken of the opening 𝆷 𝆸 𝆸 𝆷 and later repetitions of the same pattern. Anglés, in his 1943 transcription, assigns temporal values of /2,1,1,2/, that is, without perfection or alteration; this relies, however, on a corroborative but incorrect reading of the palaeography of *To*, which Anglés here gives as 𝆸 𝆹 𝆹 𝆸 .[3] When a correct reading of *To*— 𝆸 𝆹 𝆸 𝆷 — is taken into account, the results are far-reaching, for the only feasible understanding of this string in *To* is as a cell of Mode III followed by a note of 3*t*, that is with values of /3,1,2/3/.[4] The resultant rhythm is compatible with the notation of the Escorial codices where *LBBL* appears, provided that both perfection and alteration are

[1] The analogy with the Rosetta Stone is not intended to be watertight. Indeed, as will be seen, there are cases where the elucidation of rhythm derives not from confronting two sources, but from comparing two or more occurrences of the same phrase in a single source.

[2] *See* Ferreira 2010, to be discussed below. The opening of this subsection necessarily echoes the exposition of basic data on which both the present analysis and that of Ferreira rely.

[3] The incorrect reading of *To* cannot in this instance be traced to the pseudo-facsimile of Ribera (1922); it appears, rather, to originate with Anglés himself, possibly as a back-formation expressing a particular supposed meaning of *T* (or, in this case, *E*). The same untenable reading of *To* also abets Wulstan's transcription in choriambic rhythm — repetitions of /2,1,1,2/ — of the outer sections of this piece; *see* Wulstan 2000, p. 52 and ex. 14, p. 52, enlarged in Wulstan 2001, ex. 2.9, p. 56, with further comments on pp. 76–7 and p. 310. *See also* Wulstan 2009, p. 212, where the choriambic view persists. The presence of third-mode cells, and hence of dotted rhythms, is, for Wulstan, thus limited to the longer chains in the middle section or *mudanza* of the melody; *see also* n. 8 below.

[4] Phrases b and g in *To* begin with a notational variant 𝆷 𝆹 𝆸 𝆷 whose first component makes even more explicit the third-mode pattern. For a brief comment on the Mode-III character of the notation of the version found in *To*, *see* Ferreira 1993, p. 589, n. 51.

applied. So it is that at first sight, taking an overview based on all sources, this *cantiga* appears to be broadly characterised by cells of Mode III rhythm alternating with isolated perfect longs, and longer chains of third-mode cells in the middle section. Such may be appreciated from the conservative reading provided in Example 9.[5]

Not all, however, is straightforward. We need look no further than the second half of the first phrase (*see* a.5-6-7 in Ex. 9) to find a context in which, in the understanding offered by Ferreira, a cell of Mode III occurs in the Escorial sources, implying /3,1,2/ — a total of six *tempora* —, whilst *To* gives ♦ ♦ ♦ (a cell of Mode VI if we wish to see it in such terms), amounting to a mere 3*t*.[6] When the view is widened to take in the penultimate

EXAMPLE 9
Conservative reading of *Cantiga* 162
barred to show occurrences of cells of third-mode rhythm.

[5] In his 1958 revisions, Anglés unusually offers this piece in two possible new readings, of which the first corresponds broadly to the interpretation just described. *See* Anglés 1958, vol. II, no. 162*a* on p. 25 of the musical section. Whether this reading was influenced by a greater reliance on *To* is not clear, since the only palæography supplied is that of *E*. The reading given as no. 162*b* persists without perfection or alteration in the opening string and its repetitions.

[6] The durational non-correspondence is encapsulated diagrammatically in Ferreira 2000 *ter*, ex. 9.7, p. 154.

rhythmic cell of every phrase, the non-correspondence is endemic, both within individual sources, between sources, and most especially between the two notational codes (*i.e.*, between *To* on the one hand, and the Escorial sources on the other). As will be appreciated from Example 9, there is disagreement between sources as to note length in the penultimate cell of almost every phrase. (It must be borne in mind that the figure ▪̩ , in *To*, is ambiguous: in the sequence ▪̩ ♦ ♦ it must be read as a plication of ♦, and so = 1*t*; in the sequence ▪̩ ♦ ▪ , however, it must be interpreted as a plication of ▪ or ▪̩ , and so of duration 3*t* in the context.) The picture becomes even more complex when we import further variant readings from source *E* (*see* the boxed panel after the main transcription), where the presence of ▪▪̩ at b.5 and h.5 has the effect of adding a third-mode cell not present in *T*. The divergence between the sources has led Ferreira to speak of real rhythmic variants as part of a process of evolution, beginning with *To* and ending with the version found in *E*. What is more, variability in phrase length occurs within individual sources, such that the various phrases, as presented in *T*, display lengths varying (according to Ferreira's computations) within the range of 15–18–21 *tempora* per phrase.[7]

Thus do things stand. Is there another way?

Cantiga 162: Another View

Let us return to the penultimate bar in the first phrase of Ex. 9. Here, as already noted, *T* has ▪̩ ▪ ▪ , which (with perfection of the ▪̩ and alteration of the second ▪) gives six *tempora*, whilst *To* gives ♦ ♦ ♦ , totalling three *tempora*. Can these be reconciled? Or, to rephrase the question: When and how can 6*t* = 3*t*? Answer: when the former is *dimidiated*. In other words, the *dimidiation* of time-values in a third-mode cell provides a ready means of reconciling the overall duration of this cell in the two sources. This leads to the conviction that, instead of two substantively different rhythmic variants, one double the duration of the other, we are dealing with essentially the same rhythmic component; the only difference is that it acquires a slightly more 'decorated' (in this case, dotted) form in one case than in the other (that is, ♩. ♪♩ as against ♩♩♩). This, then, is our 'Rosetta moment': the reading of *To* has been applied to a segment of *T* in a way that elucidates the 'meaning' (that is, the duration of the components of a rhythmic cell) of the latter.

Following the logic of the situation, the application of dimidiation must now be extended not only to all those cells showing variation (that is, the penultimate rhythmic cell of each phrase), but also to other cells displaying apparent Mode III notation. This latter category includes both the first cell of each phrase (which now, therefore, contracts to a duration of 3*t*), and the longer, triple chains of third-mode cells in phrases d and f.[8] And so it has been done in the final full transcription (below). As regards the penultimate rhythmic cells (the second-last bars, in the transcription) of each phrase, what emerges is an apparently free variation between the dotted (after dimidiation) and undotted variants of the various phrases, but with no variation in the overall duration of that cell, either

[7] These data are taken from Ferreira's detailed discussion of this piece (2010; the tabulation of varied phrase-lengths is given on p. 293).

[8] Wulstan, in his transcription of this piece, also sees dotted rhythms — 'Bagpipe rhythm', in his terminology — in these two phrases, although confining it to only *two* cells in each (b.1–6 and f.1–6); *see again* Wulstan (2001), p. 56, and note 3 above.

between sources or between different phrases within the same source. We may speculate on whether this reflects fluidity in performance practice, with an otherwise undecorated tribrachic segment being rendered as a dotted variant introduced sporadically and perhaps spontaneously by the performer.

More remarkable, perhaps, is that the dimidiation applied in the middle section (phrases d and f) has brought about a reduction in overall length of the phrases in question, such that *all* phrases of the melody are now of equal length. This was in no way a preconceived aim, but it is certainly an outcome which allows symmetry of structure to be perceived in the piece as a whole.[9]

This leads on to consideration once again of the important rôle of tri-membered cells (whether expressed as ♩ ♩ ♩ or as ♩. ♪♩) in contexts where the textual syllable-count varies between lines. If we take the present case, we are dealing with stanzas in whose *mudanza* or middle section, lines containing eight (real) syllables alternate with lines of ten syllables:

c.	Ca en onrá-las dereit' é	(8 syllables)
d.	e en lles avermos gran devoçón,	(10 syllables)
e.	non ja por elas, a la fe,	(8 syllables)
f.	mas pola figura da en que son…	(10 syllables)

The presence of an additional tri-membered cell in phrases d and f, in comparison to other phrases of the melody, allows the extra syllables to be 'mopped up' whilst averting the need to extend musical phrase-length.[10] This 'syllable-absorption capacity', already mentioned in relation to *Cantiga* 20, appears to be an important functional aspect of the introduction of dotted rhythmic cells in particular, and will be noticed in several pieces in this collection.

Cantiga 162: Further Considerations

Whilst the main outlines of the rationale behind the transcription are established, there remain three further aspects of the notation that require comment.

First, there are two occurrences in *To* of rhythmic cells notated ■ ♦ ♦ rather than the expected ■ ♦ ■ or ■ ♦ ■ ; these are the first group in phrase c (c.1–3) and the penultimate in phrase f (f.7–9). What are we to make of the second ♦? Ferreira, commenting on the latter case, proposes that it can hardly be understood other than as representing

[9] In computational terms, what Ferreira has seen as a variability of phrase length which in *T* ranges from 15 to 18 to 21 *tempora* (*see* note 7 above) is commuted by the procedures here adopted to a standard phrase length of 12 *tempora*.

[10] Behind these observations there lurks a problem of inconsistency of metrical structure in *Cantiga* 162. Whilst the stanza that is underlaid to the melody in all sources has a last line of eight syllables (phrase h), this is the case only for the first two stanzas; the remaining six stanzas have ten syllables in this line. On this subject *see* Parkinson 2010, pp. 322–24. For Ferreira (2010, pp. 293–4), the variability of musical phrase-lengths may in part be a response to the need to accommodate the longer line in later stanzas; whilst I do not share this view, the stanzas with the long line remain a problem, especially for the performer. No solution seems available without some radical editorial intervention — perhaps involving the break-up of the ligature at h.4? Into a dotted rhythm? This proposed solution is taken up again in the 'Metrical Note' to the textual edition (*see* Appendix).

CANTIGA 162

(*To* App. VI)

COMO SANTA MARIA FEZ QUE A SUA OMAGEN
QUE MUDARAN DUN ALTAR A OUTRO
QUE SE TORNASS' A SEU LOGAR
ONDE A TOLLERAN

HOW HOLY MARY GOT HER STATUE
WHICH THEY HAD MOVED FROM ONE ALTAR TO ANOTHER
TO RETURN TO THE PLACE
THEY HAD TAKEN IT FROM

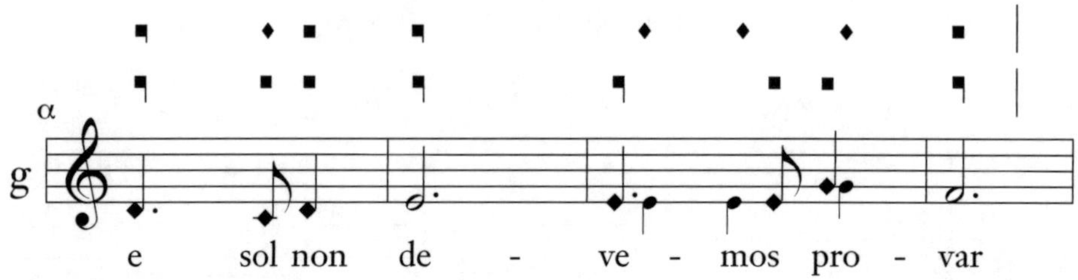

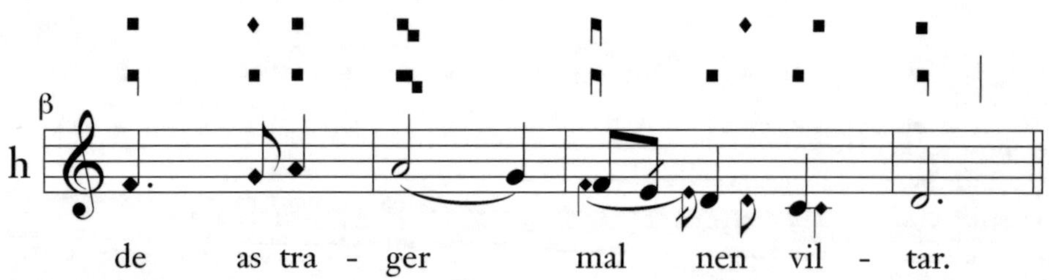

CSM 162: Musical palæography

To App. VI, f. 152r	*T* 162, f. 217v	*E* 162, f. 156r–v
Notated: ℜ-0; I *only*.	Notated: ℜ-0; I, *incipit* of ℜ-I.	Notated: ℜ-0; I, ℜ-I.
	The brief repeated section (five notes) yields no notational variants.	*Notational variance from T:* a.8, c.8, d.8, e.8: *tractulus* rather than bar b.5, h.5: (at b.5 in ℜ-I) d.3, f.9: *Further variants in* ℜ-I: a.5: with *tractulus* (!) b.4:

two *tempora*, and so taken as a case of alteration.[11] On the one hand, this appears to swim against the general understanding of the notation of *To* as being innocent of alteration;[12] indeed, the explicitness with which *To* notates the duration of third component in a Mode III group is on occasion useful in pointing up instances of alteration in *T* or *E*. On the other hand, it must be recalled that this *cantiga* is a very late inclusion in Codex *To* — one of the very last pieces, indeed —, and its notation may perhaps bear traces of transitional features that anticipate Escorial practice which was even at that moment in the very process of being adopted.[13] The question of alteration in *To* thus takes us into difficult waters. But there is another possible explanation. It would be comfortable to think that, where cases of dimidiation of an apparently third-mode cell are concerned, the three notational components would be ring-fenced to ensure their treatment as an indivisible group; but the third component, though it 'ought' to be notated as double its performed duration, corresponds in reality to a length that can also be notated in 'real time'; in other words, there is no reason why the notator cannot abandon this doubling of temporal values after only two notes. This is untidy, if it occurs; but the piece will not be the only *cantiga* in which there may be a suspicion that 'early exit from dimidiation' underlies an apparent notational anomaly. If this is what is at work here, then the second ♦ in the ▪ ♦ ♦ groups identified above differs from the note before it *not* because the second ♦ is subject to alteration, but because the first ♦ is subject to dimidiation.

Second, much has already been said about the ambiguity of the figure ╕ in *To*, whose duration is dependent on the context, and in the present piece is sometimes 1*t* (*i.e.*, a *plica brevis*), sometimes 3*t* (*i.e.*, a perfected *plica longa*). If we accept the view that *To* is the primitive notated version, and *T* (and *E*) in some sense 'translations' into a more 'modern' notational code, that process of translation must have involved decisions over whether *To*'s ╕ should emerge in *T* and *E* as *B* or *L* (*i.e.*, as ╕ or as ▪╕). Can we rely on the process of re-notation always to produce the correct result? Or are we faced with cases of the phenomenon already described in Section II as 'plica confusion' — 'scribal inertia' in Ferreira's terminology —, leaving the ╕ as ╕ even though that might represent a duration not originally intended?[14] If so, then there are, in *T* (and *E*), cases of ╕ that should be ▪╕. Indeed, there are cases (b.5, h.5) where *E* has ▪╕ against *T*'s ╕, and we must suspect that *E*'s reading is correct. There is, of course, no way of proving that this is the case; but we are left with a suspicion that, in those locations where *To* has third-mode notation beginning with a plica (╕ ♦ ▪), and *T* has *BBB* of which the first is plicated, then the notation of *T* may be awry; that the cell might more carefully have been notated as *LBB* (with implications, moreover, of alteration); and that the two versions should perhaps have been identical in their rhythm. The locations in question are c.5-6-7, d.5-6-7, e.5-6-7 and h.5-6-7.[15]

---

[11] *See* Ferreira (2010), p. 293 and Ex. 7.

[12] *See* Section II above.

[13] This argument of course relies on an understanding of *To* as predating the Escorial codices.

[14] *See again* Ferreira 2000, pp. 13–14; *see again also* p. 15 above.

[15] The explanation given here for the 'plica confusion' relies on acceptance of the chronological priority of *To* over *T* and *E*. But more: the confusion in *T* surely provides an important corroborative argument for that precedence. If *To* came first, the plica confusion in *T* is explainable; if on the contrary *T* came first, it is difficult to accept that a faulty aspect of its notation could suddenly be put right by translation into a less specific code such as that found in *To*.

Third, the rhythmic variants provided by the various sources suggest a degree of free variability in the execution of tri-membered cells, rendered now as ♩♩♩, now as ♩. ♪♩. Whilst the Escorial sources are able to provide specific notational strings to cover these variants, Toledo notation is in general more reliant on context to provide durational information; one wonders, therefore, whether the apparently undotted string ♦ ♦ ♦ may not in fact also imply dotted rhythm when such rhythm is present in a given piece — a sort of 'approximative' notational usage where the context allows nuancing. This possibility is raised now in passing, but will acquire greater feasibility in some pieces yet to be discussed.

CANTIGA 162: CONCLUSIONS

The three sources for this *cantiga* provide a complex picture of disagreement in certain segments which sometimes appear as cells notated as Mode III, with a written duration of six *tempora*, whilst other occurrences comprise three even notes totalling three *tempora*. The discrepancy occurs not only between sources, but can also be seen between repetitions of the same phrase within the same source. The solution invoked here for the resolution of this conflict sees all occurrences of the cells in question as occupying three *tempora*, requiring those notated as cells of Mode III to undergo editorial dimidiation. The clearly ternary nature of the cells notated as three even notes is taken as implying that no binary subdivision can subsist in the cells notated as Mode III once they have been halved in duration. What emerges is a variation between simple ternary and dotted ternary rhythmic segments.

A BRIEF EXCURSUS ON BINARY SUBDIVISION

An important consideration in relation to the internal binary structure of third-mode cells, and the possibility that such binary subdivision subsists even when the cell is dimidiated or 'compressed', arose in relation to the analysis of *Cantiga* 20 offered by Ferreira. The additional information provided by the notation of *Cantiga* 162 renders any such subdivision unlikely if not impossible, since in this case the dotted rhythm emerging from the halved durations appears in free alternation with a rhythm notated ♦ ♦ ♦ in *To*, clearly representing a simple triple structure (call it a tribrach, call it a cell of Mode VI) where the question of internal binary subdivision simply does not arise.

Further corroborative evidence may be uncovered by analysing the dotted cells from the point of view of word-stress. In the case of *Cantiga* 162 it might be pointed out that the short middle note of the dotted cell bears predominantly unstressed syllables, and, far from being accented — the only possible physical manifestation of binary subdivision —, the middle note appears weak.

The conclusion to be drawn — namely, that any question of binary subdivision (with the concomitant need to transcribe such cells in 6/8 time) is illusory — must be understood to apply not only to cases in which there exists parallel notation in another source giving a simple ternary rhythm, but to extend to all others in which 'dotted rhythm by dimidiation' is found — including, in retrospect, to *Cantiga* 20.

CANTIGA 38

CANTIGA 38: READING THE NOTATION

The general rhythmic profile of this *cantiga* does not seem in doubt: it presents as cells of Mode III-type, sometimes singly, sometimes in lengthy encadenations; when single, the cells are interspersed with others consisting of a single perfect *L* (as at a.4 *etc.*[16]) or of Mode I-type at intermediate cadences (a.8–9 *etc.*). This understanding is entrenched by two factors: first, the presence of a *tractulus* or a bar at strategic points particularly in *To*: the *tractulus* at e.3 is particularly important at the start of a long chain of Mode-III cells; that at h.4, together with the longer bars at a.4 and b.4, help to section off the perfect *L*; and second, the use in *To* of the short-stemmed *virga*, found both in the position of the isolated *L* (as at c.4, g.4, i.4) and as the first component of a third-mode cell (as at a.1, b.1, h.1 and i.1). These features ought to rule out any attempt to read the cells in question in quintuple metre — or, indeed, (given *T*'s use of *LBB*) as binary.[17] Thus we arrive at a provisional interpretation of the outer sections of this piece as exhibiting Mode III rhythm 'with interruptions', these being in the form of a single perfect *L*, or else cells of Mode I at the cadences.[18]

But not all is so straightforward, as will be seen from a careful analysis of the notation of the α-phrase (*see* transcription). This phrase occurs twice in the Refrain and twice in the *vuelta* (phrases a and c, g and i); of particular interest is the way figures 5-6-7 are represented, both within each ms, and between mss. The notation of *T* is internally consistent, with *LBB* on each occasion, and that of *E* mirrors this faithfully. The possibility of a binary interpretation having already been dismissed, given the general context, we conclude that this is a third-mode cell, to be read with durations of /3,1,2/ — in other words, with perfection and alteration. The three figures in question thus represent a total duration of six *tempora*.

When we turn to the α-phrase in *To*, however, we find a discrepancy: in the Refrain, the three figures are ▪ ♦ ▪ (allowing a Mode-III reading in 6*t*), whereas in the *vuelta* (phrases g and i) we have ♦ ♦ ♦ , effectively a cell of Mode VI, occupying only 3*t*. Once again we must ask the question of whether, or how, 6*t* can equal 3*t*. This, then, is the 'Rosetta moment', when the reading of *To* dictates the interpretation of duration in *T*; once again reconciliation of the two readings can only be achieved by dimidiation of the longer, and there thus emerges a dotted rhythm in both occurrences of the α-phrase of the

[16] It will perhaps not have escaped the reader that this rhythmic pattern is similar to that of the provisional reading of *CSM* 162 just discussed (*see* Ex. 9 above).

[17] The interpretation offered by Anglés (1943) is essentially binary, with unperfected Longs, though only at the cost of ignoring *To*; there is no corrected reading in the 1958 revisions, where Anglés generally takes greater account of *To*. The reading of Elmes (2014), by contrast, treats the third-mode cells as quintuple, though likewise in defiance of *To*.

[18] Such, broadly, is the understanding that underlies the transcription offered in Ferreira 1986, p. [190], and reproduced partially in Ferreira 1993 *bis*, ex. 2a, p. 469; in a later footnote Ferreira posits a minor correction (2009, p. 195, n.37). Attention had already been drawn to the Mode III characteristic of the rhythm in *To* by Ferreira (1993, p. 589, n. 51). Ferreira also comments (2000, p. 16) that the notation admits either quintuple or Mode III interpretation; this applies, however, only to some phrases, and the possibility of transcribing in quintuple metre only in isolated phrases must be weighed against other possibilities (Ferreira 2013, 137–8 and n. 26): the notation of *To* 'allows us to identify third-mode patterns…defining the metrical framework' (Ferreira 2015, p. 22).

vuelta. The logic of the situation demands that this must at the very least be imported into occurrences of the same phrase elsewhere: in the refrain (phrases a and c), in occurrences of phrases that are melodically similar if not identical (phrases b, h) — and then, by domino effect, into all segments notated as cells of Mode III.[19]

What stands out from this particular piece is, on the one hand, how minor, how late, how almost hidden, are the occurrences of the Mode VI cell in *To*; and, on the other hand, how vast are the consequences: for although the outer sections are in some sense similar to *CSM* 20 and *CSM* 162, displaying alternation between dimidiated cells and 'normal' cells, the middle section by contrast displays whole strings of dotted cells now encadenated, with phrases e and f each having eight consecutive occurrences.

One detail of the notation requires comment. The notation of Mode III in the Escorial codices oscillates between *LBB* and *LBL*, with the latter figuring particularly in the encadenations (phrases e, f), and the former in the isolated Mode III cells (phrase a, b *etc.*) before a single *L*. It is interesting, therefore, to see the use of *L* for the final note of the group in line d, when another dimidiable cell follows. What can be gleaned from this, seen in isolation, is maybe not much — except that the distribution of *LBB* and *LBL* is perhaps not so chaotic as it may seem, and may be contextually determined in ways that have yet to be defined.

Cantiga 38: Musical Accentuation of the Text

The question of the musical enhancement of word-stress may again be raised. It would be unrealistic to expect a 100% correspondence. Notably mis-stressed words in the present piece would include *pecadores* in phrase b; *pesa* in phrase d; *Fillo* in phrase e; *fazen* in phrase g. No amount of tinkering with the transcription, or abandoning dotted rhythms, will put these right. But if we focus once again on the short note in the middle of the dotted groups, we find a fair degree of correspondence with weak syllables. Let us take at random the f-phrase. Here we find, on those medial short notes, the syllables *por* (a preposition), *mui* (an adverb, and also a monosyllable), *-os* and *-dos* (unstressed final syllables), *con-* (mildly stressed, but a disyllabic preposition), *-la* (final unstressed syllable of a pronoun), *cui-* (unstressed initial syllable), and *el* (a weak pronoun). In short, not a single case that clearly cries out to be accented. If we relate this to Ferreira's requirement that cells of Mode III that are 'compressed' should maintain their internal binary subdivision, with the concomitant expectation of a medial secondary stress, then it must be concluded that the weak syllables just ennumerated most certainly do not provide supporting evidence for any such solution; rather, the present transcription, as it stands in 3/4 (and not 6/8) time, provides a happy vehicle for syllables that are *un*stressed.

[19] I know of no published transcription that responds to the challenge presented by the durational imbalance between sources. Wulstan (1998, p. 106), having supplied examples of 'bagpipe rhythm' (*i.e.*, dotted rhythm) from other pieces — *CSM* 384, 262, 367, 150 —, comments that in *CSM* 38, too, 'seemingly standard ligatures should be read in this way' as representing dotted rhythms, although without specifying *which* ligatures (the dotted rhythms are in any case represented by *simplex* notes and not by ligatures). His later comment (Wulstan 2001, p. 77) that 'bagpipe rhythm is the solution to problems caused by *LBB* figures' is undoubtedly correct, even though much of the time the rhythms in question are equally represented by *LBL*, as has been seen.

CANTIGA 38

(*To* 41)

COMO A OMAGEN DE SANTA MARIA
TENDEU O BRAÇO E TOMOU O DE SEU FILLO,
QUE QUERIA CAER DA PEDRADA
QUE LLE DERA O TAFUR, DE QUE SAIU SANGUI

HOW THE STATUE OF HOLY MARY
HELD OUT AN ARM AND TOOK THAT OF HER SON
WHICH WAS FALLING OFF
AFTER THE STONE THE GAMBLER HAD THROWN,
WHENCE CAME FORTH BLOOD

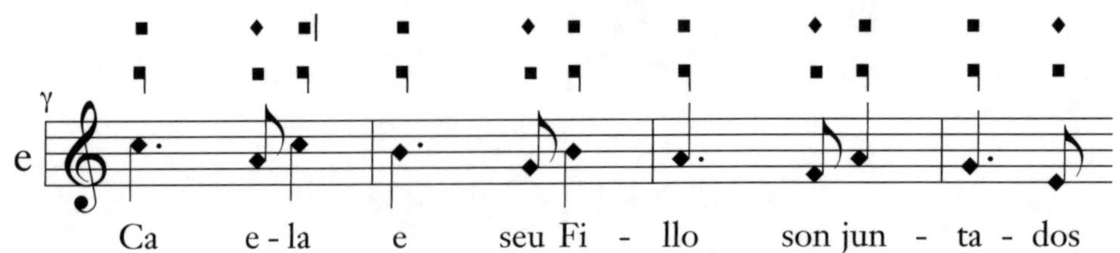
γ
e
Ca e - la e seu Fi - llo son jun - ta - dos

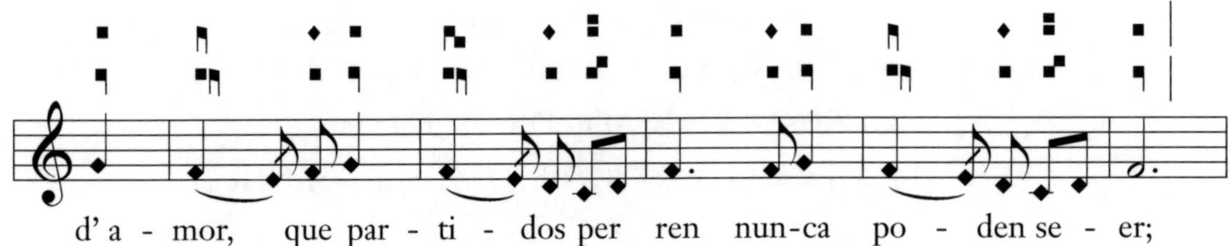
d' a - mor, que par - ti - dos per ren nun-ca po - den se - er;

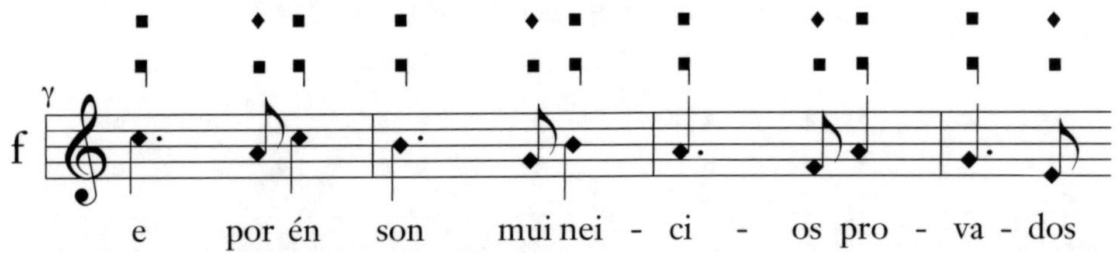
γ
f
e por én son mui nei - ci - os pro - va - dos

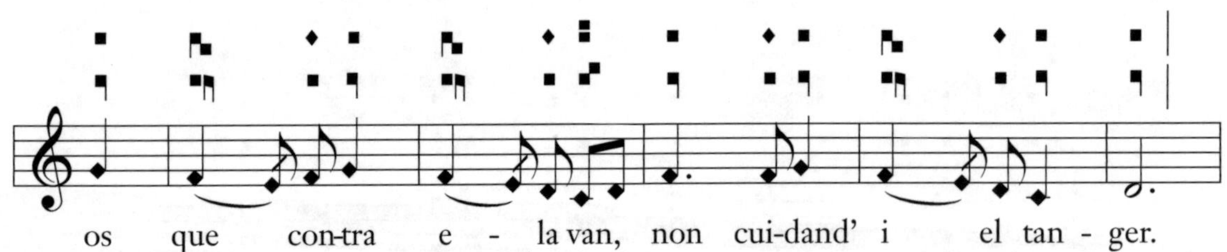
os que con-tra e - la van, non cui-dand' i el tan - ger.

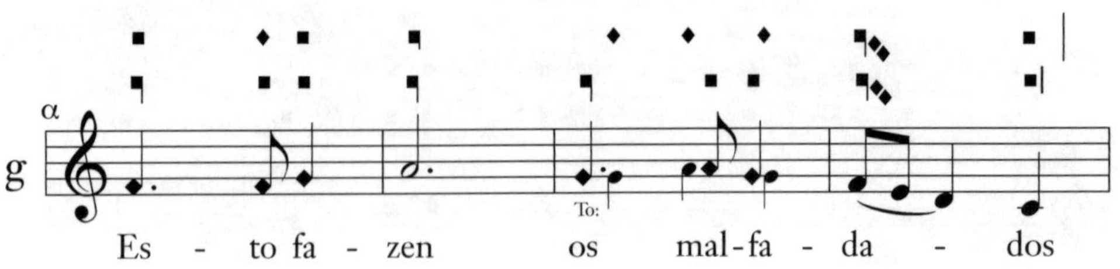
α
g
To:
Es - to fa - zen os mal-fa - da - dos

αα
h
que est' a - mor non que-ren en - ten - der

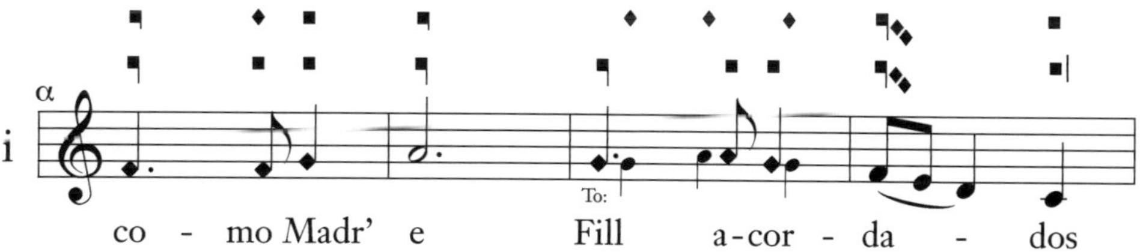

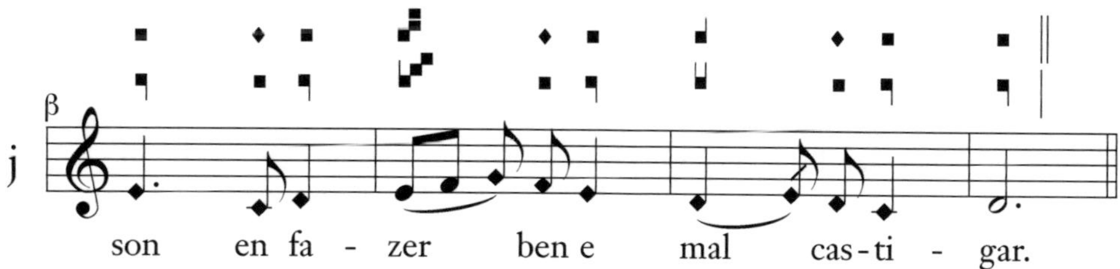

CSM 38: Musical palæography		
To 41, f. 54r–v Notated: ℜ-0; I, *first line of* II *without repetition of* ℜ. *Variant from Incipit of* II: e.3: without *tractulus.*	*T* 38, f. 56v Notated: ℜ-0; I, *incipit* of ℜ-I II, *incipit* of ℜ-II. *The repeated sections yield no notational variants.*	*E* 38, f. 61r–v Notated: ℜ-0; I *only*. *Variants in E as against T:* b.9, h.9: *B* without plication d.7: [neume] d.9: [neume] e.3: with *tractulus* f.24: *B* (*altera*) g.9: without *tractulus.*

Cantiga 38: Musical Phrase-Structure

The relationship between syllable-count and musical phrase-length is, in this piece once again, transformed by the process of dimidiation into one of unexpected symmetry. In the outer sections we find alternation of nine and ten (real) syllables per line, and this is matched by a difference in musical phrase duration: twelve *tempora* for the shorter lines and fifteen for the longer — four and five bars respectively in the transcription, a total of nine bars for each pair of lines. In the lines that make up the middle section variety in the metre of the text provides alternations of eleven and fourteen syllables — a syllable-count that contrasts hugely with that of the outer sections; yet the syllable-absorption capacity of the dotted rhythm, carrying three syllables per cell, permits the musical structure — astonishingly — to remain constant, with once again nine bars per pair of lines.

CANTIGA 97

From its position as the eighth piece in the Appendix to *To*, this *cantiga* is reallocated to a position late in the first cental of the later compilations; it is one of only half-a-dozen pieces to achieve this 'upward mobility'. From a notational and rhythmic point of view it has attracted little attention; only Ferreira has offered comments, taking the version found in *To* as Mode III mixed with Mode IV, and referring in passing to 'rhythmic variants'.[20] More recently Ferreira, in a reference to this piece and five others in the first cental, speaks of how '...nothing prepares us, after a fairly consistent use of a LBL pattern, for the sudden presence of a quaternary pattern uniquely reserved...for the cadence or its approach'.[21] As will become apparent, a different perception underlies both the transcription offered here and the response to questions of how to interpret rhythmic variants.

This piece differs from those previously considered in this section, in that the cells seemingly divergent in duration occur not in *To* but in *E*. Thus here for the first time the rhythmic discrepancy between versions does not align with the contrast between notational codes.

CANTIGA 97: AN INITIAL DIFFICULTY

The first problem that needs to be sorted out concerns the first figure of all, a.1, in the Escorial sources; the same problem recurs at b.1 and at h.1. None of the published editions of this piece, from Anglés's two bites of the cherry onwards (1943, 1958), does anything other than take this Escorial figure at face value — that is, as a *plica brevis* resolved as *SS*. The reality, however, surely lies in *To*; here, first of all, the first three figures are helpfully grouped as a threesome by the *tractulus* after a.3, with the implication that this grouping must somehow be meaningful; if we secondly recall that the figure ▜ in *To* is ambiguous and may represent a plication of ■, then the opening group of ▜ ◆ ■ emerges as a cell of Mode III — as it were, ■ ◆ ■ with the first note plicated — with values of /3,1,2/ *tempora*. And so it appears that the figure ▜ has been carried over from the earlier notation into *T* and *E* and rendered in the same *form*, without too much care over its true significance — a case of what has earlier been called plica confusion (*see* Section II above).

All the notational symmetries of the piece point to this view as being the correct solution. First, the very next cell, a.4-5-6, exhibits the confusion spread between the two Escorial sources, with *E* persisting in the error; by the time we reach the second cell in phrase b, the error in *E* (b.4) has been corrected. And second, all those phrases that begin with a *simplex* — phrases c, d, e and f — express it, in *T* and *E*, as *L*. (In passing, let the short-stemmed *virga* of *To* at c.1 be noted, confirming the three-beat start to the cell.)

The overall rhythmic structure of the piece thus emerges as being very much built around successive cells exhibiting the characteristics of Mode III. The exception — before we get into questions of apparent 'rhythmic variants' in the penultimate cell of certain phrases — is the rhythm of the second cell of each line in the stanza section. If *To* was helpful in phrase a in sectioning off the first three figures, in the stanza it is in *E* that we

---

[20] *See* Ferreira 1993, p. 589, n. 51. Mention two pages earlier of the value that should be attributed to the *porrectus* (▚) in this piece appears to be a mis-reference.

[21] *See* Ferreira 2014, p. 45. Of the six pieces mentioned, *Cantigas* 38 and 41 are also edited in the present volume.

CANTIGA 97

(*To* App. VIII)

COMO SANTA MARIA QUIS GUARDAR DE MORTE
UN PRIVADO DUN REI QUE O AVIAN MEZCRADO

HOW HOLY MARY SOUGHT TO SAVE FROM DEATH
A MAN TRUSTED BY A KING
WHEN [HIS ADVERSARIES] HAD COMPROMISED HIM

e
a Vir - gen por un o - me dun rei
f
fez, que mez - cra - ran, com' a - prés ei;
g
e ben sei
h
que o cui - da - ran a fa - zer mo - rir.

CSM 97: Musical palæography

To App. VIII, f. 153r–v
Notated: ℜ-0; I *only*.
Flat signature given once, at start of stanza (here phrase c).

T 97, f. 140v–141r
Notated: ℜ-0; I, *incipit* of ℜ-I;
II, *incipit* of ℜ-II;
III, *incipit* of ℜ-III;
IV (*stanza only*).
On the stave a flat stands before c.3.

E 97, f. 108v–109r
Notated: ℜ-0; I *only*.
Without signature or any accidentals.
Variants from T:
as shown in transcription.

Notational variants in T:

a.6: ▪ (ℜ-III)
a.10: *no bar* (ℜ-I)
c.5: ▪ (III)
d.5-6: ▪ ▪▪ (II, III, IV)
d.8: ▪ (III, IV)
e.5-6: ▪ ▪▪ (III, IV)
e.8: ▪ (III, IV)
f.5-6: ▪ ▪▪ (II, III, IV)
f.8: ▪ (III, IV)
f.9: *no tract.* (II, III, IV)
h.6: ▪ (II)
h.9: ▪ (III, IV).

find, regularly, a *tractulus* after the *fifth* note (*see* c.5, d.5, e.5, f.5), giving a cell of different chatacter, with only two figures in a Mode I pattern. The fact that the second cell in each phrase is tri-membered in the outer sections but bi-membered in the stanza section is a direct response to the differing textual syllable-count, which is a syllable shorter per line in the *mudanza* than in the refrain and *vuelta*.

CANTIGA 97: WHEN 6*t* = 3*t*

Attention may now be turned to the third cell in the phrases of the *mudanza* (c.6-7-8 *etc.*, as far as f.6-7-8).

The interpretation of the ▪ ◆ ▪ given clearly in all four phrases (c, d, e, f) in *To* can hardly be any different from that applied elsewhere throughout the piece, beginning with the first two cells of phrase a. In other words, this is once more a cell of third-mode type with values of /3,1,2/ *tempora*. In *T* the clearest exposition of a Mode III structure is found in phrase c, where the ▪▪ ▪ ▪ (the second *B* is subject to alteration) leaves no room for doubt. It is a pity that the remaining phrases in *T* lapse once more into plica confusion (d.6, e.6, f.6), giving rise to a general insecurity which the cell-final *L* (d.8, e.8, f.8) does not entirely disperse. (The disarray in *T* may be considered to begin with the note that precedes the cell in question, where ▪ is given, perhaps in error for ▪| . Indeed, the notation of *T* for these *four* figures beginning at d.5 suggests values of /2,1/1,2/, which is of no help whatsoever in the context!) Standing back from the anomalies, it must be concluded that the intention of both *To* and *T* is to present, in all four phrases of the middle section (c, d, e, f), a third cell of Mode III rhythm, with overall duration of 6*t* as written.

Not so in *E*. Here, in all four phrases, we have an identical statement consisting of *BBB* (the first of them plicated). The boundary of the cell is carefully and consistently set by the *tractulus* after the preceding note (c.5, d.5 *etc.*), so there can be no doubt about how the cell is constituted. It might be possible to take an elaborate view involving plica-confusion for the first figure and alteration for the third, making the cell conform to the third-mode reading of the other sources. But the straightforward reading of what is actually stated in *E* sees a cell with three *B*s (call it a tribrach, call it a cell of Mode VI) with a total duration of 3*t*.

To leave the two distinct readings unreconciled is to see a substantive rhythmic variant in *E* in comparison to the other two sources.[22] Reconciliation, however, is possible if the total cell duration represented by *E* is held to signify the duration implied by all sources; in other words, dimidiation of the third-mode cell found in *To* and *T* is enjoined by the apparent conflict in cell-length. And once the third cell in the four phrases of the middle section has been subjected to dimidiation, by domino effect all other cells apparently of Mode III must likewise succumb. The resultant dotted rhythms are what is shown in the accompanying transcription.

This still leaves a rhythmic variant in the relevant cells in *E*, but it is of minor degree, consisting of a straightforward tribrach in *E* where the more decorated dotted rhythm occurs in the other sources. These two variants, already seen in free alternation in other pieces, are here more strictly distributed, each source using one variant exclusively.

---

[22] This view may perhaps be behind what was meant by Ferreira in speaking of this *cantiga* as being rhythmically Mode III mixed with Mode IV 'without taking rhythmic variants into account'. *See again* Ferreira 1993, p. 589, n. 51.

CANTIGA 97: AN UNEXPECTED USE OF THE *VIRGA* IN *To*

If the second rhythmic cell of phrase c is examined in the Escorial sources, it is found to consist of the sequence *LB*, a cell of Mode I; this is particularly clear in *E* where the cell is marked off with a *tractulus*. A reading of /2,1/ *tempora* seems inescapable. When attention turns to *To*, however, we do not find the expected ■ ♦ , but instead ▜ ♦ , in which the group is begun with a short-stemmed *virga*. It appears therefore to be a case of a particular use of ▜, which here does not represent a duration of three *tempora*. Since this question has implications extending beyond any single piece, it requires treatment in more general terms.

A BRIEF EXCURSUS ON THE SHORT-STEMMED *VIRGA*

The modern understanding of the short-stemmed *virga* (herein *ssv*) has its foundation in Ferreira's 1993 description of its function. There we read that 'this shape may mean two different things, or occasionally both: either it signals the melodic importance of a note (normally at the beginnings and ends of phrases or at the highest and lowest melodic points) or it reminds the singer of a long worth three tempora'.[23] Of the two constituent parts of this encapsulation — the 'melodic' and the 'durational' —, it is I think fair to say that in ensuing studies the latter has greatly overshadowed the former; this is the case not least because the 'durational' value of the *ssv* can be used predictively, to help identify and fix rhythmic patterns, whereas any supposed 'melodic' importance attached to it remains stubbornly and merely descriptive. So it is that in a more recent formulation, Ferreira speaks of how 'duration [that is] *L* is represented by a square *punctum*, at times changed into a [short-stemmed] *virga* to denote extra duration';[24] the melodic explanation for the use of the *ssv* appears to have receded, if not fallen away completely.[25]

The *cantiga* just analysed, however, exemplifies at c.3 what I see as an important use of the *ssv* signifying a duration of only two *tempora* in a very specific context. That context is precisely the point of exit from a cell that uses dimidiation to notate dotted rhythm. Here we have a moment at which there is the greatest danger or likelihood of insecurity over beat-values and so the greatest need for clarity. In the cell requiring to be read as dimidiated, the final component in *To* is notated as ■ or its durational equivalent, with a value after dimidiation of 1*t*; but if the next note, now in 'normal' (undimidiated) values, must convey a value of 2*t*, normal usage would imply the use of the very same ■ with a 'revised' duration. This is the moment of potential confusion: it appears that a simple use of ■ in such a context is insufficient; it seems that a 'strengthened' form of the note, ▜ rather than ■ , is required to proclaim that 'normality is restored', 'normal note-values prevail from now on'.

If this understanding of the short-stemmed *virga* as representing 2*t* is correct — and the corroborative reading of the Escorial sources in this case leaves scant room for

[23] Ferreira 1993, p. 608 (Ferreira's translation; the underlying Castilian is found on pp. 592–3).

[24] '...a duração longa é significada pelo ponto quadrado (às vezes transformado em *virga* para denotar duração extra)...', Ferreira 2010, p. 288. The observation is later reinforced: '...sendo a *virga* usada apenas para clarificar, pontualmente, uma duração que exceda os dois tempos' — 'the *virga* being used only to clarify specifically a duration in excess of two *tempora*', *ibid*., p. 292.

[25] Whilst I am prepared to be corrected on infirmity of memory, I recall no specific occurrence of a *ssv* that has been satisfactorily explained purely in terms of melodic prominence.

doubt — then I believe Ferreira's formulation of the function(s) of this figure stands in need of amplification or possible revision. The short-stemmed *virga* is an 'assertive' variant of the square *punctum*; it represents three *tempora* in normal discourse, but can also be used to inculcate a value of two *tempora* in contexts of potential durational insecurity.[26]

The point of interface between a cell that is dimidiated and a following one that is not clearly involves a 'change of gear' in how the notation is processed, and a number of notational devices appear designed to draw attention to the transition. These are generally common to both notational codes and will be pointed out at the appropriate moment; the use of the short-stemmed *virga* for what we might term 'assertive normalization' of beat-values is, however, restricted (for obvious reasons) to Toledo notation.

A NOTE ON *CANTIGA* 150

To offer a full transcription of *Cantiga* 150 would be to stray beyond the remit of this volume, for whilst it undoubtedly displays dotted rhythm in ternary metre, it also relies on the semibreve, used here for the first time as a self-standing half-beat note in *E*, the only source for this piece.[27]

Even so, a glance at the notation of the middle section or *mudanza* (effectively the e- and f-phrases), as transcribed in Ex. 10 (*see* over), will suffice to illustrate how this piece, in its own way, also provides a 'Rosetta moment'. Here the notator has seen fit to use no fewer than three different ways of deploying the 'new' device, the semibreve. As marked off in the transcription with brackets over the stave, first comes (a) ▪ ♦ ♦ , which is followed by (b) ▪ ♦ ▪ ; then in the following phrase comes (c) ▪̧ ♦ ▪ . The fact that all three methods of notating the rhythm amount to the same thing illustrates how, although the problem of notating the half-beat middle note may have been solved using the semibreve, problems of how to notate the outer notes linger; indeed, they may even have been made more acute, given the absence of a specific figure for notating the 1½ beat note at the start of the group. Perhaps the most unexpected feature is the repetition of *S* as the third note of (a).

To some onlookers the committing to parchment of three different versions in such close proximity may seem profligate, or careless, or perhaps insecure. It might be more profitable, however, to view it as experimental — as if the notator were musing in terms of 'these are the ways dotted rhythm might be notated from now on'. But what hap-

26 Following the foregoing comments, it would be of great interest to know how many of Ferreira's listed 51 pieces in *To* using the *ssv* (1993, n. 63 on p. 592) would nevertheless still rely on explanations of melodic prominence for its use — another area requiring further research!

27 Anglés provided two transcriptions of this piece (1943, 1958); these are analysed and compared in Rossell 1985. Transcriptions are also offered in Ferreira 1986, p. [189], and again in Ferreira 2014, pp. 47–9; the latter version is accompanied by an analysis of both the piece's tonal structure and its notation, including comments on the inconsistent and ambiguous use of the semibreve; the notation is also briefly mentioned in Ferreira 2011, p. 200. Mention in Wulstan 1996, p. 52, relates to 'bagpipe rhythm' that is not immediately obvious; the discussion of ways of notating dotted rhythm in Wulstan 1998 includes a reproduction of part of the source of this piece. Further discussion may be found in Wulstan 2000, where there is reference (p. 41) to an anacrusis at the start of the *mudanza* — a reading I do not share —, and to the overall rhythm being in 'free pattern' (p. 55), a term Wulstan revises in later writings to 'polyschematic'. Reference to melodic motifs with 'bagpipe' associations occur in Wulstan 2000, p. 60, and are taken up again in Wulstan 2001, p. 304.

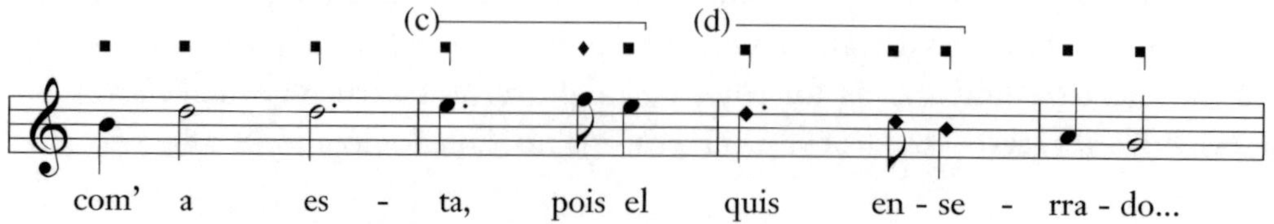

EXAMPLE 10
Cantiga 150 — Opening of Stanza (*mudanza* section)
showing diverse methods of notating dotted rhythm.

pens next is the most surprising of all: in (d) there appears a reversion to the 'old' method, with *LBL*, requiring dimidiation (it will not escape the reader that the written note-values in (d) are exactly double those found in (b) directly above it). It is, once again, as if the notator were proclaiming his thoughts: '...and *this* is how we *used* to do it'. By providing his own 'translation' of what he has just written, the notator successfully links the 'old' (breve-based) and 'new' (semibreve-based) methods of notating dotted rhythm; he also, incidentally, provides justification for the process of dimidiation of written values in the rhythmic cell at (d) — a cell which, it should be noted, is *unmarked* by the presence of any *tractulus* or other distinguishing feature of prolongation, division or separateness.

SECTION IV: FIINDA

The pieces that have been examined in this section, taken together with *Cantiga* 87 (*see* Section IX below), are the best tools at our disposal for reaching an understanding of how cells written apparently with Mode III rhythm were intended to be read with halved durational values. The existence of certain cells in parallel versions occupying now six *tempora*, now three, is the clearest proof that can be expected that dimidiation is required for the former. Further aspects of the transcriptions, in particular the musical enhancement of word-stress and the regularization of phrase-structure, provide some degree of corroboration that the transcriptions are viable. The application of dimidiation to further pieces must be done with a lesser degree of certitude, relying in large measure on what has been learned from the pieces dealt with in Section IV.

V
SIX FURTHER CANTIGAS

The previous section saw examination of three *cantigas* in which the written version of certain rhythmic cells sometimes presented a duration ostensibly of six *tempora*, whilst elsewhere — either in a different source, or even in a repetition of a particular phrase within one source — the same melodic segments clearly occupied only three *tempora*. The likelihood of such major rhythmic variability affecting whole phrase-lengths having been rejected, such notational variants were seen to be reconcilable if the rhythmic cells occupying six *tempora* were subjected to a halving — a dimidiation — of their durational values. And so it is that cells ostensibly offering a Mode III-type rhythm of /3,1,2/ *tempora* were reduced by half to give durational values of /1½,½,1/ — that is, a dotted rhythm within a single rhythmic cell in ternary metre.

Another six pieces may now be approached in which there occur cells of (apparently) Mode III rhythm that are isolated, or sporadic, or occasionally in short strings. The cells in question are written as *LBL* (whether given as ¬ ■ ¬ or else as ¬ ■ ■ with alteration of the last *B*) in the Escorial sources, and as ■ ◆ ■ (or, on occasion, ¬ ◆ ■) in the Toledo codex; in other words, a comparison of sources does not provide any clear indication that such cells should be halved in duration so as to occupy only three *tempora*. Even so, the presence particularly of isolated cells of Mode III-type rhythm is frequently found to disrupt not only the rhythmic flow of a melody (by markedly slowing progress in the relevant segments) but also the phrase-structure. We appear to have, therefore, candidates for dimidiation much like those found in *Cantiga* 20 (where the dimidiated cells are discontinuous, largely alternating with cells of Mode II-type rhythm), inviting treatment similar to that employed in the cases of the three *cantigas* just dealt with. The difference is that here, *no* source enforces dimidiation on another.

The notation in these cases thus offers little in the way of help, or any indication or even suggestion that dotted rhythm is abroad; the only possible exception is — sometimes — the presence of a *tractulus*, with the function of assisting in the grouping of figures. Though by no means a firm indication of dotted rhythm, such a *tractulus* can at least help by marking out clearly the presence of a third-mode cell. Other associated uses of the *tractulus* will be further commented on in the appropriate contexts. The related features of regularity of phrase-structure and respect for textual stress provide important corroborative input in evaluating the application of dimidiation; indeed, judgements on the success of the whole process may well rest on how these 'related features' are seen to fare after dimidiation has been selectively applied.

The cases analysed in this section are ones in which the notation of dotted rhythm may be seen as functioning in a relatively straightforward manner; pieces presenting additional difficulties, or of especial interest, are dealt with in later sections. Three of the six pieces (255, 407, 415) have been briefly mentioned by Wulstan in association with 'bagpipe' rhythm, although no dotted-rhythm transcriptions are available. For the remaining pieces, this section breaks new ground.

Cantiga 15

This piece is one of the 'long' *cantigas*, moved from its miscellaneous position in *To*, where it is no. 33, to a quintal position (*i.e.*, a position whose number ends in -5; *cf* no. 255 below) during the reorganization that accompanied the expansion of the repertoire found in the later sources. Unusually, *T* and *E* differ in the numerical placing of this piece.

Apart from the unsatisfactory transcriptions available in the usual editions, the notation and rhythm of this *cantiga* appear to have attracted no consideration beyond two brief comments offered in 1993 by Ferreira. These refer to the presence of Mode III elements in *To* — an observation whose relevance must surely be enlarged to elucidate the intention of the other sources —, and to the overall duration represented by the descending *cum-sine* binary (▸) as being 'clearly' *B* — a claim that is open to discussion.[1]

Cantiga 15: The First Half of Each Phrase

There is a strong temptation (to which Anglés succumbs) to see the notes of every phrase in pairs, reading

LB LB L'X' BL BL

the 'X' coming out as *L* or *B*, depending on which phrase is being looked at, and in which source. Not the least of the unfortunate consequences of this approach is to throw a strong accent onto the fifth syllable of each line, where generally there should be none. But there are the most obvious palæographic indications that this grouping into pairs was not what was intended (and for this reason, the transcription of this piece carries the notation of all three sources, since the evidence is scattered among them). The evidence comes in the form of a *tractulus*, inserted apparently rarely and randomly, but with the effect of grouping the opening of the line in which it occurs, not into pairs, but into a group of the first *three* or *five* figures. Thus: at c.5 we have a *tractulus* in *T* which suggests a division after the *fifth* note; at e.3, another *tractulus* in *E*, after the *third* note; at f.5, a *tractulus* after the *fifth* figure, in *E*; and at g.5, a similar suggestion of division in both *To* and *E*. The presence of these tiny indications is not systematic, nor is it exhaustive; but it is surely indicative: these are barriers that prevent mistaken grouping; the groups end after the third and fifth figures. And so, instead of the grouping by pairs given above, we have:

LBL BL

for the first five figures; this, by extension, can later be developed into a reading of the whole phrase as: *LBL BL [L]BL BL*

It is the presence of a *LBL* group that would allow, in a conservative transcription, treatment as a cell of Mode III; this reading is corroborated by the sporadic presence in *To* of a short-stemmed *virga* (▪ = 3*t*) as the first figure in the phrase (d.1, i.1).[2] If we further proceed to dimidiate durations in that first cell in each line, we have taken an important first step towards the transcription offered here (*see* facing page).

---

[1] *See* Ferreira 1993, p. 589 and n. 51 (on Mode III features in *To*) and p. 587 (on ▸).

[2] The presence of the short-stemmed *virga* in this position in *some* phrases warns against the interpretation of the first note as having a duration merely of 2*t* in *any* phrase, a warning ignored not only by Anglés, but also by Pla (2001), López Elum (2005) and Elmes (2nd. ed., 2014). This case is a good example of the way in which the notation of *To* provides information that clarifies what is intended in all sources; Ferreira's observation concerning the presence of Mode III features in *To* (*see* previous note) may thus be seen as having wider applicability than he cautiously allows.

CANTIGA 15

(*To* 33, *T* 5, *E* 15)

COMO SANTA MARIA DEFENDEU
A CIDADE DE CESAIRA DO EMPERADOR JUIÃO

HOW HOLY MARY DEFENDED THE CITY
OF CÆSAREA AGAINST THE EMPEROR JULIAN

(!)
β
e
E de lle se - e - ren ben man - da-dos,
γν
f
es - to de - reit' e ra - zón a - duz,
β
g
pois que por e - les en - cra-ve - la-dos
γχ
h
ou - ve seu Fill' os nem - bros na cruz;
αμ
i
To, E:
T:
de - mais, per e - la san - tos cha - ma-dos
αν
j
son, e de to - dos é lum' e luz;

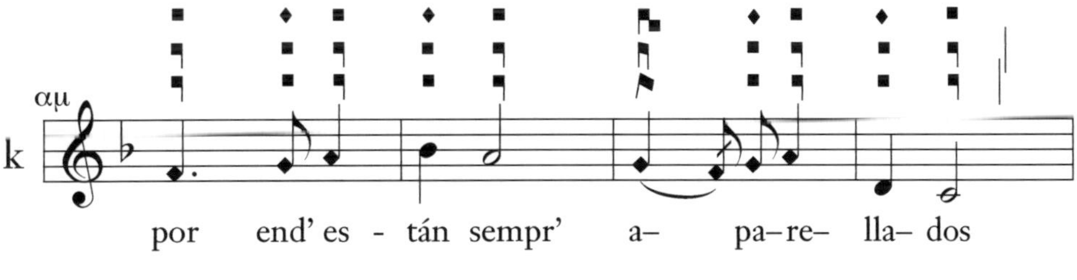

CSM 15: Musical palæography		
To 33, f. 43v–44r Notated: ℜ-0; I *only*. Flat signature throughout (missing in phrases d and h).	*T* 5, f. 10r Notated: ℜ-0; I, ℜ-I. Flat signature throughout. *Notational variants in* ℜ-I: Stems are in general very faint or near-invisible (esp. b.1, b.5, d.1). a.10: *tractulus* rather than bar. c.5: without *tractulus*. c.10: no bar.	*E* 15, f. 42v–43r Notated: ℜ-0; I *only*. Flat signature throughout.

Even so, a comparative examination of the first five figures in all phrases reveals that the notation displays some symptoms of insecurity. Whilst the general pattern of *LBL BL* (in *To*, ▪ ♦ ▪ ♦ ▪) is clearly established much of the time, deviations occur. This is particularly noticeable in *To* in the fourth figure of several phrases. Phrases b, e, g, k and l give a rhomb in *To* in this fourth position, as just exemplified, but on other occasions the position is occupied by ▪ (phrases a, d, and j), and even on two occasions by a reinforced form, the *virga* with short stem ▪ (phrases c and i). It should be noted that some of these variants are self-contradictory: phrase j replicates phrase b, but substitutes the longer note; similarly, though in reverse, phrases l and d.

What these substitutions in *To* have in common is that they all occur at the sensitive point at which, in the transcription, dimidiation ceases, and there is a reversion to 'normal' time-values. In the previous rhythmic cell, with dimidiation, the rhomb has had a value of 0.5*t*; if the next cell requires a first note with duration of 1*t*, the same rhomb, without dimidiation, ought to serve; yet this is irksome, since it relies on the same figure displaying two quite distinct durations in close proximity. It is reasonable to infer that the sudden shift in what duration the rhomb represents is what occasions insecurity, resulting in an understandable (if sporadic) reluctance to use the same note-shape with two distinct values in quick succession. This case of notational insecurity, in phrases a, c, d, i and j in

To, may be explained in terms of what can be understood as 'late exit from dimidiation'; by contrast the use of the short-stemmed *virga* to re-establish 'normal' durations at c.4 and j.4 resembles the 'assertive normalization' described in the context of *Cantiga* 97 (*see* Section IV). Though distinguishable, these two phenomena are clearly responses to the same difficult notational context just after a cell read with dimidiated values.

The other cases in *To* in which ■ appears in this critical fourth place in the line, namely f.4 and h.4, may perhaps be read as genuine rhythmic variants, with the ambiguous following *clivis* (▛▖) being taken with a value of 1*t*.

Returning to the overall interpretation of rhythm at this difficult fourth figure in the line, the notation of *T*, with its generally regular *BL* in this second cell, is more secure. Even in this source, however, the notation is somewhat awry at this point in phrases f and h, being hypermetric if taken at face value (▜ + ▛▖ = 4*t*). By way of extenuation, these two *L*s may again be attributed to a 'late exit from dimidiation'. Source *E*, more helpfully, has *B* at both these locations, and surely represents the underlying intention.

Cantiga 15: The Second Half of Each Phrase

In the foregoing subsection a case was made for reading the first five figures in all phrases as having values *LBL BL*, with a cell-division after the third figure, allowing the first segment to be read as a cell of Mode III and so inviting its subsequent dimidiation. The second half of all phrases, at first sight, would seem amenable to similar treatment (allowing room for variation at the cadences consequent upon syllable-count: *LBL BL* alternating with *LBL L*), were it not for the seemingly intractable variability of the first figure after the mid-point — the '*X*' in *XBL BL*.

A look at *To* shows that in only two lines, e and g, is the length of the sixth figure unequivocal; here the ■ ♦ ■ (*e.g.*, g.6-7-8) is certainly consistent with a reading of /3,1,2/ *tempora* and so a cell of Mode III inviting dimidiation. The remaining phrases in *To* give a durationally ambiguous *clivis* (▛▖) at this point. If *To* were the only source, there would be no hesitation in attributing to this *clivis* a length identical to that of the *simplex* in phrases e and g; such a reading would be justified as maintaining a rhythmic pattern that is already established at the start of each phrase, and is explicit in mid-phrase in e and g. But how can this be reconciled with the readings of *T* and *E*?

As far as *T* is concerned, in the two instances where this note is *simplex* (e.6, g.6) it is written *L*; these locations correspond to the unequivocal cases in *To*, and as was the case there, so also here the cell in question can be most easily read as exhibiting Mode III. In all other phrases, however, the sixth note is plicated and written *B*. If this is taken at face value, then the coherence of rhythmic structure in the whole piece collapses. There is, however, another possible explanation: that *T*'s use of a plicated *B* where we might expect *L* derives from a misreading of an underlying copy in which this note was ambiguous as to length — exactly the same ambiguity, in fact, as has already been observed in *To*'s use of the *clivis*. Whether due to a careless, merely mechanical 'translation' into a more explicit notational code, or else to a genuine misunderstanding or perplexity at how to understand the model, such 'mistranslation' resembles cases of 'plica-confusion' (*see* Section II above), even though the underlying figure may not in this case have been a plica.

Turning to *E*, we find that this troublesome sixth figure in each line reproduces the plicated *B* of *T* on only one occasion (at b.6), all other locations showing — bizarrely

— the *cum-sine* binary ♪ . We may posit that this was intended to be taken as representing *SS* (corresponding to the *supposed* reading of the ♪ in *T*), arising from a similar misunderstanding of the ambiguity of the model (be it *To* or some other intermediate copy in an earlier notation). As to its real duration, we are left with a *cum-sine* binary grotesquely representing a value of *three tempora*, to which dimidiation must then further be applied![3] If this sixth note in most phrases is durationally ambiguous in *To*, and subject to a type of plica-confusion in *T*, all we can say of the usage in *E* is that it amounts to an aberration. Of the three, paradoxically, it is the ambiguous figure that is the most secure, allowing a persistent rhythmic pattern to emerge.

A related set of observations arises in relation to figures 6-7-8 in all phrases in *T* and *E*. When the third of these is written *L*, or where both the first and third are *L*, there is surely no doubt that a dotted rhythm is intended by way of dimidiation. But where all three notes are written *B* (as in phrase f in *T*) there are two possible readings: either we take the first note as incorrectly notated and the third as a *brevis altera* (and so read the segment as a cell of Mode III), or else we take it at face value, *BBB*, a straightforward tribrach without need or possibility of dimidiation. The mystery thickens, however, when we turn to *E* at this same point and inquire whether the *cum-sine* binary ♪ should also be interpreted as *SS* — and not only here (f.6), but also at h.6, j.6 and l.6. On foot of this possibility an alternative reading of *BBB* has been included for this third cell in phrases f and h in the transcription; one advantage is that when the syllable of text that falls on the middle note of the three is stressed, the *BBB* reading accommodates it more comfortably than the dotted reading; the chief disadvantage is that, to adopt this reading, the *cum-sine* binary ♪ must be taken with two different overall values (1*t* or 3*t*) in the course of the piece as a whole. Whichever way we incline, this all serves as a reminder that the dotted rhythm ♩. ♪♩ is, in effect, merely a more elaborate version of ♩♩♩, and both are effective ways of accommodating three syllables within the same rhythmic unit.

One small corner of the notation of *To* merits mention, namely the last two figures of phrase e. The two long notes may be taken as a case of cadential lengthening (as described in Section II above), or else perhaps the first of them is due to 'late exit from dimidiation'. Either way, the anomaly is corrected in phrase g. The archaic plica that finishes both these phrases (e.10, g.10) is not here taken literally; it seems, rather, to be merely a reflection of the falling step in the melodic line.

Cantiga 15: Further Considerations

Sufficient has already been said about the rhythmic characteristics implied by the notation of this *cantiga* to justify the symmetry of phrase-lengths present in the transcription — in modern terms, an unvaried four bars per phrase throughout. Such symmetry is notably absent from previous transcriptions, not least that of Anglés; the principal cause of the irregularity is the varying length attributed to the sixth figure in each phrase, which has

---

[3] If, in the abstract, we ask the question 'Can the descending *cum-sine* binary ♪ , when *Long*, be perfect?', we would expect to hear the answer 'No!', and this impossibility has been used to argue in favour of quintuple metre when this figure comes first in an *LBL* group. But here we have a case in which — admittedly in error — repeated occurrences of ♪ head up cells of Mode III. It would be well for the possibilities raised by this case to be recalled when dealing with cases of notationally difficult *cantigas* for which no version survives in *To*.

the effect of injecting an extra *L* into some phrases but not others. The explanation given above does away with the variability by positing a value for the relevant figure in *To* which — if this transcription is correct — was overlooked or misunderstood by the scribes of *T* and *E*. The resultant symmetry may be held as corroborating that attribution of length.

Without wishing to enter into a lengthy analysis of the musical response to textual stress, it will suffice if the reader first compares the stresses of the opening words in this version — *Tó-do-los sán-tos* — with those of Anglés's version — *Tó-do-lós san-tós*. The improvement is manifest, and further examples could be adduced. It is also interesting to evaluate the correlation between textual stress and the short middle note of the dotted cells. The correlation — we would expect a weak syllable here — is not perfect, but when we rule out monosyllables,[4] discount cases of words so frequent as to admit great variability of stress,[5] and dismiss some marginal cases,[6] we find the only real misfit — in 24 underlaid cases — is the word *razón* in phrase f.[7] Here the argument may rest.

CANTIGA 15: SUMMATION

From this lengthy exposition three elements stand out as of general importance for the way ahead. The first is that the note *following* a dotted group occupies a sensitive position: its length may require the use of a figure that already appears in the preceding dimidiated cell where it has a conflicting, shorter absolute value. There may consequently be a temptation to write this sensitive note longer than what is strictly meant. This phenomenon may be seen as the reverse of what has elsewhere been referred to as '*early* exit from dimidiation'.

The second important aspect of the process of transcription thrown into sharp relief by this piece is the need to bear all available sources in mind — especially when there is a suspicion that later sources may misrepresent intentions implicit in an earlier version — and to bear in mind all *details* of the sources: a single *tractulus* can change the universe.

Third, *Cantiga* 15 illustrates once more the importance of repeated rhythmic patterns; in this case they are pervasive, each phrase being in essence a pattern and its repetition. From an editorial perspective, the *expectation of finding* repeated rhythmic patterns is likewise important in motivating exhaustive examination of the permutations of possible readings. In comparative terms, the alternation of Mode III (dimidiated) and Mode II-type cells seen here strongly recalls the pattern already found in the outer sections of *Cantiga* 20; indeed, a glance back at the pieces already presented shows that alternation of rhythmic cell-types may be emerging as an important structuring principle in a number of pieces with dotted rhythm.

[4] These include *son* (phrase a), *gran* (phrase b), *ben* (phrase e) and *lum'* (phrase j).

[5] The relevant case here is *Virgen* (phrase c). For brief comments on the general question of mobility of musical stress on some commonly-used words, *see* Wulstan 2000, p. 58.

[6] Such a case would be that of the conjunction *demais* (phrase i).

[7] Curiously, this word stands at the *only* point at which the notation of both *T* and *E* would admit interpretation as an undotted tribrach, a reading that would go some way towards provision of the syllabic enhancement felt to be missing.

CANTIGA 76

Although this piece does not figure in codex *To*, it is included here for the sake of statistical completeness in dealing with the first hundred *cantigas* in the standard numeration. It is the only piece discovered (so far!) within that first cental to display dotted rhythms in ternary metre that does not appear also in *To*. Whilst the musical palæography of *T* has been provided in the transcription in conformity with the practice followed in the other pieces included here, this piece seems to be one in which that of *E* is in some respects more reliable, and so relevant variants from *E* have also been included above the stave.

Apart from the usual editions, *Cantiga* 76 was transcribed by Huseby in his 1983 thesis;[8] his reading, offered without comment on the rhythm, is obtained at the expense of some difficulty over textual versus musical accent, especially at line-endings in the stanza. Two studies in 1987 by Fernández de la Cuesta enhanced the profile of this piece within *cantiga* studies. The first of these, after an exhaustive general study of melodic leaps and vocalic range in the *Cantigas*, provides a detailed analysis of *Cantiga* 76, looking at the correlation between textual stress on the one hand, and melodic height and duration of melodic components on the other;[9] the second has regard to the relationship, in this *cantiga* and three others, of note length and pitch to what the author calls the *accent rythmique du texte*.[10] The recent approach to this *cantiga* offered by Ferreira will be examined below.

CANTIGA 76: READING THE NOTATION

The notational mechanism involved in recording dotted rhythms is the same as already observed: the use of *LBL* groups (sometimes written *LBB*, with alteration) with double the intended durational values. In the transcription, dimidiation has been applied in the first full bar and in the penultimate bar of phrases in the outer sections (phrases a and b, e and f), but is restricted to the first full bar of the remaining phrases (c and d). All this is offered without further comment.

The notation in both *T* and *E* makes full and frequent use of both *cum-sine* binaries (▚ and ▞), which I persist in considering as durationally ambiguous figures, and here understand as *SS* (*i.e.*, with an overall value of *B*);[11] cases in *T* of interchangeability, particularly of ▞ with ▙ (compare, for example, a.1 with b.1, and reversing the correspondence, b.7 with a.7), confirm the intended duration of the former; the constant presence of the *plica brevis* at the start of all lines in *E* also confirms this value of ▞ in *T*. Such a reading of the *cum-sine* binaries allows simple tribrach groups to emerge (*e.g.*, a.4–6, c.10–12, *etc.*)

---

[8] *See* Huseby 1983, Ex. 75, p. 213.

[9] *See* Fernández de la Cuesta 1987 *bis*. Since the author spurns questions of mensural interpretation — indeed, his article includes scathing comments on *CSM* notation — his conclusions, though of interest, cannot weigh in the present context.

[10] *See* Fernández de la Cuesta 1987 *ter*. Note-length, since the author refuses to acknowledge the distinction *B* and *L*, is calculated by reference to the number of noteheads of differing pitch attached to a given syllable. How the *accent rythmique du texte* emerges or is to be recognized — it appears to be distinct from normal textual stress — is nowhere made clear (unless perhaps one should seek illumination from the preface to the *Liber usualis*).

[11] Ferreira (1993, p. 587) specifically mentions this piece as one in which the *cum-sine* binaries are clearly of overall duration *B*. *See*, however, note 9 in Section II above.

intermingled among cells displaying dotted rhythm. Between the one and the other, cells carrying three syllables appear as the norm, giving an overall impression of a Mode VI-like metre, though one in which the dotted cells provide variation and embellishment. Interruptions to this pattern (*e.g.*, c.5–6) are, of course, conditioned by the metre of the text.

The notational variants that occur both in the writing out of Stanza II in *T*, and in the single stanza given in *E*, provide much that is interesting and corroborative. At a.10 and e.9 *E* has ▪, confirming the reading of *T*'s *B* as altered. The rising plicated *B* (▪) in *E* at b.1, c.1 *etc.*, confirms the reading of *T*'s ▪ as *B*. Finally, the *B*-with-*tractulus* at c.6 and d.6 in *T* is at first sight puzzling. How are we to take the *tractulus*? Does it lengthen, or merely section? Could it perhaps represent a *rest*? The general intention — that whatever is there, it must occupy 2*t* — is clarified by the presence in *E* of ▪ at each of these points.

One point of notational confusion is the indecision at c.9 and d.9. Source *T* has ▪ in I and ▪ in II; either of these might be taken with overall value *L*, though the precise intent of the final plication remains unclear. Source *E* provides a much more straightforward reading of ▪ , which is in effect what has been transcribed here.

Two observations are also in order for the *currentes* at e.5. First, this single figure occurs at a point where in other phrases we have two syllables, and represents a clever solution to a textual difficulty: that of defective metre, which is a syllable short at this point although only in some stanzas. In other later stanzas (III, V, VI, VIII) the extra syllable is present, and the *currentes* must be split into a descending binary followed by a *B*.[12] And second: given that these *currentes* at e.5 replace a ▪ ▪ pair in an earlier statement of the same phrase (at a.5-6), the total duration can hardly be different in the two cases; and since the *currentes* are unlikely to be employed with a duration that exceeds 2*t*, it follows that the ▪ and the ▪ must occupy 1*t* each. The view that ▪ must overall be *B* is thus reinforced.

CANTIGA 76: A DIFFERING VIEW

In a recent article Ferreira provides a rhythmic scheme for the refrain of this piece which he considers can be analysed rhythmically in terms of the Arabic rhythmic cycle known as Light Ramal.[13] Ferreira's argument is based on the fact that patterns consisting of durations /1,2,2,1/ or /2,1,1,2/ beats (which Anglés would have considered as a mixture of Mode I and Mode II) are also current in Arabic music. He treats the refrain of *Cantiga* 76 as a mixture of the first of these patterns with others involving three longs,[14] giving a reading (based on *T*) of /1,2/1,2,2,1/2,2,1,1/2,2,2/1,2,2,1/[2],2,1,1/ *tempora*, justifiable in Arabic music theory and interpretable in modern terms as a combination of 6/4 and 3/2 bars.[15] Speaking for myself, I have no wish to pour cold water on the idea of Arabic rhythmic cycles in the *Cantigas*; even so, a number of aspects of this case encourage caution. First, it remains unclear whether the analysis could be extended to cover the whole piece; second, rhythms involving mixed triple and compound duple elements, effectively depend-

---

[12] Further comments on this problem accompany the textual edition (*see* Appendix). Wulstan takes a different approach to solving irregularities of syllable-count, seeking to iron them out by means of paragogic syllables. *See* Wulstan 1994, p.19, and 2001, p. 148.

[13] *See* Ferreira 2015, pp. 19–20.

[14] The last of the *L*s in a group of three can be divided, giving /2,2,1,1/ instead of /2,2,2/.

[15] A difficulty in Ferreira's presentation is that, although he inserts time-signatures, he leaves the rhythmic scheme in original notational figures; the numeric string just given is my own reading of how I understand Ferreira intends durations to be allocated.

CANTIGA 76

COMO SANTA MARIA DEU SEU FILLO
AA BÕA MOLLER, QUE ERA MORTO,
EN TAL QUE LLE DÉSSE O SEU
QUE FILLARA AA SA OMAGEN DOS BRAÇOS

HOW HOLY MARY GAVE BACK TO THE GOOD WOMAN
HER SON WHEN HE HAD DIED,
PROVIDED HE GIVE HER BACK HER OWN SON
THAT HE HAD STOLEN
FROM THE ARMS OF HER STATUE

T:
E:
α
a
Quen as sas fi - gu - ras da Vir - gen par - tir
β
b
quer das de seu Fi - llo, fol é sen men - tir.
γ
c
Por end' un mi - ra-gre vos quer' eu o - ra con - tar
γχ
d
mui ma - ra-vi - llo-so, que quis a Vir - gen mos - trar

CSM 76: Musical palæography	
T 76, f. 112v	*E* 76, f. 94r
Notated: ℜ-0; I, *incipit* of ℜ-I; II, *incipit* of ℜ-II.	Notated: ℜ-0; I *only*.
Notational variants in II: c.9, d.9: d.6: without *tractulus*.	*Notational variance from T:* a.10, e.9: b.1, c.1, d.1, f.1: b.7: c.6: with bar; d.6: c.9, d.9: e.10: without bar.

ent on hemiolic cross-play,[16] are in any case to be found in the Iberian folk tradition and Renaissance song, and may well have deeper roots than Arabic theory alone can explain; third, an application of text to the rhythmic outline shows that weak syllables would be brought to unwanted prominence, such as *sas* and *da* in *l.* 1 and *de* in *l.* 2, all of which stand first in their rhythmic group in Ferreira's schema;[17] and fourth, the irregularity in the pattern of occurrence of the different elements (as opposed, for example, to a strict alternation) is motive for doubt. For these and for other more technical reasons[18] it seems prudent to suspend judgment pending a fuller analysis of this approach to the piece.[19]

[16] 'Anacreontic–Ionic' in Wulstan's terminology. *See* Wulstan 2001, esp. pp. 49ff and 308ff.

[17] An aspect of the question on which I have seen no investigation or projection is how the shorts and longs of Arabic rhythmic cycles, such a hand-in-glove match for a language such as Arabic whose syllables are likewise short or measurably long, might cope with a language such as Galician (or indeed Castilian) which relies on syllabic stress — and *mobile* stress at that.

[18] Among the technical reasons is that Ferreira's reading appears to depend heavily on *T*. So for example the tenth figure in the refrain, in his pattern, *must* be taken as the *B* of *T*, and the *L* of *E* must be rejected; this contrasts with the situation underlying the transcription offered here, in which the *B* of *T* is read as altered, and so reconcilable with the *L* of *E*, satisfying both sources. A second technical reason is that the rhythmic compartments are not symmetrically placed with respect to the lines of text.

[19] It is my hope that these comments will not be understood as in any way dismissive, but rather as leaving Ferreira's suggestion open to further debate.

CANTIGA 76: MELODIC FEATURES

Whilst melodic analysis does not form part of the central aim of this study, two observations nevertheless seem pertinent in this case. First, the schema implied by the Greek letters sitting on the shoulders of the staves sees the first two phrases as α and β. But in reality the melody is much more unified than this simple dichotomy would suggest. In particular, the first half of the second phrase is strongly echoic of the opening of the previous one, following it at a distance of a 3rd when not exactly coinciding. It might be closer to the reality to see these as a single phrase, varied in its first half, and with *ouvert* and *clos* variants in the second half. Schematically, this would make them α and α'χ, with the *mudanza* as β and βχ — a pleasantly balanced structure.

Second: just what is the melodic mode of the present piece? Authentic tetrardus, no doubt.[20] And so with F natural? Perhaps. But this is just the sort of melody to which adherents of 'Medieval major' and 'Medieval minor' would assign a subsemitonal cadence — an F sharp, no less! Maybe not in the upper octave, but certainly at the lower end of the ambit, at and in the approaches to cadences. This idea will be anathema to some, and we are certainly navigating in deep waters; but if the dance-like dotted rhythms take us further and further from theoretically-described rhythmic models, perhaps we need to allow room for deviance also in tonal models.[21] Worth noting in this context is the family resemblance of the melody of *Cantiga* 76 to that of *Cantiga* 303,[22] in which we find a very similar first phrase notated a tone lower than here; although it cadences on F, however, the phrase does not descend semitonally below that note.

CANTIGA 76: SUMMATION

At the heart of any interpretation of the rhythm of this *cantiga* must be a resolution of the question of how to read the *cum-sine* binary ligatures. Here, arising out of a view that they are durationally ambiguous, they are read with a value of *SS*, that is, with a total value of *B*. Any attempt to fix their value as *BB* (*i.e.*, with a duration that is overall *L*) must of necessity produce results that are markedly different.

Beyond that, the transcription that is offered provides a good response to textual stress; witness the treatment of words such as *fi-gú-ras*, *Fí-llo*, *mi-rá-gre*, *ma-ra-vi-lló-so* in the refrain and *mudanza* sections; other corroborative examples could be provided, but particularly striking is the good match of weak-to-weak in the case of syllables underlaid to the short middle note in the dotted cells.[23] As regards phrase lengths, the difference in syllable-count between the outer sections (eleven syllables per line) and the *mudanza* (thirteen), coupled with the fact that there are three cells per phrase already carrying three syllables each, means that there is no scope for 'hiding' the extra two to achieve symmetry.

---

[20] For Huseby (1983, pp. 213–4) this piece is a case of modal conmixture, conforming to Mode 7, plus Mode 1 transposed to A.

[21] For a consideration of the question of tonal alteration (*i.e.*, 'accidentals') in supposedly modal melodies, *see* Wulstan 2001, pp. 317–20.

[22] For a look at the possible remote origins and family ramifications of the *Cantiga* 303 melody, as well as its compatibility with the Bergamask bass, *see* Wulstan 2005, pp. 232–3. I can find no context in which Wulstan comments directly on *Cantiga* 76, other than his efforts to resolve problems of inconstant syllable-count (*see again* n. 12 above).

[23] *See particularly* a.3, a.9, b.3, b.9, c.3, d.3, e.3 and e.8 in the refrain and first stanza.

CANTIGA 255

From its position as no. 74 in the original collection as represented by *To*, this *cantiga* appears to have been relegated and was only incorporated into the expanded collection much later as no. 255. Whether this was due to any difficulty over the rhythm or its notation, we can only speculate. The late inclusion means that it does not figure in *T*, nor was its text copied into *F*; the sources, then, are *To* and *E*.

Anglés's 1943 transcription shows that he took full cognizance of the presence of Mode III cells; Ferreira, too, comments on this piece, as it appears in *To*, as rhythmically third mode.[24] Of course neither of these scholars comtemplates any halving of time-values selectively in the relevant cells; however, a transcription dating from 1945 effectively does precisely that. The version in question is that offered in an article by Fernandes Lopes (*see* Example 11).[25] It must be admitted that Lopes's knowledge of musical palæography leaves something to be desired: he seems to have little or no grasp of how plicas work, and some of his alternative rhythms stretch the bounds of the possible. Even so, his evidently intuitive reading of the rhythm of this piece shows remarkable insight especially with regard to the presence of segments that are dotted (by dimidiation!!), and it is a pity his views, at least of this *cantiga*, have not been accorded greater attention.

EXAMPLE 11
Cantiga 255: Refrain
(Fernandes Lopes, 1945, p. [68])
Sigla: *M* = *To*; *B* = *E*

[24] *See again* Ferreira 1993, p. 589 and n. 51.

[25] *See* Fernandes Lopes 1945, p. 68. The quality of the inter-library loan photocopy from which the above scan of Lopes's transcription has had to be taken — it disappears at the right-hand edge into the gloom of a binding gutter — means that the last note and last syllable have had to be cropped.

In spite of the date of publication of his article, Lopes was working in ignorance of Anglés's monumental 1943 edition because of the vicissitudes of book distribution and postal disruption in wartime Europe. For the same reason copies of the relevant issue of the journal in which Lopes's article appeared are very hard to come by: there is, for example, no copy in Oxford.

For a rather downbeat assessment of Lopes's amateur contribution to Portuguese musicology — he was a medical doctor —, *see* Ferreira 2011 *bis*, p. [2] and n. 3.

In similar vein Huseby also perceives dotted rhythm in this piece.[26] As is usual in the case of this scholar, transcriptions are not offered primarily as rhythmic solutions — rather, as examples of melodic modality — and so his insight, unsubstantiated by rhythmic or notational analysis or discussion, has not weighed with subsequent editors. What may be pointed out is that his approach to the b-phrase (*see* second stave in Example 12) sees fewer dotted cells than Lopes's transcription previously reproduced; this difference of interpretation, and the reasons for it, will be further examined below.

EXAMPLE 12
Cantiga 255: Refrain and opening of *mudanza*
(Huseby, 1983: part of Ex. 86, p. 231)

More recently Wulstan, in the midst of a densely-packed survey of ways in which he considers that 'bag-pipe rhythm' may be notated, offers the view that 'seemingly standard ligatures should be read in this way' (*i.e.*, with dotted rhythm). He does not, however, clarify *which* ligatures (indeed, it is hard to see why the word 'ligatures' is used in the context of *CSM* 255), nor does he offer a transcription. In mentioning *Cantiga* 255 he also draws comparison with *CSM* 38, edited here in Section IV above.[27]

Of other modern editions, those of Pla (2001) and Elmes (Vol. 3, 2010) are in agreement in transcribing the piece in quintuple metre; the notational features that provoke such a response will be discussed below.

In order to facilitate analysis, the full transcription (*see* over) leaves the musical phrases short, each of four bars only. Even so, a good case could be made musically for considering each pair as a unit (*i.e.*, the α- and β-phrases to be taken in a single span, *etc.*); this procedure would simplify the overall schema, giving an elegantly simple αββα.

[26] *See* Huseby 1983, Ex. 86, p. 231.
[27] *See* Wulstan 1998, p. 106.

CANTIGA 255: QUINTUPLE RHYTHM?

The odd-numbered phrases in this piece break naturally into halves, as is indicated by the presence of a *tractulus* in *E* (at a.5, c.5 e.5 and g.5); each half is further analysable into two rhythmic cells of which the first exhibits, *prima facie*, the characteristics of Mode III. The even-numbered lines present an editorial choice that will be dealt with later; for the present, what can be offered by way of certainty is that these lines also begin with a cell seemingly of Mode III.[28]

The trouble arises if examination of the notation of these cells is restricted to that found in *E*. Here there is no indication that the cells in question, whether written *LBL* or *LBB*, have to be taken with durations of /3,1,2/ *tempora*; a conflicting view has been taken by some transcribers (Pla, Elmes) who read durations of /2,1,2/ *tempora*, casting the whole piece in a quintuple mould maintained where necessary (*i.e.*, in cells where only three beats appear) by the insertion of rests. There is one figure in the notation of *E* which is strongly corroborative of such an interpretation, namely, the *cum-sine* binary ( ) at g.1; this figure, in any conventional view, could only with difficulty be accorded the 3*t* necessary to allow a Mode III interpretation to prevail over the quintuple.[29]

Contrary evidence, however, arises if we take into account the notation of *To*. In this source, at e.1, there occurs a short-stemmed *virga* ( ) generally understood to represent an unequivocal duration of three *tempora* in a context such as this. Its position here at the start of a three-note group would thus appear to make impossible any interpretation other than Mode III; the reading of this one cell must then be taken as extrapolable to the whole piece giving a reading — provisional, in terms of this study — in which cells predominantly of Mode III-type are patterned with others of Mode II (*see* a.4–5 *etc.*) or Mode I (c.4–5 *etc.*) character.

To break the apparent impasse between two incompatible readings, recourse must again be had to the likelihood that what we have in *E* is a 'translation' from an earlier copy with earlier notation; this is made all the more probable given the presence of this piece in *To*. As has been noted in the case of plicas (*see again* Section II), such notational 'translation' does not always represent perfectly the intention of the underlying copy. What is written here in *E* at g.1 may then be taken as a 'loose' use of a descending binary figure whose most literal meaning is not to be trusted. The notation of *E* contains another such case at c.9, repeated at e.9, where descending binary whose literal meaning can only be *L* stands where in *To* there is a *plica* whose meaning can equally be *brevis*. The two figures at e.9 and g.1 in *E* may then be taken as mutually corroborative cases of mistaken use, and the latter thus seen as a shaky foundation on which to build a reading in quintuple metre. The reading of *To* at e.1, with its short-stemmed *virga*, may finally be taken as indicative of the presence of Mode III-type cells throughout, and on this basis dimidiation may be applied to such cells, as is shown in the transcription.

---

[28] It is worth noting in passing that in Escorial notation the last note of each such cell, when it occurs as a *simplex*, is written *B* (requiring alteration) before a *simplex L* (*see* c.3, d.3) but it is written *L* before anything else — which in these instances means a *simplex B* (a.3), and elsewhere would include ligatures. Although the sample is small, this pattern of choice between *LBB* and *LBL* represents a practice that is sufficiently generalised as to be considered as a weakly-enforced norm.

[29] *See again* consideration of this question in n. 3 to this section and corresponding main text.

CANTIGA 255

COMO SANTA MARIA GUARECEU
A MOLLER QUE FEZERA MATAR SEU GENRO
POLO MAL PREZ QUE LL' APÕIAN CON EL,
QUE NON ARDEU NO FOGO EN QUE A METERON

HOW HOLY MARY CURED THE WOMAN
WHO HAD HAD HER SON-IN-LAW KILLED
OVER THE ILL-REPUTE REPORTED TO HER ABOUT HIM
AND HOW SHE DID NOT BURN
IN THE FIRE IN WHICH THEY PUT HER

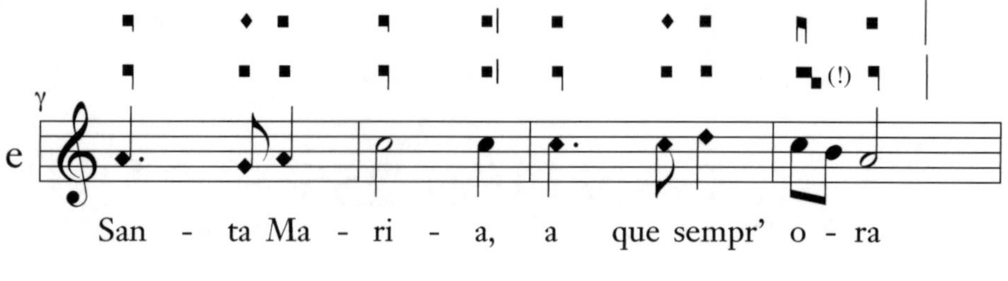

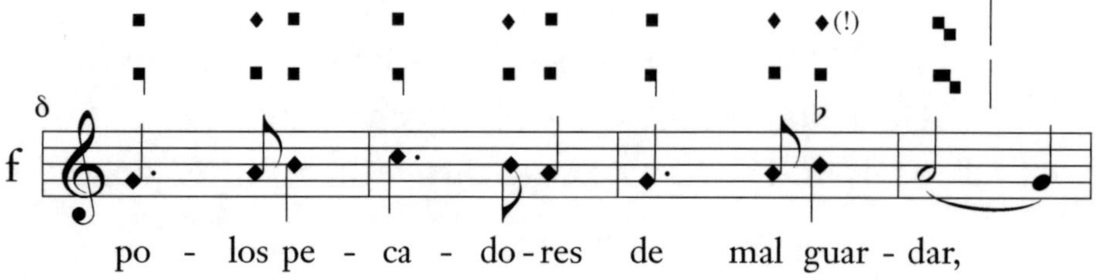

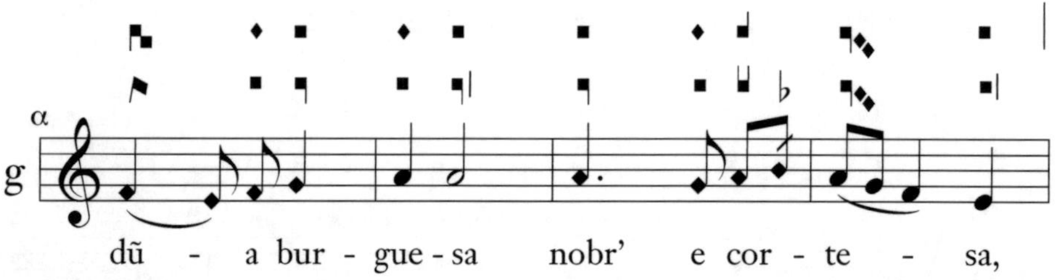

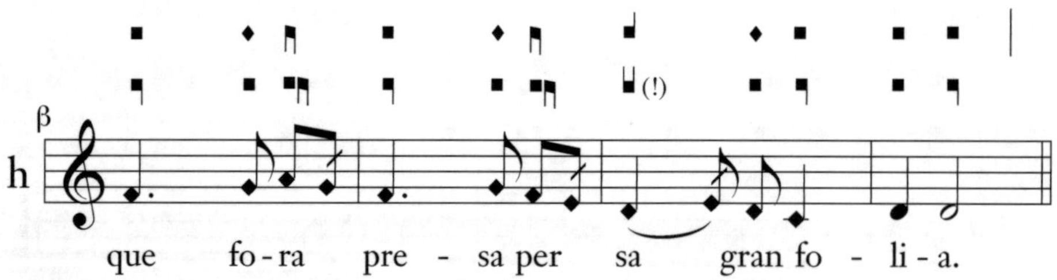

CSM 255: Musical palæography	
To 74, f. 95r Notated: ℜ-0; I *only*. Without flat signature.	*E* 255, f. 231v–232r Notated: ℜ-0; I, first phrase of ℜ-I. Without flat signature. *The repeated phrase does not yield any notational variants.* b.5: written as *L*, then corrected with a line through the stem.

CANTIGA 255: ASSERTIVE NORMALIZATION

The short-stemmed *virga* at e.1 in *To* was used above to confirm the reading of 3*t* at this point and so endorse the reading of the relevant cell, and all others likewise susceptible, as being third mode. But how is the *following* short-stemmed *virga* at e.4 (repeating that at c.4) to be understood? If a reading of 3*t* is enforced here also, it causes serious difficulty in the maintenance of any rhythmic pattern.

Such a reading is not, however, necessary; cases have earlier been encountered in which the short-stemmed *virga* is used with a value of 2*t* in very specific circumstances[30] — circumstances that have to do with the sensitivity to changing durational values at the point of exit from dimidiation, as is the case here. Whilst it may be uncomfortable to encounter two quite distinct uses of the short-stemmed *virga* at such close quarters — e.1 and e.4 —, the latter of these, along with that at c.4, must surely be read with a duration of 2*t*, constituting a case of 'assertive normalization' of temporal values at the sensitive point of exit from a dimidiated cell.

CANTIGA 255: ANOTHER NOTATIONAL CRUX

Perhaps the most serious difficulty of interpretation in *Cantiga* 255 arises from the rising plica at b.7. This is given in *E* as a *plica brevis*, a figure that is repeated at h.7. If this reading is to be respected, it becomes impossible to read this phrase as being constituted by three cells of (dimidiable) Mode III, and the phrase must be read as shown in Example 13:

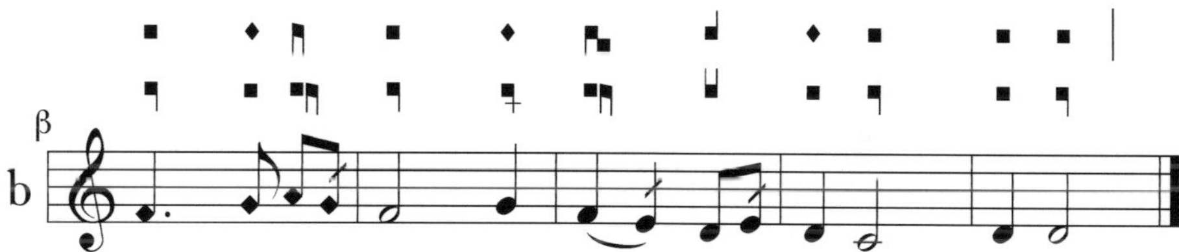

EXAMPLE 13
Cantiga 255: Transcription of the b-phrase
(and by implication the h-phrase)
respecting the ms reading of at b.7

This, it will be seen, matches the transcription given by Huseby (*see* Ex. 12 above).[31] What can be wrong with it?

Well, most obviously its failure to comply with the phrase-lengths of the rest of the piece. Throughout this *cantiga* alternate lines of text display ten syllables (the odd-numbered lines) and eleven syllables (the evens). In the melody of the middle section or *mudanza* (phrases c, d, e and f) the extra syllable is packed in by the use of a dotted cell as the second cell in the phrase (*e.g.*, d.4–5–6), which stands instead of a cell carrying only two syllables (*e.g.*, c.4-5). This use of the 'syllable absorption capacity' of dotted cells has been seen in more than one previous piece, used as a device for balancing musical phrase-lengths when the textual metre is varied. It surely cannot be the case that rhythmic design should respond in this way for part of this composition, but behave differently — spilling over into an extra, asymmetrical cell — in the refrain and *vuelta*.

A corroborative factor that helps to embolden a transcriber to disregard the clear import of the *plica brevis* here is that the notation of *E* bears signs elsewhere of being a 'poor translation' from an underlying copy. This was pointed out above in the case of the unlikely use of at g.1; the descending binary at c.9 and e.9 is another example of a

[30] *See* the Excursus on p. 52 above.
[31] It also, incidentally, matches that of Anglés (1943), except insofar as Anglés does not dimidiate the first three notes.

figure carelessly used. On this basis it can be posited that the ⊔ at b.7 and h.7 is a case of plica confusion arising in the process of translation.

The full transcription is entirely compatible with the notation of *To* at these points. It is also congruent with the version not of Huseby, but of Lopes.

CANTIGA 255: SOME FINAL DETAILS

A number of minor features of the notation of this piece may finally be dealt with.

In *E*: the rising *plica* at a.8, repeated at g.8, may be taken either as altered (can a *plica* undergo alteration?) or else as the result of 'early exit from dimidiation' (*see* the discussion in the next paragraph), or even as a case of plica-confusion; whatever the cause, the rhythmic pattern requires a reading of *L*. Before moving on, it seems appropriate to record an abiding impression of the notation of *E* as less than careful in this piece.

In *To*: the last rhythmic cell in the outer sections (lines a, b, g, h) is given in a form that appears hypermetric, undoubtedly reflecting the phenomenon that has been referred to as cadential lengthening. More worrying are two appearances of the rhomb in *To* at d.9 and f.9, which might be construed as cases of alteration. There is, however, another possible explanation arising once more from the idea of 'early exit from dimidiation'. Whilst the doubling of notated note values that gives rise to dimidiation might be expected to apply to all three notes in a cell of dotted rhythm, there appear to be cases in which the notator does not carry through the doubling right to the end of the cell, leaving the last note written in 'normal' values. Attention was drawn to a possible case in the discussion of *Cantiga* 162;[32] in the present piece, d.7-8 certainly require note-values to be read halved, but d.9, the last figure of the cell, can be understood as representing its normal, undimidiated value, the more easily because the use of a dimidiable *punctum* would conflict with the same figure in the following cell used with a different value. Though no such concern arises in the case of f.9 (because what follows is a ligature), the same understanding may still be applied. It would in any case be dangerous to attempt to build theories of 'alteration in *To*' around such cases as these when another explanation is available.

CANTIGA [407]

This *cantiga* appears in the Appendix of *To*, and — doubtless owing to a scribal lapse — it is the second piece therein to bear the number XII. The metrical asymmetry between refrain and stanza, as well as the lack of a musical *vuelta*, have claimed the attention of Parkinson (2010, p. 322), who goes on to suggest that it was the structural anomaly of this piece that led to its not being copied into the expanded repertory of *E* and *T/F*. As things stand, therefore, *To* is its unique source, and so it is the only piece in the present edition for which we must rely exclusively on *To* notation.

Anglés offers two versions of this *cantiga* (1943, 1958), both predominantly Mode I in character, with some cells of Mode III in the stanza in the later reading. For Wulstan (2001, p. 309; no transcription is offered), the refrain is in Mode I and the stanza in 'bag-

[32] *See* 162.c.3 and the discussion on pp. 38–41 above.

CANTIGA [407]

(*To* App. XII *bis*)

COMO SANTA MARIA FEZ VEER AO OME
QUE CEGARA PORQUE SE COMENDARA AO DEMO

HOW HOLY MARY GAVE SIGHT TO THE MAN
WHO HAD GONE BLIND
BECAUSE HE HAD COMMENDED HIMSELF TO THE DEVIL

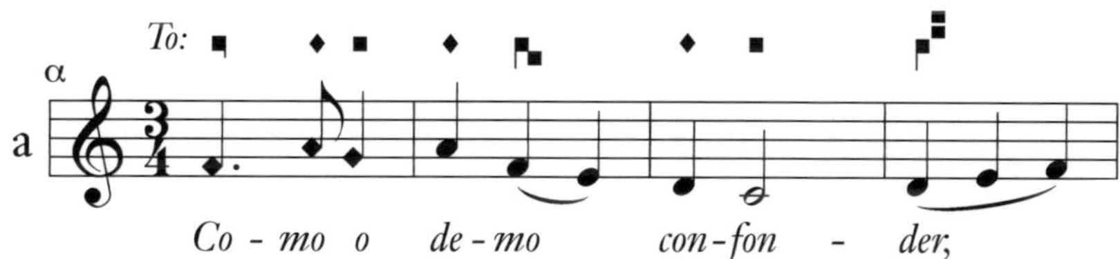
α
a
To:
Co - mo o de - mo con - fon - der,

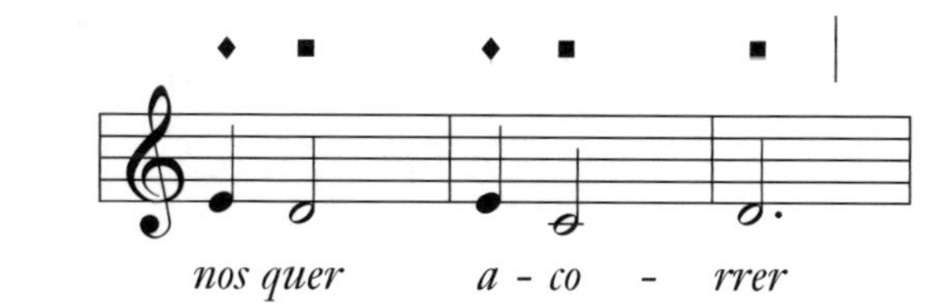
nos quer a - co - rrer

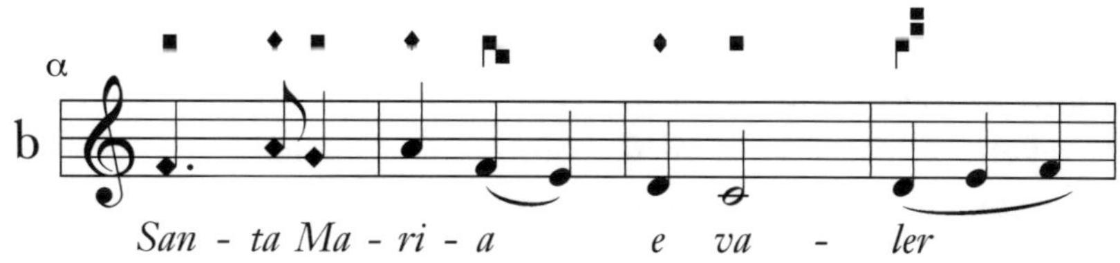
α
b
San - ta Ma - ri - a e va - ler

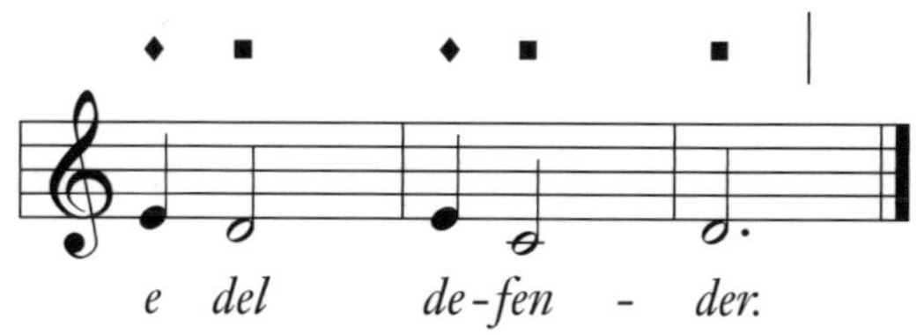
e del de - fen - der.

β
c
(!)
Dest' un mi - ra - gre vos con - ta - rei que vi

β
d
es - crit' en li - vro, e di - zi - a a - ssi

γ
e
com' o - i - re - des a - de - an - te per mi,

δ
f
que foi a Vir - gen fa - zer...

CSM [407]: Musical palæography

To, App. XII *bis*, f. 158v (unique source).
Notated: ℜ-0; I *only*. Without signature.

pipe rhythm'; but I do not find convincing the distinction in rhythmic character between the sections; nor do I find acceptable the violence done to textual stress by forcing parts of it into Mode I.

As to the refrain, a Mode I outcome is possible only if we take the notes in pairs, reading as successive repetitions of ■ ♦ . The first note of the melody (a.1) is, however, 'reinforced' with a short stem, and this is as good an indication as we are likely to get that we should treat it as having a duration of 3*t*. And so, rather than pairs of notes with values /2,1/, we must take the first *three* notes as /3,1,2/, that is, a cell of Mode III which, in the context, invites dimidiation. It should be noticed that after this 'hint' in the form of a stem has been provided once, it is not repeated except at d.1 (Ribera and Elmes are both incorrect in seeing more occurrences); the pattern, once established, must be assumed to persist. After the dotted rhythm, the remainder of the phrase resolves, not as Mode I, but predominantly as Mode II.

There are certainly dotted rhythms in the stanza, as Wulstan implies, but not to the exclusion of others, since they too give way to brief passages which must surely also be heard as Mode II. And so the same two rhythms — cells of dotted rhythm giving way to cells of Mode II — are present in the stanza as in the refrain, providing rhythmic unity to the whole melody; the difference in the number of cells of each type in the two sections is to be seen as a response to the differing syllable-count: 13 (or 8+5) in the refrain, and 11 with a final line of 7 in the stanza. It should be added that the dotted rhythm, as well as that which follows in both sections, supports textual stress in a way that could hardly be bettered.

A doubt may perhaps be expressed regarding the refrain. In the transcription, the first eight notes have been grouped

■ ♦ ■   ■ ♦ ■   ♦ ■

in other words, with the two cells of Mode III coming together at the start. There is, however, another possible grouping:

■ ♦ ■   ■ ♦   ■ ♦ ■

Why is this not preferable? The answer surely lies in the melodic contour: the three notes of identical pitch at c.4–6 are not easily split between two different rhythmic cells; moreover, if treated this way, the highest note of the phrase, c.7, loses its prominence and becomes the weak quaver in the dotted pattern. When we reach the penultimate phrase, it becomes difficult to see how we could group and dimidiate e.6–8, so awkward is the resulting rhythm. In the absence of any *tractulus* or other indication of grouping, the first option is adopted after a process of considered judgement.

One element of the musical palæography that requires comment is the rhomb at c.10. Must we consider this (yet again!) as a case of alteration in *To*? If so, it must be borne in mind that this piece occurs extremely late in *To*, and the notation may carry transitional features. But it seems unlikely, and is probably better viewed as a scribal error; it is, in any case, corrected in the following line (d.10).

Finally, with this transcription we hope to lay to rest the observation by Pla that 'the last *Cantigas* are a torment…because of the lack of a version in *E*'.[33] On the contrary; the notation of *To* is seen to be cogent, and decipherable.

CANTIGA [415]

This *cantiga* was already included in the small collection of Marian Festival pieces present in *To*, where it appears as the second of five. In the enlarged group of twelve *Festas* contained in *E* it figures as the fifth. In the conventional numeration assigned by Mettmann it becomes *Cantiga* 415. There appears to be no published musical transcription other than those available in the standard editions.

The presence of third-mode formulæ in the notation in *To* has been commented upon by Ferreira.[34] Focusing on the notation of *E*, Wulstan's comment that 'Bagpipe rhythm [*i.e.*, dotted rhythm] is the solution to problems caused by *LBB* figures' is appli-

[33] 'Las últimas Cantigas son un tormento…por falta de una versión del Códice E1', Pla 2001, p. 536.
[34] *See* Ferreira (1993), p. 589 and n. 51.

cable once again to this piece;[35] it is a view with which one may readily agree, since the reconciliation of the two notations suggests cells of Mode III inviting dimidiation, giving pockets of dotted rhythm at the start of each musical phrase.

Beyond that, however, the notation of both sources is not without difficulty.

CANTIGA [415]: TRANSITIONAL NOTATION IN *To*

A first necessary step is to seek out symptoms of Escorial features in the notation of *To*; once their presence has been acknowledged, much that would otherwise be obscure becomes clearer.

Phrases c and d — with due allowance for a *rhythmic* discrepancy at figures 4-5 —, are *melodically* identical; the notation of d, moreover, is readily comprehensible as a standard use of Toledo figures, and I submit it would be difficult to disagree with the transcription of phrase d (*see* facing page) insofar as it relies on *To*. However, an examination of the notation of phrase c, and in particular the two figures at c.6-7, and a comparison of them with d.6-7, will suggest that something is awry. The notation of *To* gives, at c.6-7, a long-stemmed, (*i.e.* 'normal') *virga* plus a *punctum*; these must be taken as a rhythmic replication of what appears as ▪ ♦ in Toledo notation in the following phrase (and, in the transcription, vertically below). To be blunt: this is *Escorial* notation in *To* — a case of *L* + *B escurialenses.*

The point having been established, it then becomes evident that the scribe is torn in two directions when he needs to write a *simplex* of duration 1*t*. Each phrase begins with a cell of Mode III (dimidiable) in which the middle note is invariably written ♦ . In phrase d he is punctilious (!) in his use of ♦ . But a look elsewhere, particularly at the final notes of many non-phrase-initial cells, shows a vacillation that is hard to pin down: in cases such as a.5, a.7, a.9, b.6, b.8, c.7 already discussed, c.9 and e.7, therefore, it will be necessary to reach a judgement on whether the notator of *To* has been seduced by 'modern' practice, and is using ▪ in an 'Escorial' sense. To complicate matters, whilst some individual cells adhere totally to one code or the other, there are cells that may be mixed (*e.g.*, c.4-5, e.6-7), and others that could equally be read in either (*e.g.*, b.5-6). In phrase f the notation is once again solidly Toledan, contrasting with that of the supposedly identical b-phrase.

CANTIGA [415]: RECONCILING THE SOURCES

A look at the f-phrase, pellucid in both notations, shows that the two sources can agree at least some of the time. It is interesting to note in passing that at f.3, *E* depends on alteration but *To* does not. The *tractulus* in *To* at f.4 is also interesting. Its function cannot be divisory; it must be taken as part of the process of normalization of beat values after the exit from the dimidiation of the previous cell; its function thus resembles that of the short-stemmed *virga* with a value of 2*t* in the same context.[36]

The principal point at which reconciliation between the two sources is difficult is the sixth and seventh figures in several phrases. Since each musical phrase occurs twice in the course of the piece, it will be easiest if each of the three is considered in turn. As regards the β-phrase, the sixth and seventh figures in both phrase b and phrase f seem to

---

[35] *See* Wulstan (2001), p. 77.

[36] *See* Excursus on p. 52 above.

CANTIGA [415]

(*To FSM* II; *E FSM* V)

COMO O ANGEO GABRIEL
VẼO SAÜDAR A SANTA MARIA
E ESTA FESTA
É NO MES DE MARÇO

HOW THE ANGEL GABRIEL
CAME TO GREET HOLY MARY
AND THIS FEAST
IS IN THE MONTH OF MARCH

CSM [415]: Musical palæography	
To, *Festas de Santa Maria* no. 2, f. 139r	*E*, *Festas de Santa Maria* no. 5, f. 6r
Notated: ℜ-0; I *only*.	Notated: ℜ-0; I *only*.
Flat signature throughout (missing in phrase e).	Flat signature throughout.
The notation dips into and out of Escorial usage, as treated in the discussion.	
b.4: The binary ligature carries two syllables and must be split; *cf* f.4–5.	b.4: The same comment made in relation to *To* applies here also.

establish a Mode I rhythm here quite clearly, even if the notation of *To* differs between the two; it is not as if ♦ and ■ (f.7 and b.7) were interchangeable, rather that the b-phrase, at this point, appears to adopt Escorial conventions. In summary: both occurrences of the β-phrase are readily interpretable as having a third cell of two components with durations of 2 + 1 *tempora*.

Turning to the γ-phrase, we find the situation is less clear-cut. Here *To* once more gives clarity, even if it switches notational code between c.6-7 and d.6-7; the durations again constitute a Mode I cell. But *E* stubbornly gives *LL*. One interpretation is that *E*'s ■ at c.7 is a response to the ■ in *To*, which, though intended with the sense of an *Escorial* breve, is nevertheless 'translated' into *E* as though it were a 'true' Toledan *punctum*. Whether such a surmise provides sufficient grounds for saying that the following d.7 is a downright error in *E* (whether by blind copying of what has just been written, or some other form of scribal insouciance) is grist for the transcriber's mill.

Finally to the α-phrase (lines a and e), where we have the clearest expression of *LL* in both sources, implying durations of /3/3/. If this is laid alongside the /2,1/ reading of the β-phrase, it is in direct contradiction, with the γ-phrase sitting somewhere between. What should be the editorial reaction?

Several choices seem to present themselves. On the one hand it would be possible to accord these sixth and seventh figures a duration of 3*t* + 3t (*i.e.*, two perfect *Ls*) in the α-phrase, and durations of 2*t* + 1*t* (*i.e.*, a cell of Mode I) in the β-phrase, even though this breaks the phrase regularity of the piece. The remaining γ-phrase is the most conflictive since the sources seem irreconcilable, but perhaps priority should be given to the version that might claim chronological priority, that is, *To*. If these decisions are implemented, we reach the reading given in partial form in Example 14.

EXAMPLE 14
Cantiga [415]
Rejected reading with unbalanced phrase-lengths

On the other hand, it could be argued that (i) since Mode I is the predominant rhythm everywhere else except in the dotted cells, and (ii) since the introduction of a /3/3/ segment would produce a disruptive sense of hiatus in the rhythmic flow, and (iii) since the extra intrusive *L* puts the phrase-lengths out of balance, and (iv) since the notational anarchy in *To* is such that any subsequent version stood little chance of being entirely cogent,[37] *then* it is more likely that the rhythmic structure of the piece was intended to be regular, as were the phrase-lengths. And so it has been rendered in the full transcription.

A third possibility is that we are actually dealing here with genuine rhythmic variants between the sources. This would allow us to take the critical cell(s) (in terms of the full transcription, the third bar of each phrase) as having a duration of 3*t* in the β-phrase in both sources, and in the α-phrase a duration of 6*t*, also in both; the variant thus comes in the γ-phrase, where we would see a duration of 6*t* in *E* but only 3*t* in *To*. But this would be to suggest that phrase-length is and always was inherently unstable in this *cantiga*. A case, then, for judgement and not proof.

[37] This supposes that the notator of *E* had the version from *To*, or some cognate version, as his model.

CANTIGA [419]

This piece is given as the last of the five *Festas* of the Virgin in *To*, and as the ninth of the enlarged set of twelve *Festas* in *E*. The notation and rhythm appear to have attracted no attention beyond the standard editions. Here Anglés takes conventional interpretations of ligatures such as and ; this reading contributes to a not untypical amalgam of binary, ternary and quaternary cells (*see* Example 15 below). And whilst in his view the group b.1-3 (his γ-phrase) may add up to a total of six *tempora*, his transcription allocates this group to two discrete cells, giving /2,1/3/, rather than seizing the opportunity of seeing a single group of /3,1,2/ in a cell of (apparently) Mode III (*see again* Ex. 15). It is this latter grouping that allows emergence of a dimidiable cell, bringing dotted-rhythm into the interpretation of this *cantiga*.

To,F.V.5,f.141 b-c
E1,F.V.9,f.8c-d-9a
To
Des quan - do Deus sa Ma-dre a - os çe -
os le - vou, de nos le - var con - si - go car - rei - ra
nos mos - trou.
etc.

EXAMPLE 15
Cantiga [419]: Refrain
(Anglés, 1943)

CANTIGA [419]: A TOUCH OF DOTTED RHYTHM

Provided the ascending *cum-sine* binary is taken with overall value of *B*, and the ternary ligature is read simply as overall *L* (rather than by segmental analysis which gives Anglés's *BBB*), the notation of *E* gives strong enough grounds for an interpretation largely in Mode I (with anacrusis), with occasional but regular intrusions of a perfect *L* (a.6, b.6, c.6 *etc.*); this leaves an *LBL* group at the start of phrases b and f. Interpreting this group at face value (*i.e.*, as a cell of Mode III) causes the melody to stall at the juncture with the previous phrase (whether or not the final note of that phrase is prolonged); more particularly, the second and third notes of the group inject a segment of Mode II-type rhythm, which is at variance with the prevailing pattern. If, on the other hand, the *LBL* group is

CANTIGA [419]

(*To FSM* V; *E FSM* IX)

COMO SANTA MARIA PASSOU DESTE MUNDO
E SE FOI AO CEO
E ESTA FESTA É NO MES D' AGOSTO MEIANTE

HOW HOLY MARY PASSED ON FROM THIS WORLD
AND WENT TO HEAVEN
AND THIS FEAST IS IN THE MIDDLE OF AUGUST

To:
E:
α
a
Des quan - do Deus sa Ma - dre
a - os ce - os le - vou
β
b
de nos le - var con - si - go
ca - rrei - ra nos mos - trou.

γ

c

Ca pois le - vou a - que - la

que nos deu por se - nnor

γ

d

e el fi - llou por ma - dre,

mos - trou - nos que a - mor

α

e

(!)

mui gran - de nos a - vi - a,

β
f
ca
pe - ra
o
seu
rei
-
no

lo - go
nos
con - vi - dou.

CSM [419]: Musical palæography	
To, *Festas de Santa Maria* no. 5, f. 141r–v Notated: ℜ-0; I *only*. Flat signature throughout. a.7: missing, as is the corresponding syllable; Anglés supplies ▪ .	*E*, *Festas de Santa Maria* no. 9, f. 8v–9r Notated: ℜ-0; I *only*. Flat signature throughout.

treated with dimidiation, the resultant cell of dotted rhythm helps to keep the phrase-structure of the whole piece tidy and in balance. Dotted rhythm is thus present in the outer sections of this *cantiga*, but in such a minor way that it is hardly surprising it does not seem previously to have been noticed or commented upon.

The notation of *To* has to work harder to give occasional hints about the interpretation of its ambiguous binary ligatures as *L* or *B*. First, we notice that the plication found at a.2, e.2 in *E* has been sacrificed in *To*, possibly because a plica here would contribute too high a degree of ambiguity; the resultant *simplex* ▪ lends greater rhythmic certainty. Then at a.9, the stem on the *podatus* adds weight, and helps to mark it as longer than the following *clivis* (*cf* e.9: the distinction in length, once stated, need not be repeated). For the inherent ambiguity of these two figures, compare b.9–10, which must be interpreted according to the prevailing rhythmic pattern. The same may be said of e.4–5, where the minor melodic variant in respect of a.5 risks total rhythmic confusion if the established pattern is not held to.

Finally, the stem at e.2 in *To* would be worrying; this is not a context in which a *virga* would be easily explainable. The following note, however, proves to be a square *punctum*, and if the two are taken together they may be seen as a cell written not in *Toledo* notation but following the conventions of the Escorial sources. This, then, is another instance, albeit a minor one, of transitional notation in *To*.

A Brief Excursus on Juncture Phenomena following Dimidiation

Attention has repeatedly been drawn to the sensitive nature of the notational environment at and near the interface between a rhythmic cell whose figures must be read with halved duration and a following cell where this does not apply. The fact that the same symbol may represent different durations according as it is used before or after the juncture-point gives rise to a number of phenomena that may now be considered together.

The first of these is a seemingly anomalous use in *To* of the short-stemmed *virga* in a position immediately after the juncture. Its appearance is due to the fact that the ordinary square *punctum*, normally of 2*t* duration, will have had a dimidiated duration of only one *tempus* if used in the preceding dotted cell; if the cell following the interface begins with a note of 2*t* duration, the use of a reinforced or strengthened note-form averts possible confusion. This process has been referred to as 'assertive normalization', and was discussed in an Excursus on p. 52 above.

Second, in the dimidiated cell itself, the expectation is that halving of temporal values will apply to all three figures, tightly bound in their common participation in a dotted group. This is not always the case, however, and it sometimes occurs that the third note in the group will be presented using a figure that represents the undimidiated or absolute duration of the note concerned. This may be in anticipation of the same figure being used with the same absolute value immediately on the other side of the juncture. The phenomenon has been referred to as 'early exit from dimidiation'; it was discussed in relation to its occurrence in *Cantiga* 162, on pp. 38–41 above. This phenomenon, when it occurs in *To*, can provide an alternative explanation for what otherwise might be taken to be cases of alteration.

Third, the reverse process, 'late exit from dimidiation' may also occur, though not as frequently. It is perhaps difficult to distinguish from another tendency that surfaces on occasion, to overstate the duration of the note immediately after the interface-point — a procedure that also has aspects in common with the first phenomenon described above.

Finally, the notation has the capacity to highlight the need to take the first figure after the juncture at full (*i.e.*, undimidiated) value by placing a *tractulus* or even a bar after it. Such a case is seen, for example, in *Cantiga* 415 following the *punctum* at f.4 in *To*. This means that a *tractulus* can be used at various points in relation to dotted rhythm, although with a meaning that also varies; after the third or fifth figure it is likely to have a divisory or grouping function; after the fourth figure, as described here (the first after the interface point), it helps enforce normalization of beat-values by suggesting 'full extension' of the duration of the figure concerned.

All of these phenomena bring an inbuilt awareness of the danger that accompanies the shift from reading figures with dimidiated or halved values, as in the dotted-rhythm cell, and reading them with full or 'normalized' durations. That danger is at its highest when a figure just before the juncture between cells would be followed by another identical one representing a different duration. Whether instinctively or by design, it seems that the notators of the *Cantigas* frequently deployed one (or sometimes more) of the above techniques in an effort to avert confusion.

VI
THREE MARGINAL CASES

In the literature dealing with notation and rhythm in the *Cantigas de Santa Maria* mention is sometimes made of specific pieces in relation to dotted rhythm or related matters. Three such references are taken up in this brief section, with a view to eliminating the pieces concerned from our enquiries.

CANTIGA 19

In a section in which he considers 'Bagpipe rhythms' in the *Cantigas*, Wulstan suggests that '*CSM* 19...has an upbeat that should probably be read as Bagpipe rhythm'.[1] If by 'upbeat' is meant an anacrusis, then I am at a loss, because I do not find one (*see* transcription of refrain in Ex. 16), nor any way of interpreting the opening figures that could be construed as providing one.

EXAMPLE 16
Cantiga 19: Refrain

Even if the search for dotted rhythm is widened, it is difficult to see where it might be found. The opening three figures cannot be pressed into a dotted cell, since the notation of *To* makes clear that the second and third notes are of equal duration — not to mention the unlikely accentuation of *san-de-cé* that would result from dotting, or the strain that would be placed on interpreting the duration of the fourth figure. Nor can the apparently opposite propriety binary ligatures (▘▀) be implicated: these are simply a notational quirk of *E*,[2] as was recognized even by Anglés who disregarded them in favour of the reading of *T*, where ▖▀ is found. All in all, and in the absence of any clearer indication, there appears to be no reason for pursuing the question of dotted rhythm in respect of this piece. The partial transcription given above is my own, but it is in essential

[1] *See* Wulstan 2001, p. 304; *see again also* n. 17 to Section I above, and corresponding main text.

[2] This feature of the notation of *E* was alluded to in Section II above.

agreement with those of Anglés, Pla and Elmes, all of whom concur in offering an irregularly mixed Mode I–Mode II interpretation, with the occasional intrusion of a perfect figure (a cell of Mode V, so to speak) in the refrain.[3] Indeed, although the terminology is different, Wulstan too allocates this piece to his 'iambo-trochaic' category, and his transcription of it is congruent with that given above, at least as far as rhythmic interpretation is concerned.[4]

CANTIGA 61

In the course of a discussion of dotted rhythm and how it is notated, Ferreira provides a list of seventeen *cantigas* in which it is found; although he is dealing essentially with the phenomenon as it occurs in pieces with binary rhythm, *Cantiga* 61 uniquely in the list is

EXAMPLE 17
Cantiga 61: Refrain

in ternary metre.[5] A glance at Example 17, however, will show that the rhythm at the end of the melodic phrase, with its *ultra mensuram* long notated with double *tractulus*, does not correspond in any way to the sort of dotted rhythm of interest in the present study, and so *Cantiga* 61 need not detain us.

CANTIGA 78

This piece is one of three dealt with briefly by Ferreira in the context of a discussion of the 'compression' of Mode III cells to match the overall duration of other cells that are

[3] The 'intrusions' that disrupt the Mode I–Mode II mould occur in the third cell of both phrases of the refrain, to accommodate text that is a syllable shorter per line than the corresponding passage in the stanza. This may be seen at the syllables *faz* and *Deus* in Ex. 16.
[4] Wulstan 2001, p. 58, and transcription, Ex. 2.12, p. 59. In his transcription Wulstan seeks to iron out the syllabic inequality between refrain and stanza (*see* preceding note) by expanding *faz* paragogically, and by splitting the diphthong of *Deus*.
[5] *See* Ferreira 2000, p. 12 and n. 30, previously mentioned in n. 11 to Section I above. From a comment given in Ferreira 2015, p. 18, I deduce that my reading given here in Ex. 17 coincides with his view, against that of Anglés (1943) and Elmes (2014) who take an essentially Mode II reading without anacrusis.

adjacent.[6] In the present case Ferreira compresses not only the first three figures (*see* Ex. 18), seen as a cell of Mode III, but also the fourth and fifth, both read with durations of three *tempora*.

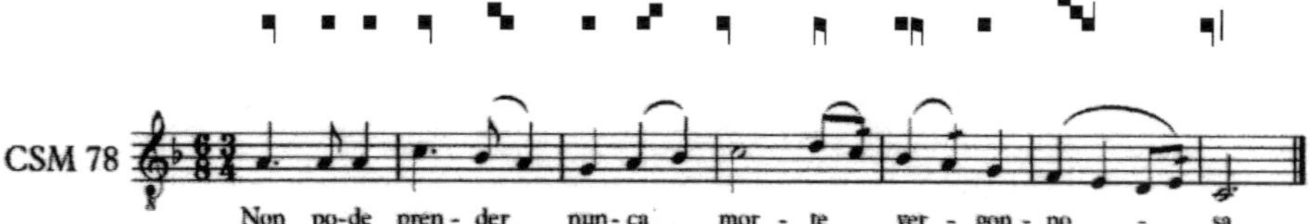

EXAMPLE 18
Cantiga 78 (First phrase)
Ferreira, 2014, Ex. 13, p. 50
The palæography of E has been suprascripted to Ferreira's transcription.

A cursory look at Ferreira's transcription might suggest that the first two bars present dotted rhythm, in the sense that the term has been used in these pages. The mixed time signature, however, brings up once again the question of the retention of binary subdivision within a cell that has been 'compressed', suggesting (though perhaps not making explicit) that the first bar must be felt in 6/8 rather than in simple triple time; this puts such a transcription at one remove from dotted rhythm in any straightforward sense. The second bar of the transcription presents a different picture, for what is being compressed here is not a cell of Mode III, but rather (should we wish to see it in such terms) two cells of Mode V, which is another way of saying two components each of the duration of a perfect *L*. Whilst there is an apparent overlap between the idea of compression and that of dotted rhythm extracted by dimidiation, the two do not mesh in this instance.

There is in any case a rather more fundamental difficulty which stands in the way of seeing this piece as in any way comparable to those with dotted rhythm, namely a doubt whether the notation of the piece really allows any interpretation — even without compression — in the way that is proposed. Problems centre on the first four figures and the

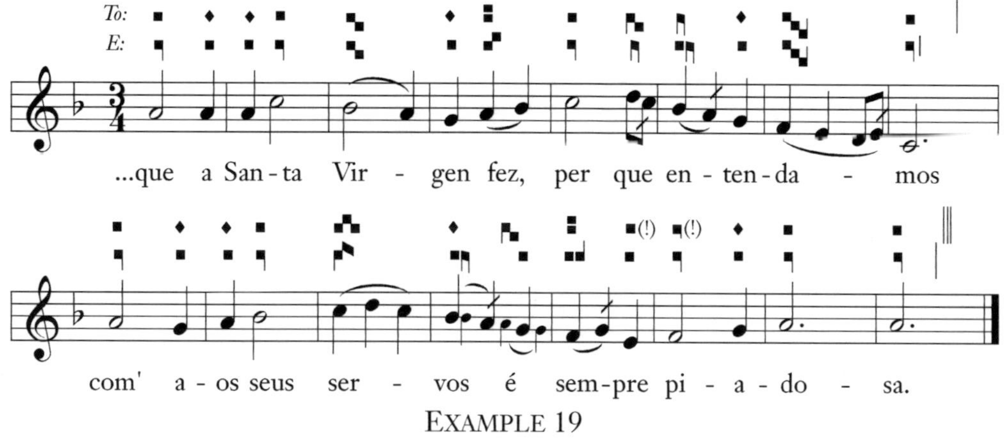

EXAMPLE 19
Cantiga 78: *Vuelta* section

[6] *See* Ferreira 2014, esp. pp. 50–1. The other two pieces considered by Ferreira, as already noted, are *CSM* 20 (*see* Section III above) and *CSM* 10 (*see* Section VII below).

way they are notated particularly in *To*. For comparative purposes a transcription is provided of the *vuelta* of this piece (*see* Ex. 19), where the notation is clearer. Here the first four figures in both phrases are given in *To* in the form ▪ ♦ ♦ ▪ , which, in view of the immovable clarity with which these things are expressed in *To*, leaves no doubt that we are *not* dealing with a cell of Mode III, but rather with an expression of /2,1/1,2/ *tempora*. A look at all phrases (there are only six) shows that they all begin rhythmically in the same way (those of the middle section substitute ▪ for the fourth figure, without disturbing the rhythmic profile) with the single exception of the first phrase. In that first phrase, *To* does indeed give ▪ ♦ ▪ , which is what appears to underlie Ferreira's transcription; it would be difficult, however, to impose this on the other five phrases, which by weight of evidence surely put the opening phrase in need of correction.[7] These considerations put this *cantiga* out of reach of any attempt to reconcile 'compression' with dimidiation.

[7] A further look at the very first note of all in *To*, which has the initial appearance of a short-stemmed *virga*, reveals that it may in fact be a square *punctum* with an appended ink-dribble. A close examination of the codex itself might be necessary to clarify this. If so, suspicion falls on the third note, given as ▪ in the first phrase but ♦ elsewhere. A scribal error? Possibly — and one that is perhaps echoed by other lapses right at the very end of the piece; here the fifth-last and fourth-last figures, given as ▪ and ▪ (*see* Ex. 19), are patently erroneous.

VII
THREE PROBLEMATIC CASES

Whether dotted rhythm is perceived in the three cases dealt with in this section raises questions particular to each that may cause doubts about such readings.

CANTIGA 25 IN ITS TOLEDO VERSION [*To* 38]

Cantiga 25 is not problematic if we restrict our attention to the Escorial codices. Here there is a general consensus that the opening *LBB* represents a dactylic binary rhythm that persists through the phrase (*see* Example 20 below);[1] virtually all the available transcriptions so interpret it, from Anglés through Huseby to Elmes, with even Pla being broadly in agreement.[2] Wulstan on two occasions provides a transcription of the refrain which is also in rhythmic agreement.[3] And Ferreira, in his treatment of Arabo-Andalusian traits in the *CSM*, gives for this piece a rhythmic schema — consistent with the reading below — which exemplifies the rhythmic cycle known in Arab theory as *thaqil thânî* or 'first thaqil'.[4]

EXAMPLE 20
Cantiga 25: Refrain
as commonly understood.

[1] The dactylic pulse is maintained by a complex interplay of textual and musical elements: at the outset in each phrase, by allocation of syllables in a dactylic pattern; throughout the phrase, by melodic movement in the second half of each cell except the last.

[2] *See* Anglés 1943; Huseby 1983, p. 125; Elmes, First and subsequent editions; Pla 2001, where the rhythm is described as 'dactylic tetrameter'; some of the foregoing editions display minor disagreement over the interpretation of the eighth figure, but without disturbance to the overall matrix. The only exception is López Elum (2005), whose transcription seems to derive at least in part from a view that the *LBB* notation represents ternary metre, with all the longs perfect, much breve alteration, and some supposedly Lambertian interpretation of ligatures with the general effect of obscuring any regular metrical profile.

[3] *See* Wulstan 2000, Ex. 1, p. 36; 2001, Ex. 2.15, p. 69. Whilst Wulstan's view of rhythmic interpretation matches that of other editors, his approach to text and its syllabification is characterized by an insistence on paragogy. On the difference between *To* and *T/E*, see Wulstan 2000 *bis*, pp. 178–9.

[4] *See* Ferreira 2000, p. 12 and Ex. 2[b], p. 13; 2015, pp. 11–12.

CANTIGA 25: NOTATION IN *To*

When the version found in *To* is examined, a rhythm different from that discussed above is implied from the very first notes of each phrase. Instead of the phrase-initial ▪̩ ▪ ▪ found in the Escorial codices, phrases in *To* begin with ▪ ♦ ▪ or on occasion ▪̩ ♦ ▪ , strongly suggesting a cell of Mode III. The presence of such Mode III formulas in the notation of this piece in *To* was flagged a quarter of a century ago by Ferreira,[5] who also makes it clear that his identification of an Arab rhythmic cycle in relation to this piece does not apply to the version found in *To*.[6] More recently, Ferreira has expressed the view that the notation of *To* allows perception of third-mode patterns 'embedded in otherwise regular binary metre'.[7] Wulstan is rather more forthright in his view: commenting on the groups ▪̩ ♦ ▪ and ▪ ♦ ▪ he observes that 'neither...makes sense in the context', and that they constitute a 'rare rhythmic misjudgment on the part of *To*';[8] 'the peculiarities of the *To* notation of *CSM* 25 are seen to be an aberration...'.[9] *To*'s chosen rhythmic scheme is 'unlikely'.[10]

There is, nevertheless, one interpretation that seems not to have been tried. It comes about by bringing together two different aspects of the notation of this piece in *To*. The first, already much aired above, is the presence of an apparent cell of Mode III at the start of each phrase, to be interpreted not at face value (such a rendering would indeed stand out as awkward in the context), but dimidiated, as a cell of dotted rhythm; the second, an interpretation of the remainder of the phrase in ternary, not binary, rhythm. This is possible thanks to the ambiguity of the plicas and *clives* which can be read with duration of one *tempus* only. Such a reading is given in the full transcription (*see* opposite).

Leaving aside for a moment problems associated with the first figure of all, it can be seen that the plicas (such as a.5 and a.7, c.7 and d.7 *etc.*) have been taken as providing a single beat as the last in three-beat cells, following the unambiguous *2t* of the square *puncta*. The two cases of *clivis* at b.5 and b.7 may be taken as examples of a similar treatment of ambiguous ligatures. One problem may be immediately dismissed, that of the line endings four of which are written ▪ ▪ ; these may be taken as cases of cadential lengthening (dealt with in Section II), allowing an interpretation in ternary metre; by contrast the cadence in phrase f, written ♦ ▪ , would be difficult to explain if a ternary reading were *not* being taken. The only real remaining obstacle to a ternary reading is the case of the *punctum* at f.5, which it must be admitted looks like one half of a binary pair. But this is only one figure in eighty; if it is taken as a scribal error, the rate of occurrence of figures at odds with a ternary reading still remains extremely low, and well within arguable limits.[11]

---

[5] *See* Ferreira 1993, p. 589 and n. 51.

[6] *See* Ferreira 2000, n. 23.

[7] Ferreira 2015, p. 22.

[8] *See again* Wulstan 2000, p. 36. It must be recalled that in Wulstan's view *To* is seen as a late copy; whilst he entertains the possibility (2001, p. 73) that *To* may be revising the rhythm of this piece, he concludes that the rhythmic difference represented by *To* comes about through a misreading or misinterpretation of an underlying exemplar.

[9] Wulstan 2000, p. 56.

[10] Wulstan 2009, p. 203.

[11] Ferreira (1993, pp. 585–6) has suggested that a tolerable level of scribal error might be 2½ %. Four other factors including cadential lengthening are also accorded a similar level of tolerance, with the figure for overall expectation of notational reliability coming out at 87½ %.

CANTIGA 25

'TOLEDO' VERSION: *To* 38

COMO A IMAGEN DE SANTA MARIA
FALOU EN TESTIMONIO
ENTRE O CRISCHÃO E O JUDEU

HOW THE STATUE OF HOLY MARY
SPOKE IN EVIDENCE
BETWEEN THE CHRISTIAN AND THE JEW

γ
e
que fe - zo a Vir - gen sen par,

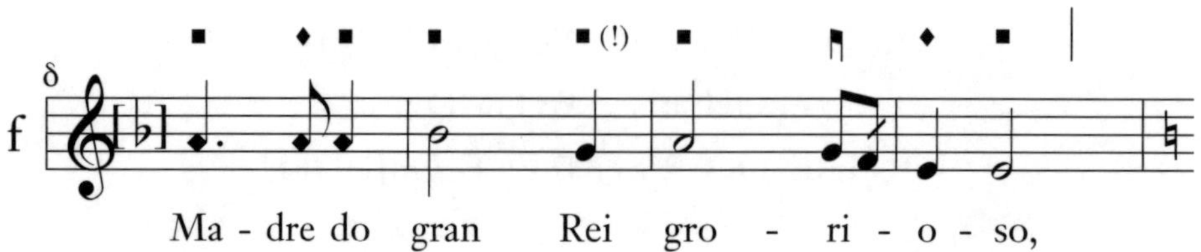
(!)
δ
f
Ma - dre do gran Rei gro - ri - o - so,

α
g
por un o - me que seu a - ver

(!)
β
h
to - do ja des - pen - dud' a - vi - a

α
i
por fa - zer ben e mais va - ler,

(!)
β
j
ca non ja en ou - tra fo - li - a.

CSM 25 (*To* 38): Musical palæography
To 38, f. 50r–v.
Notated: ℜ-0; I *only*.
A single flat signature is placed at the start of phrase e.
a.1: this figure is placed on D (*see* discussion).

Returning to the first figure, ꜝ at a.1, the codex places this on D, which at first sight seems to be at variance with the melody as known from *T* and *E*. The difficulty consists in working out what is implied by each of the two stems. It can hardly be plicated in both directions; but if the first stem is taken as a pre-plication, it is possible to understand the figure as first sounding on E (seeing it maybe as a short-stemmed *virga* which is also pre-plicated?); its melodic interpretation needs also to be taken in the context of the phrase-opening in lines c, e, g and i.

CANTIGA 25: ADDITIONAL QUESTIONS

Although questions of modality are not of primary concern here, this transcription can hardly be left without some comment on the matter. The Toledo codex places the *finalis* of this melody on C, which differs from the Escorial codices which place it on G. The most important implication of this transposition is that the Escorial version cadences with a *subfinalis* that is a whole tone below the *finalis*, whereas the Toledo version cadences subsemitonally. It is difficult to see how these versions can be reconciled without the deployment in *T* and *E* of an (unwritten) F sharp; as has been remarked elsewhere, we are navigating here in deep waters; but the broad implication is that an adherence to ecclesiastical modes and their associated expectations appears not to be reconcilable with what the manuscript sources are telling us.

CANTIGA 25: CONCLUSIONS

The reason *Cantiga* 25 is problematic is that the version contained in one of the sources, *To*, has been viewed as somehow incomprehensible and so not admitted for consideration. In the foregoing analysis an attempt has been made to demonstrate that, while parts of the version contained in *To* — generally the cells *after* the first in each phrase — are compatible with the generally accepted transcription, because of inbuilt ambiguities they also have a life of their own and contribute to a previously unrecovered rhythm.

By way of conclusion, then, let there be no diffidence. This is a viable transcription, and if *To* were the only source it is difficult to see how any different understanding could be arrived at. It presupposes that *To* on the one hand and *T* and *E* on the other record different rhythmic versions of this piece; this would not be the only *cantiga* for which this is true, although by presenting a ternary version of what in the Escorial sources appears as binary, it might be seen as swimming against the tide of progressive ternarization of *cantiga* metre.[12]

[12] Ferreira (1994, p. 87, n. 79) points out six *cantigas* binary in *To* but with ‘isochronous movement’ in *T* / *E*.

CANTIGA 10

Cantiga 10 must surely be one of the best-known and most recorded pieces in the whole corpus.[13] Even so, in spite of the fact that numerous differing musical versions have been published, it is still possible to agree with Ferreira's comment that it is among those *cantigas* that 'have so far resisted a satisfying modern transcription'.[14] Whether the application of dimidiation can provide a suitable remedy will depend at least in part on how well the resultant dotted rhythms match patterns of textual stress — a question that, as will be seen, is not without its difficulties.

CANTIGA 10: METRICAL MATTERS

Before proceeding, a word on textual metre. Whilst that of the stanzas presents no difficulty,[15] that of the refrain must be seen as problematic in two regards. First, in his recent edition Parkinson presents the metre of the refrain as being based not as usual on syllable-count, but as 'accentual', with four metrical accents per line (this explains the apparently miscellaneous number of syllables in the first line); and second, as a consequence, he suppresses the conjunction *e*, as an intrusive attempt to regularise the syllable-count.[16] Whilst these views are undoubtedly helpful in explaining anomalous aspects of the first line, they also raise editorial problems from a musical perspective. If metrical accent is of importance in the text, to what extent should we expect it to be enhanced musically? And should the unstressed conjunction *e*, which occupies a strongly accented note no matter how the phrase is edited, be suppressed in a musical edition also? Given the imponderable nature of some of the implications — we cannot know whether the melody as we have it was a response to the text with or without the conjunction, much less whether those responsible for combining text and melody were aware of a layer of metrical accent in its genesis — it has been decided that for present purposes the suppression of a syllable is something that cannot be undertaken, lest problems be compounded rather than solved.[17] Another layer of the question is revealed if the first two lines of the first stanza are examined, for in them the conjunction *e* appears a further three times; the two occurrences in line 2, moreover, are musically accented, with no other interpretation of the notation possible. One might wonder, therefore, whether the musical accenting of the unstressed conjunction, far from being a problem, was in fact an intended feature — even in the refrain.

---

[13] It is also a piece much analysed and commented on from textual, literary and musical standpoints: no fewer than 71 references are given for *CSM* 10 in Snow's *Bibliography* (2012).

[14] Ferreira 2014, p, 50. Ten versions of *Cantiga* 10 are collated and discussed by Katz (1990). Early attention includes a transcription by Aubry (1907) and melodic analysis Collet and Villalba (1911). Ferreira (2015, p. 3, n. 9) refers to a 1924 transcription by no less a figure than Ludwig, of whom Anglés was a student. Astonishingly, that by Lopes (1945) anticipates dimidiation, as with *CSM* 255.

[15] The form is that of a straightforward *zéjel* rhyming *aaab*, with ten (metrical) syllables per line (the fourth line, being *grave*, has an eleventh *real* syllable).

[16] *See* Parkinson 2015, p. 52. Wulstan also comments on the metrical scheme of *CSM* 10 as possibly *sui generis*, with Adonean (= dactyl + spondee) features; he further comments on the conjunction *e* in the first line, and its position on the musical accent. *See* Wulstan 2000, p. 53, 58; 2001, p. 57, 97, 115, 148, 280, 283, 299 and 309.

[17] Questions such as the need to group notational figures if a syllable is suppressed are alluded to in a note after the textual edition of this piece; *see* Appendix.

CANTIGA 10: READING THE NOTATION

The question of rhythmic interpretation may be approached in the first instance by revisiting the reading offered by Anglés (*see* first line of Ex. 21). Here we find a strongly characterised Mode III interpretation, including the second rhythmic cell which is interpreted with an overall value of 6*t*, and so compatible with the surrounding Mode III.[18] The following line of the Example gives my own transcription;[19] here the first cell is no different, but the total duration of the second rhythmic cell is halved, in the belief that the version provided by Anglés could surely not be what the notation says. I was not the first to take this view; a glance at Katz's 'stack' of versions shows that even Anglés himself

(i)
Ro - sa das ro - sas e Fror das fro - res
(ii)
Ro - sa das ro - sas e Fror das frores
(iii)
Ro - sa das ro - sas e Fror das fro - res

EXAMPLE 21

Cantiga 10: Three readings of the opening phrase
(i) Anglés 1943; (ii) Cunningham 2000; (iii) with dimidiation.

had experimented with shortening the duration attributed to the fourth figure.[20] A disadvantage of the transcription, however, is the sudden change in speed of textual enunciation, which passes from a leisurely first three syllables to an unprepared lurch forward with the fourth.

And so to the question of dimidiation. Are the Mode III cells here susceptible? The third line of Ex. 21 incorporates dimidiation of the first and third cells; both of these are still understood as exhibiting an underlying Mode III pattern, but are now presented with halved values, giving a dotted rhythm in ternary metre. For the first two bars the 3/4 time signature ensures deployment of musical accents in a way that complements the distribution of stressed and unstressed syllables, such as could hardly be bettered. For the

[18] Anglés's insistence on the Mode III basis for the rhythm is evident from his unpublished jottings, as examined by Rosell (1985, p. 529). The Mode III reading was further propounded by Ferreira (1993, p. 589, n. 51), although Ferreira was later to observe that the notation is as compatible with a reading in five beats as in six (2000, p. 16). Transcriptions in quintuple metre have been offered by Pla (2001) and, with acknowledgment to Ferreira, by Elmes (2004 and later editions).

[19] *See again* Cunningham 2000; time values have been doubled with respect to those used in the original publication.

[20] *See again* Katz 1990, pp. 174 *ff.*

second half of the phrase, however, the conjunction *e*, acknowledged above to be problematic, takes the principal musical accent, whilst the noun *Fror* is placed on the short unaccented note in the middle of the dotted group. Any attempt to judge the satisfactoriness of the dimidiation in this first phrase thus comes up against the brick wall of the conjunction *e*, and questions ranging from whether it should legitimately be accented, to whether it should be there at all. An unhelpful situation.

CANTIGA 10: EXTENSION OF THE PROCESS

Attention may now pass to the full transcription (*see* opposite) in which dimidiation has been applied to the Mode III cells throughout the whole piece, as witnessed by the plethora of rhombic noteheads. The time-signature is given as 3 /4, which ensures that the dotted rhythms may be perceived as such, implying no accent on the middle short note.

Problems immediately surface if this dotted pattern, with its associated musical accents, is enforced. The difficulties are seen most acutely in respect of the fifth syllable in several lines: in phrases c and d this syllable is textually stressed, but not only is it musically unaccented, but it is also crammed into the weakest short note of the cell. In phrases b and f similar problems arise, with the rhythmic environment crowded by melodic movement on frational beats, such that — particularly in phrase f — the supposedly stressed syllable at f.5 is submerged in the unaccented semiquaver detail.[21] In several pieces previously examined there has been a good weak-to-weak correlation between textually unstressed syllables and the short unaccented middle note of the dotted group. But not here, at least not in the first stanza.

What would be needed in this case for a good accentual correspondence? Since the musical phrases that carry the stanza consist of three consecutive dotted cells before the cadence, a textual pattern with stressed syllables in fourth and seventh positions in the line would be ideal. Although Galician versification does not come with made-to-measure stress-patterns, there are nevertheless passages of this text that constitute a very good match indeed; such, for example, is the fourth stanza, once we get beyond the first line:

...e de que q<u>e</u> - ro se - <u>e</u>r tro - ba - d<u>o</u>r
se eu per r<u>e</u>n p<u>o</u>ss' a - v<u>e</u>r seu a - m<u>o</u>r
d<u>ou</u> a - o d<u>e</u> - mo os <u>ou</u> - tros a - m<u>o</u> - res.[22]

Such a passage fits the dimidiated reading of the melody hand-in-glove.

What emerges, then, is a mixed picture. As has been repeatedly observed, it is not feasible to expect a complete correspondence between textual stress and musical accent, quite simply because of the way Galician versification allows freedom in the placement of the former. Even so, the difficulty experienced in this case with the first stanza raises a question mark over the viability of the dotted reading.

---

[21] By way of mitigation, infinitives (such as here) seem to be a class of words regularly treated with misplaced musical accent, though this is an area in need of fuller study.

[22] Textually stressed syllables are underscored. The two syllables *ren poss'* from the middle line of the quotation are both marked as textually stressed, raising a number of questions in this difficult field. If taken as an indefinite pronoun, the *ren* is perhaps a dubious case for consideration as stressed, but given the sense it bears the accent well. The *poss'* is denied musical accentuation, but without causing too much worry given its syntactic function as an auxiliary. The infinitives *se-ér* and *a-vér* are (for once!) correctly supported by the musical accent.

CANTIGA 10

DE LOOR DE SANTA MARIA
COM' É FREMOSA E BÕA E Á GRAN PODER

IN PRAISE OF HOLY MARY
FOR HER BEAUTY AND GOODNESS AND GREAT POWER

Sixteen «Cantigas»

δ
e
Do - na en mui pi - a - do - sa se - er,
β
f
Se - nnor en to - ller coi - tas e do - o - res.

CSM 10: Musical palæography		
To 10, f. 20v Notated: ℜ-0; I *only*. Notated a fourth higher than the other sources (*finalis* on G). Flat signature throughout.	*T* 10, f. 17v Notated: ℜ-0; I, *incipit* of ℜ-I. II, *incipit* of ℜ-II. III, *incipit* of ℜ-III. IV, *incipit* of ℜ-IV. Without signature. *Notational variants*: Stems are sometimes very faint or near-invisible. e.7: the initial plica is faint or missing in some stanzas.	*E* 10, f. 39v Notated: ℜ-0; I *only*. Without signature. *Without significant variants in respect of T.*

CANTIGA 10: COMPRESSION?

This piece has also been the object of a brief analysis and partial transcription by Ferreira, who includes it as one of three *cantigas* that, in his view, might benefit from a compression of Mode III cells to occupy the same duration as surrounding cells.[23] In the case of *Cantiga* 10 the transcription covers the first three phrases, that is, as far as the first line of the stanza ('…de parecer', here phrase c). Leaving aside a small divergence of opinion on the inner detail of how to transcribe the at a.4, Ferreira's version, with 'compression' of all the third-mode cells, *appears* identical in note-values (though not in the beaming of quavers) to that offered here. There is, however, one important difference: the 'mixed' time signature, 6/8 followed by 3/4, the latter enclosed in parentheses.

[23] *See again* Fereira 2014, esp. pp. 50–1 and Ex. 15. The other two pieces discussed by Ferreira have already featured in the present volume: *Cantiga* 20 in Section III and *Cantiga* 78 in Section VI.

The text for Ferreira's partial edition is provided by Parkinson (*see again* n. 15 above and corresponding text) who not only suppresses the conjunction *e* in the refrain, but supplies in its stead an extra (paragogic) vowel *after* 'flor', allowing two syllables 'flo-re' at a.6–7 (the extra vowel is written superscript). It is not clear why, if one vowel is suppressed as intrusive, there should be a need to compensate, especially if it is postulated that the verse-form does not rely on syllable-count. And whilst it is refreshing to have an explicit 'phonetic' spelling-out of a case of paragogy (as opposed to a dot on a consonant), this whole area remains as one that could do with a proper airing — and not merely from the standpoint of its supposed historical relationship with the notational im*plica*tions of liquescence.

An initial uncertainty arises over whether the 6/8 is intended to be invoked every time there is a compressed Mode III cell, or whether the two signatures may be applied in free variation. It would be important to know, for example, how the very first bar is to be felt: if in 6/8, a secondary accent appears on *Rǒ*-sà. If my reading of Ferreira's text is correct, then it is indeed so, for he speaks (in relation to *Cantiga* 20) of 'an invariable pulse with flexible subdivision (alternating 6/8 for compressed third mode, and 3 /4 for second mode)'.[24] His later observation on 'elasticity of subdivision within a period'[25] would therefore appear to be subject to the constraint of binary subdivision in the compressed Mode III cells. It is a pity, then, that his example from *Cantiga* 10 is too short to show problems of misaccentuation: the grouping of quavers at c.4–6 and c.7–9 certainly shows binary subdivision (*i.e.*, the bars are felt in 6/8) which happens to suit the text at this point; a longer sample, however, would certainly show misaccented counter-examples.

It must also be stressed that this piece differs fundamentally from *Cantiga* 20, in that, far from presenting alternations of second- and third-mode cells, *Cantiga* 10 is expressed almost entirely as Mode III. Given the almost complete lack of reference in the form of any *uncompressed* cells (the solitary exception being the second cell of the first phrase), it must be wondered what purpose is served by compression, more particularly if binary subdivision is maintained. When everything is compressed, nothing is compressed.

Cantiga 10: Toledo Version

A different set of problems feeds into the general question when the version contained in *To* is brought into consideration (*see* transcription, Example 22 overleaf). In particular, the question that arises is whether the more ambiguous notation of *To* is sufficiently robust to constitute a rhythmically different version. Two focal points emerge for consideration.

The first of these concerns cells such as c.4-5-6, d.4-5-6 and e.7-8-9. In all cases the outer components of these cells are ambiguous plicated figures that can be taken with overall values either of ▪ or of ♦ . If the longer reading is taken, it gives cells of Mode III, dimidiable as in the Escorial sources. But if we take the shorter reading (as in Ex. 22) each of these cells comes out as simple tribrach (or cell of Mode VI); this alleviates not only syllable-crowding (as at e.7-8-9), but more particularly the problem of stressed syllables on very short unaccented notes, in the Escorial version at c.5 and d.5. Such readings also make greater provision of reference-points in 'normal' note values, against which the surrounding dimidiated cells stand in contrast. But whether it is legitimate to read thus, in defiance of a possible reading common to all sources, is a question that raises doubts.

The second focus of attention relates to phrase-endings, which are open to debate in those phrases that carry a *grave* final syllable (lines a, b and f). The ▪ ▪ of phrase a *may* be a case of cadential lengthening, to be read (as in Ex. 22) as ▪ ♦ or ♦ ▪ , but it may perhaps be taken at face value, giving durations of /3/3/; similarly the rising plica at the ends of b and f may be plications of ♦ (as read in Ex. 22), but equally might be read as plications of ▪ , again giving two perfect figures at the end of the line. The point here is that if the longer readings are taken, they sit uncomfortably unless the surrounding cells of Mode III are left undimidiated or uncompressed.

---

[24] Ferreira, *ibid.*, p. 50.

[25] Ferreira, *ibid.*, p. 51.

CANTIGA 10: SOME CONSIDERATIONS

The outcome of the exercise of applying dimidiation to *Cantiga* 10, as far as ameliorating the melodic-textual relationship is concerned, is undoubtedly patchy in its success, making this piece by far the least satisfying in the present collection. Even so, there are aspects of the exercise that prove instructive. Among these is that the rhythm at points such as c.4–5–6 seems unsuited to carry a stressed syllable on the supposedly weak half-beat note, which it sometimes has to do if dimidiation is applied; one might further wonder whether a rhythm such as that at b.4-5-6 is suitable for interpretation as a dotted rhythm in any case. It is almost as if there were an inbuilt resistance to such rhythmic treatment. This is, then, not a piece on which one would attempt to build a strong case in favour of 'dotted rhythms by dimidiation', and it has been included with some misgivings.

To end, three sets of thoughts may be offered. The first seeks a middle ground. If dimidiation produces awkward accentuation, and if compression — assuming retention of binary subdivision — hardly changes the essential Mode III character of the rhythm, perhaps a solution might be found in halving values in the Mode III cells, but allowing freedom in the placement of secondary musical accents such as might be suggested by patterns of word-stress. In that way Ferreira's 'elasticity of sub-division' might be achieved, although in a sense that he perhaps did not intend. This is not, of course, dotted rhythm as understood elsewhere in this collection; rather, a sort of rolling hemiolic cross-play, perhaps applied differently from stanza to stanza and even from line to line.

The second concerns a possible interpretation in quintuple metre, with ▪ ▪ ▪ taken to have durations of /2,1,2/, as has been offered by two editors.[26] This, always supposing that the figure at d.1 in *To* is a *punctum* with a following ink-dribble, and not a short-stemmed *virga* (which would rule out quintuple solutions not only for *To*) as might appear from the facsimile edition or from Ribera. A quintuple reading allows grouping of beats into either 2+3 or 3+2, greatly assisting the flexible allocation of secondary accents.

The third proposal focuses on the troublesome second rhythmic cell in phrase a. This cell provides the only anchor-point for 'normal' durations if either dimidiation or compression is applied, with the concomitant difficulty that its usefulness as a reference point decreases the further the melody moves on. Seventeen years ago I persuaded myself that this was a cell of Mode II, but I now feel the matter is still open to debate. The notation of *To* might again be useful; here the cell is given as ▪ ⬩ — ambiguous, yes, but with a first component that could more easily be read as 3*t*, giving the whole group a duration of 6*t* compatible with the Mode III context. Can the Escorial sources also be similarly read? If the ▪ at a.4 in *T* and *E* were interpretable as *SSL*, any rationale for dimidiation or compression would disappear. Back to Anglés?

CANTIGA 10: PARTIAL TRANSPOSITION?

A question not broached in the foregoing (lest the discussion of *Cantiga* 10 become over-burdened with too many questions open simultaneously) is that of transposition of the middle section with respect to the outer sections. My previous edition of this piece[27] embodied such a transposition, arising from a perceived need to respond to what I called

[26] These are Pla and Elmes; *see again* n. 17 above.

[27] *See* Cunningham 2000, pp. 90–4.

the 'inconsequential' plica at b.11; the approach, however, was not well received.[28] Even so, while I acknowledge that the question cannot be proven beyond doubt, I consider that a case can still be made for lowering the pitch of the *mudanza* by a fifth; the argument is based not only on the extraordinary plica, but on an analysis of the whole melody as plagal protus (clearly discernible in the outer sections), and the impossibility of solmization of the middle section if the lowest note of the melody is a *major third* below the *finalis*. I hope to be able to develop these arguments at some future date.

EXAMPLE 22

Cantiga 10: A possible reading of the Toledo version maximising simple tribrachic (*i.e.*, undotted) interpretation of certain cells

[28] Alison Campbell (2011, n. 9, p. 56), for example, offers the view that 'Martin Cunningham is ...wrong...to argue for the transposition of the refrain and *vuelta*'. In a fuller exposition of the question I would hope to make clearer that this is *not* what I am arguing for; rather, that the middle section or *mudanza* is what causes difficulty in notation, and that it is placed a fifth higher in the sources so as to provide notes otherwise unavailable at the base of the thumb on a Guidonian hand.

CANTIGA 4

What is problematic in the case of *Cantiga* 4 is the evident disjunction between the rhythm as heard, and the rhythm as usually transcribed.[1] The problem arises right from the opening phrase (see Ex. 23):

EXAMPLE 23
Cantiga 4: Opening of refrain (unbarred)

Here it is the second syllable which takes prominence, for three reasons: first, it bears the textual stress; second, it is, melodically, the highest note; and third, the plicated *L* has twice the duration of the surrounding figures. Our auditory impression thus invites us to hear the F as bearing the primary beat, and if we were to write this down from dictation, it might well appear as in Ex. 24:

EXAMPLE 24
Cantiga 4: Opening of refrain
(barred to respect the prominence of the second syllable)

Such a transcription, however, is in sharp contrast to what seems to have become accepted as the only cogent reading of the notation: that is, to take the rhythm overall in a Mode II pattern, starting as in Ex. 25:

EXAMPLE 25
Cantiga 4: Opening of refrain
(as commonly accepted)

[1] The impersonal presentation of what I consider problematic in this piece encapsulates an autobiographical reality. I have been worried by *Cantiga* 4 ever since as a student I first heard it on an LP recording by the Studio der Frühen Musik under Thomas Binkley, with *mezzo* Andrea von Ramm as vocalist, and then confronted what I heard with Anglés's transcription. I still have my vinyl LP., catalogue no. EMI J 063-20.114; according to the sticker it still bears, it cost me 310 pts in the Corte Inglés, probably in 1971 or '72. The track assuredly reproduces items 19 and 20 in Tinnell's *Discography*, even though the record label (EMI) is distinct.

This is the solution offered by Anglés, and endorsed by Ferreira who finds the melody as given in *To* to be in Mode II; it also underlies the transcriptions offered by Elmes, and even coincides with that of Pla, for whom the metre is 'pure iambic tetrameter'.[2] Yet this is hardly satisfactory. The brief opening phrase given in Example 25 shows the violence done by mis-stressing *A Madre* as *á Ma-dré*, and this is not the only instance; another prominent case occurs in the second phrase of the refrain, where *fogo* is accented as *fo-gó*. Is there another way?

CANTIGA 4: REGROUPING

A reading in Mode II depends on grouping the various figures into pairs, each consisting of underlying durations *BL*. The opening of the first phrase, then, is read as

BL BL BL L

But this is not the only possible grouping; it is also possible to begin with an anacrusis, and divide into groups as follows:

B LB LBL L

What leaps out from this string is the *LBL* group, interpretable as a cell of Mode III and a candidate for dimidiation, which gives a dotted rhythm. This has been applied in Ex. 26:

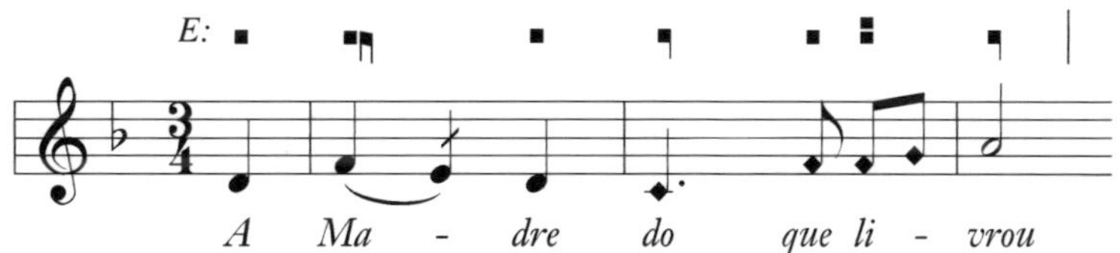
E:
A
Ma
dre
do
que
li
vrou

EXAMPLE 26
Cantiga 4: Opening of refrain
interpreted with dotted rhythm

As far as the correspondence between textual stress and musical accent is concerned, this appears to be an improvement. But how is it to continue? The second half of the phrase is also susceptible to the same treatment (*i.e.*, grouping as *B.LB.LBL.L*), as may be seen below in Ex. 27: but this is much less satisfactory, with its distortion of *leões* into *lé-õ-és*.

E.
dos
le
õ
es
Da
ni
el

EXAMPLE 27
Cantiga 4: Continuation of refrain
interpreted with dotted rhythm

[2] *See* Anglés 1943; Ferreira 1993, p. 589, n. 51; Elmes 2004 and later editions; Pla 2001, p. 121.

It would be possible to go through the whole piece line by line, examining the pros and cons of applying this grouping to each half-phrase in turn. But so that musical examples do not become burdensome, a general overview is provided in the table below, showing in summary form the effect on the text of reading the rhythm in this way. As the caption states, syllables that are naturally stressed are indicated by being underlined, and those that bear a musical accentuation, if the same rhythmic interpretation as given above for the first line is applied throughout, are given a written acute accent.[3] In an ideal world, it might be hoped that there would be a perfect coincidence; given the mobility of stress-patterns within Galician verse, one might at best hope for some reasonable degree of correspondence. But a glance at the table shows that words where underlining and acute accent are in conflict considerably outnumber words that are 'properly' accented (*lé-õ-és, mé-ni-nnó, Bé-or-gés, ou-vé, fá-zer, vi-dró, etc.*). It might not be an exaggeration to say that the experiment has proved a disaster.

	♩	𝅗𝅥	♩	♩.	♪	♩	𝅗𝅥	𝅗𝅥.	𝅗𝅥
	A	má-	dre	dó	que	li-	vróu		
	dos	lé-	õ-	és	Da-	ni-	él,		
	e-	ssá	do	fó-	go	guar–	dóu		
4	un	mé-	ni-	nnó	d'I-	rra-	él.		
	En	Bé-	or-	gés	un	ju-	déu		
	ou-	vé	que	fá-	zer	sa-		bí-	a
	vi-	dró,	e	ún	fi-	llo	seu		
8	(ca	énd'	el	máis	non	a-		ví-	a
	per	quánt'	end'	á-	pren-	di	eu)		
	ontr'	ós	cris-	chá-	os	li-		í-	a
	na	és-	col';	e	e-	ra	gréu		
12	a	séu	pa-	dré	Sa-	mu-	él.		

EXAMPLE 28
Cantiga 4: Text of Refrain and Stanza I
interpreted with dotted rhythm in every line
(underlining = natural text stress;
acute accent = musically accented syllables)[4]

---

[3] As always, any attempt to mark up textual stress runs into problems of word-categories that do not attract stress. Here, for example, line 8 is complicated by the presence of the partitive particle *end'* and the comparative adverb *mais*, neither of which, it could be argued, is susceptible of being stressed. A better approach, however, might be to apply the principle of words on which stress (as brought by musical accentuation) is *not unwelcome*, thereby allowing possessives and certain types of pronoun, as well as the two words mentioned, into the class of words not irksome if accented. Words unhappy if accented would include articles and monosyllabic prepositions.

[4] *Para quienes necesitaren saber la clave del Ejemplo, sépase que las sílabas textualmente acentuadas están subrayadas; las que llevarían el acento musical van con tilde.*

CANTIGA 4

COMO SANTA MARIA GUARDOU AO FILLO DO JUDEU
QUE NON ARDESSE
QUE SEU PADRE DEITARA NO FORNO

*HOW HOLY MARY SAVED THE JEW'S SON FROM BURNING
WHEN HIS FATHER HAD LEFT HIM IN THE FURNACE*

To:
T:
α
a
A Ma - dre do que li - vrou
(!)
dos le - õ - es Da - ni - el,
β
b
e - ssa do fo - go guar - dou
un me - ni - nno d' I - rra el.

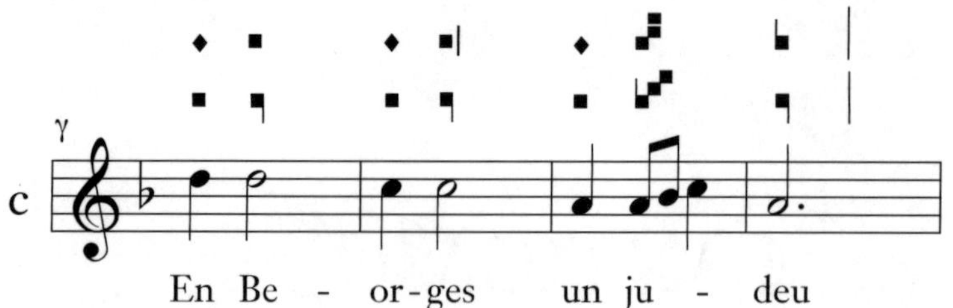
γ
c
En Be - or-ges un ju - deu

ou-ve que fa - zer sa - bi - a

γ
d
vi-dro, e un fi-llo seu

(ca end' el máis non a vi - a

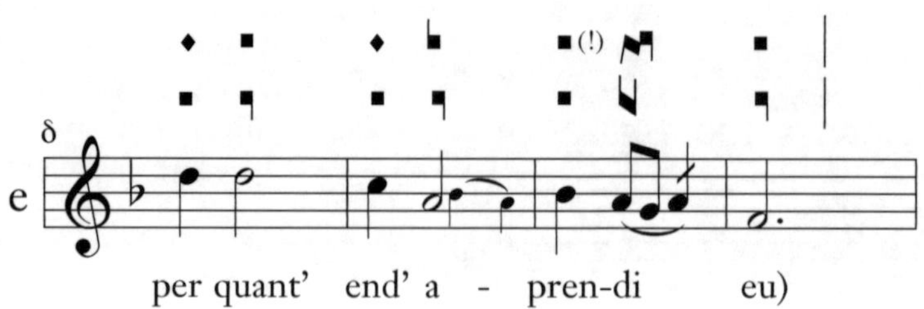
(!)
δ
e
per quant' end' a - pren-di eu)

ontr' os cris-chã - os li - i - a

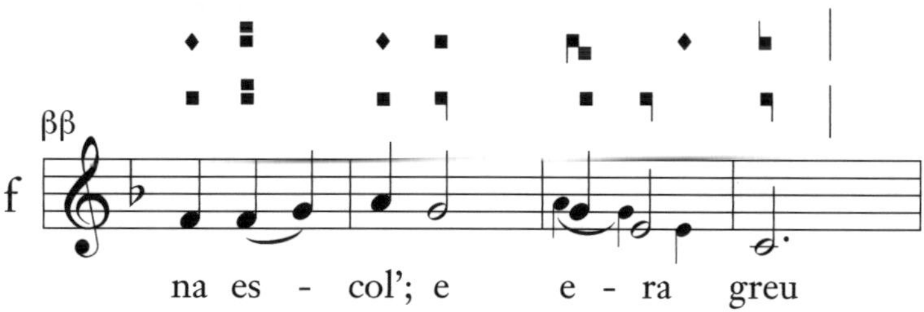
ββ
f
na es - col'; e e - ra greu

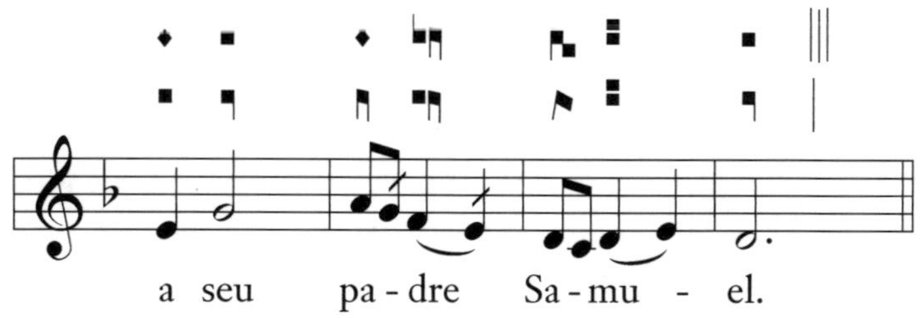
a seu pa - dre Sa - mu - el.

CSM 4: Musical palæography		
To 4, f. 12v–13r Notated: ℜ-0; I *only*. Flat signature (missing a.1–a.7 and from phrase f).	*T* 4, f. 8v Notated: ℜ-0; I, *incipit* of ℜ-I; II, *incipit* of ℜ-II. Flat signature (missing a.1–a.8 and the repeat of a.1–a.7 in ℜ-II). *Variants in repeated sections:* ℜ-I: *First four figures not inserted.* ℜ-I, a.6: *The remaining variants concern insertion or omission of bars at the ends of half-phrases or full phrases*: ℜ-I, a.7: *with bar.* ℜ-I, a.14; II, e.7, f.7; ℜ-II, a.14: *without bar.* ℜ-I, a.14: *with tractulus.*	*E* 4, f. 31v Notated: ℜ-0; I *only*. Flat signature for the third system (a.6 to a.14), and from the start of the stanza onwards. *Variants in respect of E:* a.13, e.6: b.10–11, f.10–11: (*cf To*). a.7, b.7: *with bar.* a.14, e.15, f.7: *without bar.*

CANTIGA 4: A *TRACTULUS*!

There might the matter rest but for one small mark: a *tractulus* in *To* after the figure at c.4. This seems a curious, a miscellaneous point at which to include a *tractulus*, and its meaning must be carefully teased out. It appears to have a grouping function, keeping the first four figures in the phrase together. From this a first inference may be drawn: that the Mode II reading of this phrase-initial (and stanza-initial) group is correct and the foregoing efforts to impose a different rhythm were ill-advised. But why point out a Mode II grouping at *this* point? The answer can only be that such a rhythm needs to be asserted at this point because it *contrasts* with what went before. The *tractulus* at c.4 in *To* is cautionary, not to say preventative, guarding against the continuation of a rhythmic reading previously intended.

To deal with specifics: the *tractulus* at c.4 must be taken as enforcing groups in the following pattern

BL BL BL L

since there is no other viable grouping that complies with the need for a cell-boundary after the fourth figure. This means that, if the diagnosis is correct, a different grouping must be applied in the preceding phrases, and this can surely only be

B LB LBL L

which brings us back to where we began. It must be concluded, then, that whilst the Mode II rhythm may remain in the stanza, there must be a revision of the commonly-accepted rhythm in the refrain. A little further experimentation leads to the conclusion that the rhythm concerned, the one with the dimidiable *LBL* group, can only realistically be applied in the first half of the phrases in the refrain, for reasons of respect for textual stress. In the full transcription, then, a dimidiated cell is found at a.4-5-6 and b.4-5-6 *only*; the familiar Mode II interpretation must stand everywhere else. Whilst the occasional bumpy accentuation is only to be expected (*crís-chã-ós* is the only one in the first stanza), the Mode II reading supports the text very well. As does, of course, the dotted rhythm in the refrain.

One corroborative detail serves to put into context the fact that a.1–7 and c.1–7 display a different rhythmic character from the rest of the piece: namely, the fact that neither of these two half-lines is repeated as a *vuelta* at the end of the stanza. After its single appearance in the refrain, the α-phrase is absent entirely, its expected position being occupied by a replacement δ-phrase (phrase e); and whilst the melody does come full circle, with the stanza ending in the same way as the refrain, it is only the second half of the β-phrase that is kept, the first half having been remodelled (here it is labeled as the ββ-phrase). It may be surmised that these melodic substitutions are made because of the need to discard the *rhythms* of the lines as they occur in the refrain.

VIII
TWO INSEPARABLE CASES

The two *cantigas* included in this section, *Cantiga* 41 and *Cantiga* 58, are dealt with together because of their obvious melodic relationship. It is not merely a question of family similarity; although the refrain has two phrases in one and four phrases in the other, the first phrase is identical in both, and the second phrase is a very close copy at an interval of a third. What is of great interest in confronting these two pieces, however, is that one of them moves in and out of dotted rhythm, allowing cells with and without dimidiation to be clearly distinguishable, whereas in the other we find a piece written entirely (or almost entirely) as cells with an apparent Mode III rhythm. At issue, then, is the question of whether dimidiation is meaningful in the second piece; this in turn prompts even deeper questions about the very nature of Mode III.

The melodic relationship has been commented on by Wulstan, who widens the family to include not only *Cantigas* 41 and 58, but also nos. 126, 142 and 144. Taking them all as displaying Mode III rhythm, Wulstan uses particularly the two dealt with here as exemplifying the inconsistent way in which Mode III is notated.[1] Because the remaining three pieces are not present in the Toledo codex, they will not be further dealt with here, although it may be observed in passing that none of them is exempt from consideration as embodying dotted rhythm.

Cantiga 41

General questions posed by this piece have centred particularly on questions of its *rondeau* form;[2] on its melodic relationship to possible plainsong models (in particular the *Victimæ Paschali laudes*);[3] and on the presence of short melodic formulæ that link it to various categories of melody.[4] Questions of rhythmic interpretation, however, have figured largely; in addition to the comments by Wulstan already noted above, this piece is offered, in the assembling of his statistics on rhythmic types, an exemplar of Mode III rhythm.[5] Ferreira too, referring to this piece as it is given in *To*, points to the Mode III nature of the rhythm except at the cadences.[6] More recently Ferreira has referred to isolated phrases notated in such a way as to admit 6-beat or 5-beat interpretation — a question that arises not infrequently in the context of apparently Mode III notation.[7] Finally, in a comment that

[1] *See* Wulstan 2001, p. 40, with *incipits* of all five pieces transcribed in Ex. 2.5, p. 45.
[2] This is discussed in Wulstan 1996, pp. 37-9. *See also* Ferreira 2011, pp. 196–7.
[3] *See* Katz 1990, where another eight *cantigas* with similar *incipit* are brought together. For Ferreira (2000 *bis*) it is a question of general affinity with chant rather than influence of a specific melody.
[4] Wulstan (2001, p. 64) isolates one motif that links this *cantiga* to Galician melodies, and another it holds in common with other Mode III melodies.
[5] *See* Wulstan 2000, p. 45.
[6] *See* Ferreira 1993, p. 589, n. 51.
[7] *See* Ferreira 2000, p. 16; the question is taken up again in Ferreira 2013, pp. 137–8 and n. 26.

provides much food for thought, Ferreira refers to 'the sudden presence of a quaternary pattern uniquely reserved…for the cadence or its approach', a feature he finds in five other pieces and relates to the possibility, allowed in Arabic music theory, of combining contrasting cycles within the same rhythmic period.[8]

CANTIGA 41: DIMIDIATION?

There can be no doubt that the notation in all sources represents for the most part either a Mode III or a quintuple pulse; that in *To* is unvaryingly ▪ ♦ ▪ when expressed as *simplices*, with no short-stemmed *virga* to oblige an interpretation in six rather than five beats. The notation of *T* gives typically *LBL*, but if Ferreira's allusion to 'quaternary groups in the approach to cadences' refers to a possible four-beat reading of a group such as a.7-8-9, then I must demur: this is surely no different from the earlier groups in the phrase, except in the requirement for alteration (a control is provided by the group at c.7-8-9, in which the last figure, being plicated, is written *L*, whereas a.9, being *simplex*, has *B*). This pattern of writing Mode III, *LBL LBL LBB L*, has earlier been commented upon (*see* Section II).

It is, however, difficult to disagree that there is a new departure of some sort at *some* (though not all) cadences, a sort of 'change of gear' in the notational pattern. Specifically, it may be seen at the ends of the β- and δ-phrases. But it does not need justification from Arabic theory, being more easily interpreted as the point of return to 'normal' temporal values after cells of dotted rhythm interpreted with dimidiated values. And so it has been put into effect in the full transcription opposite.

Apart from a subjective impression that this transcription must be correct *because it works*, there are four corroborative reasons for adopting it. The first concerns the *tractulus* in *T* at j.4, otiose unless its sense is to draw out the *L* to its full 'normal' duration at the point of exit from a dimidiated cell. The second is the short-stemmed *virga* at l.4 in *To*, not to be taken in any literal sense, nor even as a case of 'assertive normalization' (in which case it would have a value of *2t*), merely as a typical overstatement of duration also just after exit from dimidiation. The third reason relates to the equalization of phrase-lengths brought about by dimidiating the apparently Mode III cells, in a context in which the syllable count differs between lines. Here, in the refrain, the first and third phrases have ten (real) syllables, but the second and fourth carry only seven; the use of cells that carry three syllables each in the odd-numbered lines allows the extra syllables to be absorbed whilst not over-extending the line; the even-numbered lines, by contrast, can extend their syllables, after the first dotted cell, over a cell of Mode II and two perfect *L*s.

The last reason relates to textual stress and musical accentuation — or more exactly, to the good weak-to-weak correlation on the short unaccented notes in the middle of the dotted cells. Here in the refrain we find the *-dre* of *Madre*, the *-tro* of *Nostro*, in line c an article and a monosyllabic adverb, then in d, the unstressed *a-* of *aver*. The correlation, as usual, is not perfect, but a glance down the stack of syllables under the fifth figure in each phrase on the second page will convince that the attempt to retain a binary subdivision of the (formerly) Mode III cells would not be an advantage; these are dotted cells with a seamless transition to normal time-values at the ends of the β- and δ-phrases.

[8] Ferreira 2014, p. 45.

CANTIGA 41

(*To* 44)

COMO SANTA MARIA
GUARECEU O QUE ERA SANDEU

HOW HOLY MARY
CURED THE FOOLISH MAN

δ'
e
To:
En Sei-xons fez a Ga - rín cam-bïa - dor
δ'
f
a Vir-gen Ma - dre de Nos - tro Se - nnor,
δ'
g
que tant'ou - ve de o ti - rar sa - bor
δ'
h
a Virgen Ma - dre de Nos - tro Se - nnor
α
i
do po-der do de-mo, ca de pa - vor
β
j
del per-de - ra o si - so;

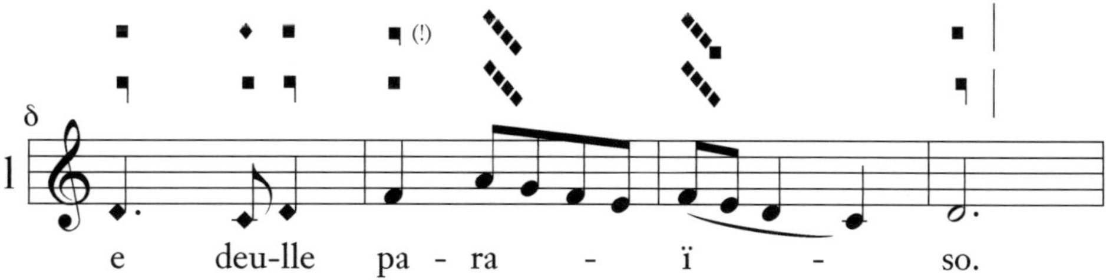

CSM 41: Musical palæography

In all sources the repeated phrase (lines f, h) is included in the notated stanza(s).

To 44, f. 58v–59r	*T* 41, f. 59r	*E* 41, f. 63r–v
Notated: ℜ-0; I *only*.	Notated: ℜ-0; I, *incipit* of ℜ-I II, *incipit* of ℜ-II. III, *incipit* of ℜ-III. *Variants in later stanzas*: II g.9: ▪ i.3: ▪ l.7: without bar III j.4: without *tractulus* l.7: without bar.	Notated: ℜ-0; I *only*. *Variants with respect to T*: d.6: with *tractulus* g.9: ▪ i.3: ▪ i.6: ▪▪ (!) j.7: *tractulus* rather than bar l.6: with *tractulus*.

Cantiga 41: Two Minor Notational Matters

Once the principle of dimidiation has been conceded, the notation in both sources offers few problems or surprises. Two small matters in *To* nevertheless deserve mention.

The first is the use of the descending pre-plicated figure ▪ , found at positions such as a.5, e.5, f.5 *etc*. It is unclear whether this should be taken at face value, or merely as a conventional allograph of a *simplex*, since it appears to be in free variation with the *simplex* rhomb at g.5. It has here been transcribed as a true plication, since it is also seems interchangeable with the more usual form ▪ found in the next piece (58.a.5, 58.e.5).

The other concerns the interpretation of the group ▪ ◆ ▪ , as at c.7-8-9. These may, as here, be read in parallel with the Escorial forms where the two outer figures are clearly *L*; but sight must not be lost of the fact that the two outer figures are ambiguous, and may be read as plications of ◆ , giving durations for the cell of /1,1,1/, and reminding of the often hazy distinction between a dotted cell and an undecorated tribrach.

CANTIGA 58

For ease of comparison with the foregoing piece, the transcription of *Cantiga* 58 given here is placed with *finalis* on D, the pitch at which it is written in *E*, even though the two sources for which original notation is given above the stave write it a fifth higher.

Much of the general comment given for the previous piece applies here also, in particular those relating to the family resemblance of the melody as dealt with by Wulstan,[9] and the presence of certain melodic motifs. The Mode III character of the notation is also pointed out by both Wulstan and Ferreira.[10] Most recently Ferreira points specifically to the notation of *To* as allowing identification of third-mode patterns that define the metrical framework.[11]

CANTIGA 58: TO DIMIDIATE OR NOT TO DIMIDIATE?

There can be no doubt that the notation of *To* encodes a durational pattern of /3,1,2/, right from the first two cells headed up by short-stemmed *virga*. The notation of *T*, meanwhile, displays instructive variability — contrast the *LBB* of a.1-2-3 with the *LBL* of the opening of the d-phrase.

And so if this piece existed in isolation, and if the notation were read as in the full transcription (*see* opposite), there is surely no doubt that it would be considered to exhibit a Mode III rhythm, complete with binary internal division in each cell. The problems begin when we bring *Cantiga* 41 into the picture. Can the dimidiation in that piece (which seems beyond doubt given the necessary transition after 41.b.3) 'rub off' onto this one? That possibility perhaps becomes a desirability if we look at word-stress, at least in the refrain, where weak syllables have a close correspondance with what would be read as the short middle note of dotted groups.

The plot thickens if we admit an alternative reading for the three figurse at b.7–9. In the full transcription these are read with relative durations of /3,1,2/, a cell of Mode III (whether or not values are dimidiated); but in Example 29 they are read as /1,1,1/, giving a simple tribrachic pattern that provides a point of reference with 'normal' durations if the

EXAMPLE 29
Cantiga 58: Alternative reading of the β-phrase

[9] *See again* note 1 above. In the case of *CSM* 58, Wulstan (1998, p. 95) additionally points out that the similarity of the melodic opening to that of *Cantiga* 92 is 'illusory'.
[10] Wulstan 2000, pp. 34, 36, 45–6; 2001, pp. 40, 45, 51; Ferreira 1993, p. 589, n. 51. *See also* Llorens 1987, p. 216, reporting the view of K. Paulsmeier that this melody exemplifies Mode III.
[11] *See* Ferreira 2015, p. 22.

CANTIGA 58

(*To* 73)

COMO SANTA MARIA DESVIOU A MONJA
QUE SE NON FOSSE CON UN CAVALEIRO
CON QUE POSERA DE S' IR

HOW HOLY MARY DISSUADED THE NUN
FROM GOING OFF WITH A KNIGHT
WITH WHOM SHE HAD PROPOSED TO ELOPE

Tò:
T:
α
a
De mui - tas gui - sas nos guar - da de mal
β
b
San - ta Ma - ri - a, tan muit' é le - al.
αα
c
E dest' un mi - ra-gre vos con-ta - rei
αα
d
que San-ta Ma - ri - a fez, com'eu sei,

α
e
dũ - a mon - ja, se-gund es - crit' a - chei,
β
f
que d' a - mor lle mos-trou mui gran si - nal.

CSM 58: Musical palæography		
To 73, f. 94r Notated: ℜ-0; I *only*.	*T* 58, f. 85r Notated: ℜ-0; I, *incipit* of ℜ-I II, … *The repeated sections yield no notational variants.*	*E* 58, f. 78r Notated: ℜ-0; I *only*. b.9: Anglés reads erroneously as *Variants with respect to T*: c.3, d.3: e.10: *tractulus* rather than bar f.3:

rest of the piece, consisting entirely of third-mode cells, is dimidiated.[12] One contributory factor is that the dotted reading supports word-stress tolerably well in the stanza, though perhaps not so well as in the case of *Cantiga* 41. The questions begged by this state of affairs are far-reaching. Does the dotted reading of *Cantiga* 58 (*i.e.*, a reading in 3/4 that dispenses with the cells' binary internal division) arise from cross-fertilization with the previous piece? Is the alternative reading for the β-phrase (Ex. 29) an absolute necessity before the dotted reading can be applied? *Or is the Mode III notation in itself simply being used as a way of notating dotted rhythm throughout?* One might add: Only for this piece? Or in any case where Mode III is pervasively present?

This is seditious talk, for it might mean the abolition of Mode III as we know it. Meanwhile, without on this occasion broaching the wider questions,[13] we appear to have a piece whose rhythm is simultaneously dotted (in 3/4) and not dotted (in 6/8) depending on whether or not the observer views it through the prism of *Cantiga* 38 — rather like a notational version of Schrödinger's cat.

[12] It may be noted in passing that the choice between readings depends on how the *cum-sine* binary ligature is understood. For the Mode III interpretation the must be taken with a value of 3*t*, which itself raises problems (on this *see again* n. 3 to Section V above). The alternative reading (Ex. 29) supposes internal values of *SS*. As to the inherent ambiguity of , this figure is probably best viewed as an unthinking, reflex translation of an underlying ambiguous in another code, as here.

[13] Some brief comments will be offered in Section X, 'Conclusions'.

IX
ONE MORE 'ROSETTA' PIECE

Cantiga 87 is present in the first cental both of *To* and of the later re-structured and expanded Escorial codices, although it occupies a widely differing position in the order (it is no. 21 in *To* but no. 87 in *T* and *E*). This, we may speculate, may have had something to do either with uncertainty as to its textual structure, or perplexity at two highly unusual features in its musical notation in *To*, or both. As regards the structure of the text, this is a matter on which, even in modern times, differing views have been advanced.[1] The textual edition offered here (*see* Appendix), and the structuring of the whole piece, parallels Parkinson's view: that we are (a) dealing with a variable refrain, which (b) unusually rhymes partially with the preceding stanza, (c) must be sung to the first two musical phrases, and (d) does not require the further repetition of any fixed refrain.[2]

As regards the first of the 'highly unusual' aspects of the notation of *To*, this is a reference to the presence of a *cum opposita proprietate* stem at b.5 and f.5. We may pass over this feature without further comment — it is not a major obstacle to transcription —, except to observe that this piece is unique in *To* in providing a case of a *c.o.p.* ligature.[3] The second 'highly unusual' feature will be dealt with in the next subsection.

For the rest, it must be observed that the notation of this *cantiga* bristles with problems. These will be dealt with under the heading of 'Cumulative Ambiguities' .

CANTIGA 87: DOTTED RHYTHM

Attention may first be focused on the opening rhythmic cell of phrases d and e. Here, in *To*, the string ♦ ♦ ▜ occurs; of this group the third component can only realistically be treated as a plication of ♦ (the following figure in both cases makes its treatment as a plication of ▪ difficult), and the whole group may thus be taken as a single cell representing a total duration of 3 *tempora* within the conventions of the notation of *To*. The corresponding string in *T*, however, gives ▜ ▪ ▪▜ — *LBL*, the third component being plicated —, whose only feasible interpretation gives values of /3,1,2/ *tempora* (a cell of Mode III), totalling *6t*. This, I submit, is our 'Rosetta moment', when 3*t* = 6*t*, and the only possible reconciliation of the two is the dimidiation of the temporal values given by *T*. We arrive, then, in the process of transcription, at a bar of dotted rhythm as supplied by *T*, occupying an overall total temporal value of 3*t* as represented in *To*.

---

[1] The difficulty appears most acutely in *E*, where the variable refrain is taken as a sort of additional shortened stanza, itself requiring the repetition of *the* refrain. The text is given in this form as early as the edition by Valmar (1889), and is reflected in the musical transcription by Anglés (1943) and in both of Mettmann's textual editions. Studies by Parkinson (1987, pp. 28–35; 2000 *ter*, n. 2) provide a necessary corrective. A different view, attributing the muddle to *To* and offering a different solution to the problem of textual structure, is offered by Wulstan (1996, p. 56).

[2] *See* the recent edition in Parkinson 2015, pp. 70–1, esp. the helpful note on 'Metrics' on p. 70. Observation (c) above is a logical musical outcome of this perception of the textual structure; observation (d) consolidates the implications of Parkinson's observations on Metrics.

[3] This observation is owed to Ferreira (1994, p. 94).

If this works for phrases d and e, in phrases a and c we must confront the second 'highly unusual' aspect of the notation of *To*, for, instead of ♦ ♦ ⊓ we find ♦̩ ♦ ⊓ — that is, the first rhomb has acquired a stem. This is a figure that appears in only two *cantigas* in the notation of *To*.[4] What is to be made of it? Whilst I know of no study that seeks to elucidate the meaning of this figure,[5] I believe the context, with its dotted rhythm clearly visible in the Escorial versions paralleling that of other phrases, allows some light to be shed. It must first be recalled what the effect is of adding a stem in another different case, that of the transformation of ▪ into ▪̩ ; here, the note becomes 'strengthened', and (at least in most cases) its temporal value is confirmed as one-and-a-half times that of the simple note. Well, cannot that apply here also, in the case of ♦ and ♦̩ ? By viewing the figure in this way, we can interpret that the notator — astonishingly — has created a note worth 1½*t* in a notational system that 'does not do halves'. Looking then at the cell as a whole, the ♦̩ ♦ ⊓ can be read with values of /1½, ½, 1/, the middle note ♦ (the smallest note-value available separately) being used in an approximative way to supply the necessary half-value. I offer this interpretation of the stemmed rhomb, as a remarkable example of resourceful notating, to represent the first element in a dotted rhythmic pattern.[6]

A look may now be taken at how the first rhythmic cell is notated in all occurrences of the α- and αα-phrases. At the start of phrases that begin sections (phrases a and c) this first rhythmic cell is notated as ♦̩ ♦ ⊓ ; but the stem is omitted — ♦ ♦ ⊓ — in phrases occupying less prominent positions in the structure (here, d and e). The assumption must be that, once the dotted pattern has been established, it may be repeated in subsequent occurrences using less precise notation. (This reflects what often happens in the case of ▪̩ , which may be given early in a particular piece to establish a note of 3*t*, when repetitions are given with a less precise ▪ .) *But this means that* ♦ ♦ ♦ (or, as here, ♦ ♦ ⊓) *can have the value of a dotted rhythm*, albeit one notated imprecisely, approximatively. And thus has it been interpreted in the transcription. The implications of this reading are wide, and will be addressed in more general terms below in a dedicated excursus.

CANTIGA 87: CONFLICTIVE READINGS

If so much is clear, the rest of the notation of *CSM* 87 is fraught with difficulties. This is as much to do with conflicts between sources as with the presence of a high proportion of figures ambiguous as to duration — and not only in *To*. The plicated figure at a.6 may serve as an example: the figure ⊓ is inherently ambiguous in *To*, but its 'translation' into

---

[4] The other is *CSM* 27 (*To* 25), according to information supplied by Ferreira (1994, pp. 93–4). The existence of this figure goes unnoticed by Anglés, as also by Ribera in his pseudo-facsimile (1922).

[5] Ferreira (2013, p. 136) speaks of the stem as a 'method of clarifying or introducing long durational values', but does not elaborate. He also suggests that this figure may belong to a 'second layer' of notation, making it a late emendation; to my eye the nibwork does not suggest discontinuity of entry, but were it so the figure might not be viewable as a remarkable early use of the stem to imply additional length, but instead would suggest an equally remarkable case of 'performance memory', in which the memory of dotted execution persisted until the notation could be adapted to reflect it.

The comments by Wulstan (1998, pp. 94–5) on the opening of this piece have more to do with whether, in the Escorial versions, the plicated figures must be read as long or short.

[6] Whilst I believe this interpretation of the stemmed rhomb works for *CSM* 87 (*To* 21), it does not seem applicable in the other case, *CSM* 27 (*To* 25), for which I cannot at present offer an explanation — indeed, if anything, the stems in that case appear otiose if the *To* version is read alongside the Escorial versions. Unless, perhaps, it is a nonce form of plicated rhomb?

CANTIGA 87
(*To* 21)

COMO SANTA MARIA MANDOU
QUE FEZESSEN BISPO AO CRÉRIGO
QUE DIZIA [SEMPRE] SAS ORAS

HOW HOLY MARY ORDERED
THE CLERIC WHO ALWAYS SAID HER OFFICE
TO BE MADE BISHOP

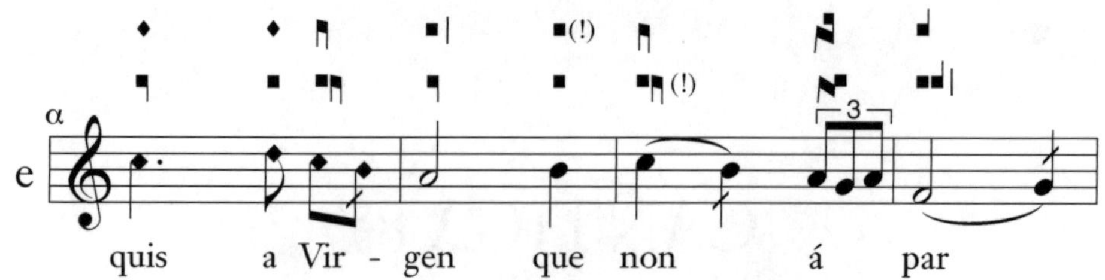

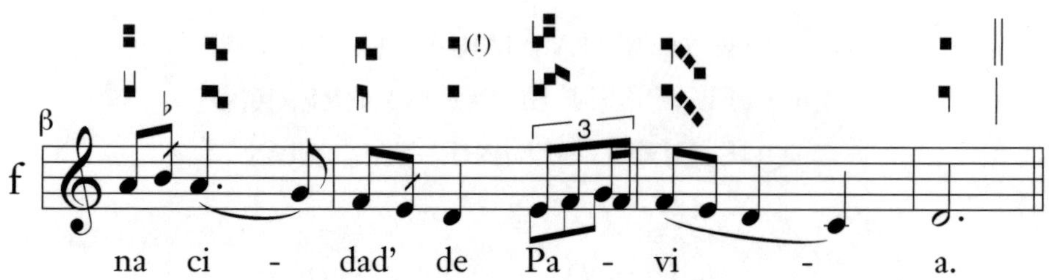

CSM 87: Musical palæography

To 21, f. 31r–59r	*E* 87, f. 101r–102r
Notated: ℜ-0; I *only*.	Notated: *This cantiga is written out in extenso, in a way that misunderstands its structure: for every stanza after the first, the first refrain* (ℜ-0) *is repeated as a fixed refrain both before* (ℜ-a) *and after* (ℜ-b) *the variable refrain* (𝔳), *which thereby takes on the function of a stanza of different length. Thus:*
T 87, f. 127v Notated: ℜ-0; I, ℜ-I. *Notational variants from repetition of* ℜ: b.4: with *tractulus* b.7: with bar.	ℜ-0; I, ℜ-I; II, ℜ-IIa, 𝔳-II, ℜ-IIb; III, ℜ-IIIa, 𝔳 -III, ℜ-IIIb; IV, ℜ-IVa, 𝔳 -IV, ℜ-IVb; V, ℜ-Va, 𝔳 -V, ℜ-Vb; VI, ℜ-VIa, 𝔳 -VI, ℜ-VIb; VII, ℜ-VIIa, 𝔳 -VII, ℜ-VIIb.

Synopsis of variants in *E* with respect to *T*

Phrases a and b (20 occurrences*):

- a.3: (!) once (in 𝔳-II)
- a.4: *with tractulus* (6 times) — *cf* e.4 ➔
- a.6: *on every occasion* — *cf* c.6 *etc.* ➔
- a.7: (13), (7) — *cf* e.7 ➔
- a.8: *bar missing* (8)
- b.2: (6)
- b.4: (11), (2), (7) — *cf* f.4 ➔
- b.6: *with tractulus* (once)
- b.7: *tight spacing means the stem is not always perceptible.*

Phrases c, d, e, f (seven occurrences):

- c.6, d.6 and e.6: *on every occasion*
- d.8, e.8, f.8: *the bar is occasionally missing*
- e.4: *with tractulus* (once)
- e.7: (4), (3)
- f.4: (3), (1), (3)
- f.7: *the stem, and sometimes even the notehead, is not always visible due to crowding.*

*This is accounted for by the fact that these two phrases carry every occurrence of both the 'fixed refrain' and the 'variable refrain' (ℜ and 𝔳 — see panel above). Hence there are two occurrences framing the first stanza, and *three each* for the remaining six stanzas. It should further be noted that phrases e and f repeat phrases a and b.

Escorial notation does not clarify its duration, since *T* has a *plica longa* whereas *E* has a *plica brevis*. It might be thought that the massive number of *twenty* repetitions of this phrase written out in *E* — 27 if the identical phrase e is included — might serve to add weight to the interpretation of this figure, but this is not really so: for all the unanimity of its *brevis* readings of this figure, codex *E* is only offering repetitions — carefully copying *itself* — that in effect constitute no more than a single witness.[7] With this in mind, the phrases that make up the melody, essentially only two in number, may be examined in turn.

CANTIGA 78: THE α- AND αα-PHRASES

First, the α-phrase in the Escorial sources. After the dotted rhythm of the first three figures (a.1–3), the reading of the α-phrase (phrases a and e) given in *T* proves the more straightforward, and can be read as continuing with two cells of Mode I (the figure ◆■ at a.7 is ambiguous, but a reading of 1*t* is certainly possible[8]). Other options get bogged down in various ways. The *L* at a.4 and e.4 is provided with a *tractulus* in *E* on about a third of its many repetitions in that source; this may perhaps suggest perfection, but two considerations militate against taking this option: first, to preserve the ternary metre the next three figures would have to be spread over two whole cells, and a line that began with sprightly dotted rhythm becomes torpid and unlikely; and second, the *tractulus* has an alternative explanation as a marker of return to 'normal' temporal values after the exit (in this source) from dimidiation. The *plica brevis* in *E* at a.6 and e.6, on *every* occasion, is at first sight more difficult to argue away, but surely cannot be other than a recidivist case of plica-confusion. The reading of *E*, then, although unsteady, can be reconciled with the more reliable reading suggested by *T*. Noteworthy in passing is the plicated variant of a.7 that occurs sometimes in *E*. A final question concerns whether the last plicated *L* in the phrase should be imperfect or perfect — a question that depends on whether the next line begins with an anacrusis, on which subject more later.

Following on from this the αα-phrase (lines c and d) presents no new difficulties, with the perpetuation of the *plica brevis* in *E* at c.6 and d.6 essentially repeating an element already dealt with. As far as the Escorial versions are concerned, then, these four phrases need no further comment.

In comparison with the Escorial sources, the Toledo codex appears not to know its own mind. The fifth figure is ◆ in line a, but ■ elsewhere; the fourth figure is given three times as ■ but once as ■ , three times with *tractulus* and once without, in various permutations amounting to three different cases in four occurrences. A first reaction to the ■| (short-stemmed *virga* with *tractulus*) at a.4 is that it appears about as assertive a statement of three *tempora* as is possible in Toledo notation. Yet such a reading, apart from being in conflict with what has been decided about the other two sources, causes immense knock-on difficulties further along; most importantly, it cannot be compatible with a 2*t* reading of a.6 without breaking the ternary mould. It must, then, be taken as a *double* statement of assertion of normal temporal values after the dotted cell, even though this is strictly not necessary, since in *To* there has been no dimidiation. The notation of *To* is perhaps understandably jittery at this point, following the unusual symbology of the preceding cell.

---

[7] Wulstan (2000, pp. 34–5) makes a similar point, with more general applicability.

[8] *See* the chart of triplet figures with duration 1*t* in Cunningham 2000, p. 47.

CANTIGA 78: THE β-PHRASE — CUMULATIVE AMBIGUITIES

Any difficulties arising from notational ambiguity present in the α- and αα-phrases pale into insignificance when the β-phrase is contemplated. Here the ambiguities in all sources are of such complexity that a solution satisfying all sources is difficult to achieve.

Example 30 below gives a synopsis both of relevant notational figures in all manuscripts, and some possible durational resolutions. The most obvious point of conflict between the sources arises at figure b.4, where *To* gives a note apparently of $3t$, but *T* gives *B*; *E* cannot make up its mind — out of 27 copyings of this phrase, *E* gives ▪ on fourteen occasions, and ▪ on thirteen (of which ten are with *tractulus*). The Table is constructed in the first instance around possible readings for the figure at b.4, with a value of $3t$ at the top, giving way to $2t$ in the middle of the table, and $1t$ in the bottom lines.

Working backwards from b.4, the figure at b.3 and that at b.1 are given as a *plica brevis* in the two Escorial sources (which do not disagree at this point), and if taken at face value are not in conflict with the *podatus* (b.1) and *clivis* (b.3) of *To*. The figure at b.2, however, presents more of a problem, since its asymmetricality might be seen as presupposing an overall value of $3t$ (resolved as $2 + 1t$); it is so treated in some of the solutions in Ex. 30,

b.1 b.2 b.3 b.4 b.5 b.6 b.7

To:

T:

E: (14) (3) (10)

(i)

(ii) 3

(iii)

(iv) 3

(v)

(vi) 3

(vii)

EXAMPLE 30

Cantiga 87: β-phrase (lines b and f)

Table exploring some rhythmic interpretations

but where not, it demands more imaginative treatment if its asymmetrical character is to be respected within an overall reading of 2*t*.[9] The *clivis* sometimes present in *E* at b.2 does not help to resolve the problem; indeed, its *cum proprietate* stem may be seen as running counter to the implication of the figure. In all of this, the question of whether the figure at b.2 binds with the following figure to form a cell, or with the preceding figure, or indeed whether it constitutes of itself an entity with duration of 3*t* — these are among the variables that are explored in the Table.

With respect to the Table, it should be pointed out that the first four solutions contemplated in it, and the last, require the presence of an anacrusis whose duration must be wrested from the preceding phrase — unsatisfactorily, perhaps, since the β- phrase would then be the only one in the piece to start with an upbeat.

Perhaps the most intractable problem, however, lies in the ligature at b.5, which in lines (i), (iii) and (v) of the Table has been given its maximum possible duration of 3*t* (even Anglés gives it only 2*t*, extending the effect of opposite propriety through the whole ligature). Yet the form given in *To* can hardly be 3*t* in duration; if it is assumed that the opposite propriety stem means what it says, a reading in *To* of 3*t* overall would in effect imply *SSL* — an unlikely resolution. But a reading with 2*t* is very difficult to square with the neighbouring figures; the only possibility, seemingly, would be the reading of line (vii) with b.4 as *B* (−1*t*), in which case b.5 can be given 2*t*.

Overall, two approaches seem to offer the best prospects of satisfactory resolution of all the collected ambiguities and uncertainties. The first of these is that taken in line (vi) of the Table, where the oblique component of the at b.5 is read as a single rather than a double time-unit within the ligature, and the whole is interpreted as a triplet with opposite propriety; in other words, it is treated as though it were .[10] This is the approach taken in the main transcription. Alternatively line (iii) provides a more spacious reading (*see* Example 31), although with a possibly undesirable anacrusis, and at the expense of no clear indication of what to do with the *c.o.p.* ligature in *To*.

EXAMPLE 31
Cantiga 87: An alternative reading of the β-phrase

[9] Whilst Anglés paid no heed to the distinction between and , Ferreira (2011, pp. 200–2) lays stress on the need to recognize as having a first component longer in duration than the second. The problem of respecting the distinction if the ligature is not perfect is confronted in the main transcription at b.2, f.2.

[10] This is not the place to enter a lengthy digression on the semantics of obliquity; let it suffice if I assert that there are other contexts in which I believe this reading provides rhythmically cogent solutions. The subject of descending oblique components in longer ligatures is another that would benefit from a dedicated study.

CANTIGA 87: A FINAL OVERVIEW
The rhythmic solution proposed in the transcription of this cantiga clearly relies on a lot of judgement rather than on unequivocal durational values; even so, it has been possible to keep the rhythmic structure of similar phrases alike, and within the bounds of possible interpretation. But amid all the uncertainty, it would be easy to lose sight of the point that is central to the present purpose: that beyond all reasonable doubt, at the opening of four of the phrases, a cell of dotted rhythm is present, notated in the Toledo source in a way that cannot but provoke surprise and admiration. A jewel in the crown.

A BRIEF EXCURSUS ON APPROXIMATIVE NOTATION OF DOTTED RHYTHM

The notation of *Cantiga* 87 provides examples of what may be called an 'approximative notation' of dotted rhythm in the Toledo source, in two different regards.

First, the occurrence of cells written ⧫ ♦ ▜ was interpreted as representing dotted rhythm, diagnosed by inference from the correspondence with the other sources, and from the use of what seems to be a specialised figure — a stemmed rhomb — as the first component. But this means that the *second* figure, normally representing a duration of 1*t*, must in this group stand for a half-beat note for which there is no separate figure in Toledo notation. The middle rhomb, in this context, is being used approximatively, with a value it does not normally have, to help complete the expression of a dotted rhythm.

Further to that, although the cell in question is written ⧫ ♦ ▜ twice, on other occasions this group is replaced by ♦ ♦ ▜ , apparently with the same value. This suggests that the group ♦ ♦ ♦ (or, as here, ♦ ♦ ▜) *can be used with the meaning of a dotted cell.* Such usage may well be described as 'approximative' since the graphic forms give no indication of differentiation of duration.

The question arises whether groups written as ♦ ♦ ♦ in other *cantigas* may not also be 'approximative' representations of dotted rhythm.[11] Among relevant pieces are *CSM* 162 and 38 (*see* Section IV): in them, at points where *T* and *E* have dotted rhythm by dimidiation, the ♦ ♦ ♦ appearing in *To* was used as a durational 'control' to establish and limit the overall duration to 3*t*; it now seems, however, that the apparent simple tribrach, as notated in *To*, may itself be susceptible of being read as dotted. If so, the correspondence between the sources no longer embodies a minor rhythmic variant (♩ ♩ ♩ in *To* as against ♩. ♪♩); instead the reading of *To* may itself be viewed as a simpler if less precise way of notating dotted rhythm than doubling values and relying on dimidiation; if so, such a reading of *To* converges with what the other sources say, with a dotted rhythm in all.

The question of whether the group ▪ ▪ ▪ in Escorial notation may also represent dotted rhythm will not be broached on this occasion.

[11] The notation of the tribrach group, given *exempli gratiâ* in its simplest form ♦ ♦ ♦ , must be understood to stand also for more elaborate versions in which one or other of the *simplex* notes might appear plicated, or substituted by a ligature of equivalent duration.

X
CONCLUSIONS

Rhythmic Elements

The most obvious conclusion to be drawn from the transcriptions provided in this volume is that the cell of dotted rhythm | ♩. ♪♩ | must take its place, alongside cells with the characteristics of Mode I (trochaic), Mode II (iambic), Mode V (isolated perfect *L*) and Mode VI (tribrachic), as one of the fundamental building-blocks of rhythmic patterns in ternary metre in the *Cantigas de Santa Maria*. An inventory of these rhythmic elements, with their transcriptional equivalents, is given as Example 32 (*see* overleaf). Whilst the modal terminology employed is familiar, the presence of dotted cells makes it clear that we are far from dealing with cases of modal rhythm *per se*.

For convenience, and likewise without any suggestion of origin in or dependence on modal rhythm, the cell of dotted rhythm will in what follows be referred to by the designation 'IIId' (*i.e.*, an apparent cell of Mode III, with temporal values dimidiated).

Rhythmic Patterns

The cell of dotted rhythm is used with the other rhythmic elements in a great variety of permutations. At one extreme it makes a single appearance in only one of the musical phrases that comprise a melody (the β-phrase of *CSM* 419); at the other end of the spectrum lengthy encadenations of dotted cells form entire phrases (*CSM* 38, where the e- and f-phrases have eight dotted cells without interruption).

Between these two extremes it is frequent for dotted cells to alternate with cells of a different composition. Thus *CSM* 255 has IIId–I–IIId–I, while in *CSM* 15 we see IIId–II–IIId–II, and so forth. Other patterns are also possible: the middle section of *CSM* 407 gives IIId–IIId–II–II–V, with the two dotted cells coming together, while in *CSM* 20 we have IIId–II–IIId–II–IIId–I–V–V, in which the dotting subsides in the cadential approach. Finally, in some cases it seems that a dotted cell may be used in apparently free variation with an undotted tribrach; so, for example, in *CSM* 162 the opening phrase is given as IIId–V–IIId–V in *E*, whereas *To* appears to have IIId–V–VI–V (though it can be argued that the cell of VI in such cases may be an 'approximative notation' for a dotted rhythm).

A cell-by-cell table of the rhythmic schemes that result from the perspective developed in this volume is provided below (*see* pp. 129–30); in it the great diversity of combinations that the dotted cell allows may readily be appreciated.

Notational Mechanisms

The mechanism for recording dotted rhythm without recourse to the semibreve, used in identical fashion in all the pieces transcribed here, relies on writing the dotted cell with doubled time-values, giving the appearance of a cell of Mode III. To recover the dotted rhythm the process must be put into reverse and the relevant cell(s) read with note-values halved ('dimidiated') with respect to other ('normal') cells. Whilst from an editorial perspective this procedure may appear counter-intuitive, the notational method itself is, on the other hand, disarmingly simple.

Mode I (trochaic)	| 𝅗𝅥 ♩ |	
Mode II (iambic)	| ♩ 𝅗𝅥 |	
Mode V (isolated perfect *L*)	| 𝅗𝅥. |	
Mode VI (tribrachic)	| ♩ ♩ ♩ |	
IIId	| ♩. ♪♩ |	(Cell of dotted rhythm, expressed as Mode III dimidiated)
a'	♩ |	(Anacrusis or upbeat)
L"	| 𝅗𝅥 …	(Phrase-final *L*, imperfected by a following anacrusis)

EXAMPLE 32
Inventory of rhythmic cell-types and other rhythmic components occurring in this volume.
Note: an imperfect L" at a phrase-end followed by an anacrusis a' in the next phrase gives the effect of a cell of Mode I disjuncted by the phrase-break.

Such difficulties as arise centre around the cell-boundary between a dotted cell and the cell that follows it, especially when the same notational figure might be used on either side of that boundary with different temporal values (*i.e.*, dimidiated and 'normal' durations). The peculiarities that may arise at this sensitive moment were dealt with in an Excursus on 'Juncture Phenomena', and range from 'early exit from dimidiation' to overstatement of the length of the note following the sensitive cell-boundary.

The notation of dotted rhythm throws up two particular features of the notation that, so far as I am aware, have not previously been analysed. Both concern the first note *after* the dotted cell. First, the need to assert the re-establishment of 'normal' durational values sometimes provokes, in the notation of *To*, the use of a short-stemmed *virga* even when the required duration is only of two *tempora*; and second, attention may be drawn to the 'real' or 'normalized' temporal value of a note in this context by the addition of a *tractulus*, even in mid-cell, to emphasize the note's full (undimidiated) value.

One feature of the process of reading with halved values emerged as essential: that it should be achieved *without* retention of any internal rhythmic features — real or imagined — of Mode III. This marks an important divergence between dotted rhythm on the one hand, and the concept of 'compression' of Mode III on the other.

PHRASE SYMMETRY

An important aspect of dotted rhythm is the rôle it can play in bringing about symmetry of musical phrase-lengths, particularly in cases in which the metre of the text provides lines with differing syllable-count. The mechanism whereby musical phrases are equalized in length relies upon the three-syllable capacity of a dotted cell which allows syllables to be accommodated at a faster rate than in most other types of cell; this allows the overall length of musical phrases to be kept in balance by the judicious use of cells that carry one, two or three syllables. The phenomenon was first analysed in detail in the case of *Cantiga* 20, in which phrases of identical length carry lines of 17 or 12 syllables (*see* Section III); among other notable cases are *Cantiga* 162 (where lines of 8 and 10 syllables are balanced

Table of Rhythmic Schemes

The schemata given below relate to rhythms as transcribed in this volume.

CSM

20

α: IIId - II - IIId - II - IIId - I - V - V
β: II - I - V - V - I - I - V - V

162

α: IIId - V - IIId (VI) - V
β: IIId V - VI - V

γ: IIId - V - IIId (VI) - V
δ: IIId - IIId - IIId (VI) - V

Noteworthy is the apparent free variation between cells of IIId and cells of VI.

38

α: IIId - V - IIId (VI) - I
αα: IIId - V - IIId - I - V
β: IIId - IIId - IIId - V

γ: IIId - IIId - IIId - IIId - IIId - IIId - IIId - IIId - V

97

αγ: IIId - IIId - IIId - V
αχ: IIId - IIId - IIId - V

β: IIId - I - IIId (VI) - V
βχ: IIId - I - IIId (VI) - V

The short γ-phrase comprises the second half of a cell of IIId, followed by a cadential V.

15

Odd-numbered phrases: IIId - II - IIId - II
Even-numbered phrases: IIId - II - IIId - V
Occasionally the penultimate cell of the latter replaces IIId with VI.

76

α: *a'* - IIId - VI - IIId - *L"*
β: *a'* - IIId - VI - IIId - *L"*

γ: *a'* - IIId - II - VI - VI - *L"*
γχ: *a'* - IIId - II - VI VI - *L"*

255

αγ: IIId - II - IIId - I
αχ: IIId - IIId - IIId - II

β: IIId - I - IIId - II
βχ: IIId - IIId - IIId - V

407

α: IIId - II - II -- V - II - II - V

β: IIId - IIId - II - II -- V
γ: IIId - IIId - II - II -- V
δ: II - II - II -- V

415

α: IIId - I - I - I - V
(IIId - I - V - V - I - V)

β: IIId - I - I - I - V

γ: IIId - I - I - I - V
(IIId - I - V - V - I - V)

419

α: *a'* - I - I - V - I - I - I - V
β: IIId - I - V - I - I - I - *L"*

γ: *a'* - I - I - V - I - I - I - *L"*

25
[*To* 38]

α: IIId - I - I - V
β: IIId - I - I - II

γ: IIId - I - I - V
δ: IIId - I - I - II

10
(main transcription)

α: IIId - II - IIId - II
β: IIId - II - IIId - II

γ: IIId - IIId - IIId - V
δ: IIId - IIId - IIId - V

4

α: *a'* - I - IIId - V , II - II - I - *L"*
β: *a'* - I - IIId - V , II - II - I - V

γ: II - II - II - V , II - II - II - V - V
δ: II - II - II - V , II - II - II - V - V
ββ: II - II - II - V , II - II - II - V

41

α: IIId - IIId - IIId - V
β: IIId - I - V - V
γ: IIId - IIId - IIId - V
δ: IIId - I - V - V

The stanza consists of melodically varied repetitions of δ.

58

All phrases: IIId - IIId - IIId - V
(The last phrase, possibly IIId - IIId - VI - V)

87

α: IIId - I - I - V
β: II - VI - V - V

αα: IIId - I - I - V

by the use of an extra dotted cell for the longer lines), *Cantiga* 41 (in which lines of 10 and 7 syllables are likewise musically equalized), and *Cantiga* 38 (where the enormously long lines of the stanza are accommodated using long chains of dotted cells). A contrary effect may be seen in *Cantiga* 4, where, if the proposed reading is accepted, the dotted cells have the effect of introducing phrase asymmetry between the refrain and the stanza.

Rhythm and Text

In a context in which textual stress-patterns are not fixed between stanza and stanza, or even between lines of text accommodated to rhythmically identical musical phrases, it has to be acknowledged that a perfect correspondence between textual stress and musical accent cannot be expected. An additional difficulty arises from the lack of basic background studies delimiting the parameters of what expectations there should be about the level of such correspondence. Even so, in the cases studied here there emerged a high level of satisfactory musical accentuation of textually stressed syllables. Seen inversely, there was also a particularly good weak-to-weak correspondence (*i.e.*, unstressed syllables occurring on musically unaccented notes) in the case of the middle half-beat note in cells with dotted rhythm, a feature that might well be regarded as a hallmark of many of the pieces edited here.

Rhythmic Paradigms

Recent work on the *Cantigas* has sought to rehabilitate consideration of rhythmic patterns of Arab (or Arabo-Andalusian) origin, such patterns being seen in contrast to the paradigm represented by the (Parisian) rhythmic modes. But the additional availability of ternary rhythms with dotted components highlights the fact that the *Cantigas* cannot simply be seen in terms of 'modal or Arabic'. It seems very likely that at least some of the rhythms uncovered in this volume derive from popular origins, and if we push the question further, it would be necessary to contemplate the possibility that they are basically dance rhythms.

General Notational Issues

The analyses undertaken offered plenty of scope for observing problematic aspects of the notation with relevance that goes beyond the particular questions of dotted rhythms under discussion. Prominent among such aspects were plica-confusion, and the presence in some of the later pieces in *To* of notational features more proper to Escorial notation. Both of these aspects were viewed as being more easily explicable if the chronological primacy of the Toledo codex was assumed. Further to that, the investigation threw into sharp focus the need to be aware of periodization and 'layering' of the notation, in all sources.

No verdict was reached on the question of whether alteration occurs in *To*; it was, however, suggested that apparent cases, arising as the third note of a cell here transcribed as dotted, were susceptible of an alternative explanation in the form of 'early exit from dimidiation'.

Mode III

The case of *Cantiga* 58, traditionally regarded as exhibiting a Mode III rhythm, and to a lesser extent that of the middle section of *Cantiga* 38 with its chains of (notationally) Mode III cells, raise profound questions about whether the traditional approach to Mode III, with its implications of a bipartite division in each cell, is correct in all cases. Of particular interest is the musical response to textually unstressed syllables on the middle note of each cell. The question thus arises whether some or all cases of pieces written wholly with an ostensibly Mode III rhythm might rather be justifiably interpreted in dotted rhythm, without any suggestion of medial secondary accentuation (*i.e.*, without maintaining bipartite internal subdivision of successive cells); or, whether again, some more fluid solution should be sought, offering freely variable accentual patterns within successive cells, as appeared to be called for in the case of *Cantiga* 10. These are questions with far-reaching implications that would benefit from a dedicated study — beginning, perhaps, with pieces such as *CSM* 17 and *CSM* 93, either of which might not have been out of place in this volume.

STATISTICS

As was stated in Section I above, the available statistical tabulation of rhythmic types, as provided by Wulstan, deals with the corpus in groups of one hundred pieces or 'centals', according to the standard numeration. The only possible point of contact with the present study, therefore, is the first cental. Wulstan's figure for dotted-rhythm pieces in that group is 3%, or three pieces. But in the present volume no fewer than eleven pieces edited with dotted rhythm (including *Cantiga* 76) fall within that numerical scope. Admittedly some of them have been described as 'difficult' cases; but even if some of these latter were to be discounted, the conclusion could still be drawn that the proportion of pieces exhibiting dotted rhythms in ternary metre has hitherto been underestimated — and *seriously* so.

Looked at another way, the statistics derivable from all sixteen *cantigas* edited in this volume provide the opportunity for a speculative statistical projection. With one exception these pieces are taken from the Toledo codex, which represents approximately 30% of the total repertoire of the *Cantigas*. If the same proportion of pieces with dotted rhythm in ternary metre were to obtain throughout the whole corpus, the total number of such pieces might ultimately rise towards four dozen — a truly arresting prospect!

All that is for the future. But even without the weight of additional evidence that such an outcome would provide, it is hoped that the pieces edited in this volume have sufficed to convince that dotted rhythms are not marginal in the *Cantigas de Santa Maria*, but appear in a significant number of pieces; and that the analyses performed on them have contributed to an understanding of how notational systems that are not fully mensural can be used to convey both intricacy of rhythm and diversity of rhythmic pattern.

APPENDIX

TEXTS

EDITORIAL CRITERIA[1]

The texts are here edited in normative spelling, with the source that offers the soundest readings (generally *To* or *T*) for each piece being used as the basis for the edition.

The following changes are effected without being recorded in the apparatus: vocalic and consonantal uses of graphic *u* and *i* are processed as *u* or *v*, and *i* or *j* respectively; standard abbreviations are expanded; consonants redundantly written doubled are simplified, and manuscript *ç* is rendered as *c* before front vowels; the *tilde* implying nasalisation is retained or commuted to a nasal consonant as appropriate, and nasal consonants are homologated to a following consonant without comment. Emendations which do not fit any of these categories are italicised in the case of text in Roman, or underlined in the case of Italic text. The aim of these procedures is to provide a readable and singable text in which editorial intervention other than the purely mechanical (as just outlined) is perceptible but not interruptive.

No distinction has been maintained between forms ending *-inno* and those in *-ĩo*, the former being generalized throughout, although with the ms form recorded in the apparatus. The practice of allowing or enforcing 'fonética sintáctica' has not been adopted, and so *log' i* and not *logu' i*.

The use of both accents and hyphens is designed both to maximise comprehensibility and assist in syllabic division for those not thoroughly versed in the interpretation of Early Galician. Written accents have been added with three functions: (i) to distinguish between words otherwise identical in appearance (*e.g.*, the preposition *en* and the partitive *én*);[2] (ii) to mark cases of diphthongs or hiatus when these are not otherwise predictable, as will be further expounded below; and (iii) to mark textual stress, also when not predictable.

As regards the hyphen, it is provided (i) when conjunctive object pronouns are added to a verb; thus *deu-lle*, *meteu-o* (examples from *CSM* 4); (ii) to link an infinitive after the loss of final *-r* to a following pronoun;[3] (iii) in the case of mesoclitic pronouns (split futures and split conditionals); and (iv) in other cases involving phonetic or other interference between adjacent items, often involving the suppression of an *-s*: thus *poi-lo*, *sobe-lo*, *todo-los*, and the nonce form of the article in *el-conde* and *el-rei* (*CSM* 38).

Word separation has been applied in the case of *por én*, but contraction has generally been allowed in the case of prepositions. The name *Jesucristo* has been standardized with that form, written as one word except when occurring at a line-break.

Except where questions of syllable-count are involved, variation in form has not been allowed to stand within a text, and the most frequent form has been generalized (*e.g.*, *vingança* in *CSM* 15); no attempt has been made, however, to achieve standardization between texts. Words relating to Mary and the Deity — including pronouns and possessives — have been capitalized, not for any reason of piety, but as an aid to comprehension. Upper case is not, however, used at the start of a stanza when the syntax runs on from the previous. Punctuation is generous, given the need in a musical edition to mark breathing-points and sense-groups for phrasing.

---

[1] The norms for the presentation of texts proposed by Ferreiro *et al.* (2007) have been kept in mind, whilst not being followed in every detail. In particular the need for foreign musicians to syllabify and place tonic stress correctly has led to the use of written accents in a variety of functions. Other decisions (as, for example, the use of hyphens to append clitic pronouns) have likewise been taken in the interests of international comprehensibility.

[2] A list of relevant words will be found in Cunningham 2000, p. 65.

[3] One of the most perplexing features of Western Iberian languages for those who are not primarily linguists is the loss of final *-r* from the infinitive — rendering it unrecognizable — before an enclitic pronoun which, as part of the same process, acquires an initial *l-*. For 'outsiders' a spelling such as *fazelo* lacks the morphemic boundaries necessary for understanding. In this edition, such infinitives are separated from the pronoun by a hyphen, and are further given a written accent to show the textual stress. Thus: *onrá-las*, *queimá-la*, *fazê-lo*, and (though strictly unnecessary as regards the marking of the stress) *vestí-los*;

SYLLABIC DIVISION; STRESS

Correct division of the text into syllables is of course necessary for its accommodation to the melody; it also allows the position of the main stress on a word to be determined. The principal difficulty arises when two or more vowels occur adjacent. The following observations apply (examples are drawn as far as possible from *Cantiga* 4):

a) The 'strong vowels' *a*, *e*, *o*, when adjacent, always stand in separate syllables; thus *Beorges* (three syllables). This includes cases of identical vowels; thus *aa* (two syllables).

b) Nasal vowels also stand in a separate syllable from any adjacent vowel; thus *leões* (three syllables). This includes cases where a nasal vowel stands next to its non-nasal counterpart; thus *vĩir* (two syllables),

c) Two *identical* weak vowels also stand in separate syllables.

d) The 'weak vowels' *i*, *u*, also remain separate when they occur *before* a strong vowel; thus *via* (two syllables), *Daniel* (three syllables). The infrequent instances where this is not the case are marked, in this edition, with a micron, implying 'lack of length'; thus *mĭa* (one syllable).

e) When a 'weak vowel' occurs *after* another vowel, it generally unites with it in the *same* syllable, creating a 'falling diphthong', so typical of the language, in which the second element recedes in prominence; thus *seu* (one syllable), *entrou* (two syllables), *Reinna* (two syllables). Cases where this is not so are marked, in this edition, with a diaeresis, implying 'separateness'. Thus, occasionally, *Reïnna* (three syllables), *creüdo* (three syllables).

f) Two *different* weak vowels standing together naturally fall into the same syllable, with the *first* of them more prominent; thus *viu* (impressionistically: 'viii^{w}').

The main stress falls on the second-last syllable of a word ending in a strong vowel, or a strong vowel followed by *-n* or *-s*. Thus *vidro*, *crischãos*, *sabia*, *deron*.
The main stress falls on the *last* syllable of other words, including those ending in a weak vowel, a diphthong, or a diphthong followed by *-s*. Thus *aprendi*, *dali*, *livrou*, *demais*.
Cases that fall outside these two rules are regarded as having unpredictable stress, which in this edition is then marked with an acute accent.

Cases in which three vowels occur together can generally be worked out using the rules already given (thus *leeu*, two syllables, by rule a then rule e); but complexities arise when a weak vowel (generally *-i-*) occurs in the middle of the group. The following cases arise:

i) Middle vowel separate. Thus *liia* (three syllables by applying rules c and d above). Where it is necessary to bring this about, the middle vowel is marked with a diæresis; thus *oïa* (*o-ï-a*, to prevent *oi-a*); similarly *saïa* (also three syllables).

ii) Middle vowel forms diphthong with preceding vowel: *peior* (two syllables: *pei-or*[4])

iii) Middle vowel forms diphthong with following vowel: *saíu* (two syllables, *sa-íu*, with the second stressed); similarly *oíu*.

More complex cases will be found to comply with the basic principles; so the name *Juião* (*CSM* 15) breaks down as *Jui* (rule f) *ã* (main stress) *-o*.

Finally, the allocation of consonants to particular syllables responds to two criteria:

a) a single consonant between vowels adheres to the *following* vowel; (since *ch*, *rr*, *ll* and *nn* each represent a single sound, they must not be separated across a syllable-boundary); thus *me-ni-nno*, *me-llor*;

b) where two (or more) consonants occur together, they will both adhere to the following vowel *provided* the same combination could also begin a word. So *ei-gre-ja*, *vi-dro*. But if the consonantal group in question cannot stand as word-initial, the group must be split between syllables. Thus *con-tar*, *cris-chã-os*, *al-tar*.

---

[4] This way of presenting the case circumvents the question of ambisyllabicity, a technical matter not productive in this context.

PRONUNCIATION[5]

The sounds of Medieval Galician-Portuguese may usefully be dealt with in the following groups:

	Spelling:	*Rendered as:*
Sibilants:	*s-*, *-ss-* , *-s*	[s] (as in Modern Castilian *casa*)
	-s- (single intervocalic *s*)	[z] (as in Modern Italian *casa*)
	ch	[tʃ] (as in English *cheap*)
	x	[ʃ] (as in English *sheep*)
	j; *g* before *e* or *i*	[ʒ] (as in French *j'ai*) or perhaps [dʒ] (English *jay*); academic opinion is not consolidated.
	ç; *c* before *e* or *i*	[ts] (as in English *pats*, *cats*)
	z	[dz] (as in English *pads*, *cads*)
Non-sibilant palatal consonants:	*ll*	As for Castilian *ll*, *ñ*, Portuguese *lh*, *nh*, Italian *gl*, *gn*.
	nn	Both sounds are pronounced with the flat of the tongue pressed firmly into the palate.
Other consonants	*b* and *v*	These sounds are to be kept separate, pronounced as written.
	b, *d*, *g*	These sounds have not yet acquired their 'relaxed' (technically: fricative) quality when they occur between vowels (later [β], [ð], [γ]).
	que, *qui* *gue*, *gui*	The vowel *u* is not pronounced in these combinations, serving merely to keep the consonantal sound 'hard'.
Vowels:	*i*, *e*, *a*, *o*, *u*	The vowels are to be pronounced clearly, with what may approximately be termed 'Latin' values. When stressed, *e* and *o* are articulated either as more close ([e], [o]) or more open ([ɛ], [ɔ]), with no indication from the spelling which is required.[6]
Nasal vowels:	*ĩ*, *ẽ*, *ã*, *õ*, *ũ*	The presence of nasality does not affect the underlying vowel quality (as distinct, for example, from what happens in French). Whilst opinions differ, it is likely that the *tilde* also represents the presence of a following nasal consonant resembling a lightly-articulated English *ng* sound [ŋ].

TEXTS AND TRANSLATIONS

It must be recalled that the texts given here are the product of the society and the period in which they were written. This is evident most particularly in the casual disregard for racial groups and religious beliefs different from those represented by the authorial viewpoint. In other words, certain of these texts do not conform to norms or sensibilities built on tolerance and respect. This may be a factor in assessing their suitability for performance.

In an effort to aid word-by-word comprehension of the Galician text, an attempt is made in the translations to keep as closely as possible to the original, even in some instances permitting mild syntactic distortion in the English version. The translations are thus meant as a study-aid for performers; it is not intended that they themselves be performed.

[5] Only the briefest treatment of some salient points can be given here. For fuller treatment *see* Cunningham 2000, pp. 59–66. The section on pronunciation on the cantigasdesantamaria website (*see* Bibliography) has very helpful comments and advice.

[6] It has not been possible to include such an indication in the texts that are edited here. Performers who wish to strive for accuracy in this particular will find the necessary information, indicated by written accents, in the texts as prresented by Stephen Casson on the cantigasdesantamaria website.

CANTIGA 4

SOURCES: *To*, n° 4, f. 12v–14r
T, n° 4, f. 8v–9r
E, n° 4, f. 31r–32r

The young son of a Jewish glassmaker in Bourges receives Communion in the company of his Christian classmates, with a statue of the Virgin and Child looking on. His father, infuriated, puts his son into the blazing furnace. Shielded by the Lady and her Son, the boy is delivered unharmed. A narrative that recalls two episodes from the Book of Daniel.

Syllable-count (real syllables): ℜ: 7 - 7 - 7 - 7
Stanza: 7 - 8 - 7 - 8 - 7 - 8 - 7 - 7

ℜ *A Madre do que livrou*
dos leões Daniel,
essa do fogo gŭardou
un meninno d' Irrael.

The Mother of Him who freed
Daniel from the lions,
She [also] kept from the fire
a child of Israel.

I En Beorges un judeu
ouve, que fazer sabia
vidro; e un fillo seu
(ca end' el máis non avia,
per quant' end' aprendi eu)
ontr' os crischãos liia
na escol'; e era greu
a seu padre Samuel. ℜ

In Bourges there was a Jew
who knew how to make
glass; and a son of his
(for more than that he did not have,
by all I have learned of it)
studied among the Christians
at school; and this went hard
with his father Samuel. ℜ

II O meninno o mellor
leeu que leer podia,
e d' aprender gran sabor
ouve de quanto oïa;
e por esto tal amor
con esses moços collia
con que era leedor,
que ia en seu tropel. ℜ

The boy studied
as hard as he could study,
and had a great liking
for learning from all he heard;
and for that reason he formed
such a friendship with those boys
with whom he was a student
that he went [round with them] in their group. ℜ

III Por én vos quero contar
o que ll' avẽo un dia
de Pascŏa, que foi entrar
na eigreja, u viia
o abad' ant' o altar;
e aos moços dand' ia
óstias de comungar
e vinn' en un cález bel. ℜ

And so I want to tell you
what happened to him one day
at Easter, when he went into
the church where he could see
the abbot at the altar;
he was giving the boys
communion wafers,
and wine from a beautiful chalice. ℜ

IV O judeucin*n*o prazer
ouve, ca lle parecia
que óstias a comer
lles dava Santa Maria,
que v*i*a resprandecer
eno altar u siia
e enos braços tẽer
seu Fillo Emanuel. ℜ

The little Jew took
delight, for it seemed to him
that Holy Mary was giving them
hosts to consume,
[She] whom he could see in splendour
on the altar where She sat
holding in Her arms
Her Son Emmanuel. ℜ

V Quand' o moç' esta visón
viu, tan muito lle prazia,
que por fillar seu quin*n*ón
ant' os outros se metia.
Santa Maria entón
a mão lle porregia,
e deu-lle tal comun*n*ón
que foi máis doce ca mel. ℜ

When the lad saw this vision,
so much did it please him
that, in order to get his portion,
he placed himself in front of the others.
Holy Mary then
stretched out Her hand to him,
and gave him communion
which was sweeter than honey. ℜ

VI Poi-la comun*n*ón fillou,
logo dali se partia
e en cas' seu padr' e*n*trou
como xe fazer soïa.
E ele lle preguntou
que fezera; el dizia:
«A Dona me comungou
que vi so o chapitel.» ℜ

When he had received communion,
he went straight off
and entered his father's house
as he was accustomed to do.
And he asked him
what he had been doing; he replied:
"The Lady I saw on the capital [of the pillar]
gave me communion." ℜ

VII O padre, quand' est' oíu,
creceu-lli tal felonia
que de seu siso saíu;
e seu fill entón prendia
e u o forn' arder viu
mete*u*-o dentr' e choïa
o forn', e mui mal faliu
como traedor cruel. ℜ

The father, when he heard this,
[felt] such a rage come over him
that he went out of his mind;
he at once seized his son,
and when he saw the furnace blazing
he put him in and closed
the furnace, and [so] sinned greatly,
like a cruel traitor. ℜ

VIII *Raqu*el, sa madre, que ben
grand' a seu fillo queria,
cuidando sen outra ren
que lle no forno ardia,
deu grandes vozes por én
e ena rua saïa;
e aqué a gente ven
ao doo de Ra*qu*el. ℜ

Rachel, [the boy's] mother who indeed
loved her son greatly,
believing quite simply
that he was burning in the furnace,
cried out aloud on that account
and ran out into the street;
and here are the people coming
[in response] to Rachel's grieving. ℜ

IX Pois souberon sen mentir
o por que ela carpia,
foron log' o forn' abrir
en que o moço jazia,
que a Virgen quis guarir
como guardou Anania
Deus, seu Fill', e sen falir
Azari' e Misael. ℜ

When they found out for certain
what it was she was bewailing,
they went at once to open
the furnace in which the boy lay,
[the boy] whom the Virgin saw fit to save,
just as God, Her Son, saved
Hananiah, and certainly also
Azariah and Mishael. ℜ

X O moço logo dali
sacaron con alegria,
e preguntaron-ll' assi
se se d' algún mal sentia.
Diss' el «Non, ca eu cobri
o que a Dona cobria
que sobe-lo altar vi,
con seu Fillo, bon donzel.» ℜ

They brought the lad out
from there with rejoicing,
and asked him
if he felt any pain.
He said: "No, for I cloaked [myself in]
what the Lady wore
that I saw on the altar
with Her beautiful young Son." ℜ

XI Por este miragr' atal
log' a judea criia,
e o menin*no* sen al
o batismo recebia;
e o padre, que o mal
fezera per sa folia,
deron-ll' entón morte qual
quis dar a seu fill' Abel. ℜ

Because of this miracle
the Jewess then [came to] believe,
and the boy forthwith
received baptism;
and [as for] the father, who in his folly
had committed the evil deed,
they then gave him a death like
[that] he had tried to give to his son Abel. ℜ

Biblical Resonances

The epigraph to this text alludes to the freeing of Daniel unscathed from the lion's den, where he had been imprisoned by King Darius for his persistence in worshipping the God of the Hebrews (Dan 6:1–28). Of perhaps greater pertinence to the present narrative is the mention in Stanza IX of the three young men Hananiah, Azariah and Mishael (referred to in the biblical passage in question by their Chaldean names, Shadrach, Abednego and Meshach) who, for their refusal to worship the golden image set up by King Nebuchadnezzar, are enclosed in the Fiery Furnace from which they likewise emerge unharmed (Dan 3:1–30). The episodes have in common that deliverance comes through adherence to what, from the narrator's perspective, is seen as right. Viewed in the light of this parallel, the *cantiga* text amounts to a championing of Christian beliefs, with Jewish beliefs being represented by implication as false.

Metrical Note: *l.* 23

The word 'Pascoa' has only two syllables — a fact not predictable from the spelling.

CSM 4: Apparatus

Text edition based on *T*.

The beginning of the Epigraph has been abbreviated: Como] [ ]ſta e como 'This [piece] is [about] how…' *T*; Eſta quarta e como 'This fourth [piece] is [about] how…' *To*; Eſta e como *E*.
2 leões] Lẽoes *E* — 4 *meninno*] menỹo *T*, mınỹo *To*, Menỹo *E* — 8 ca end' el] que el en *To*, ca el en *E* — 10 liia] leẏa *To* — 13 meninno] Menınno *T*, mınỹo *To*, Menỹo *E* — 28 vinn' en] uỹen *To*, vỹen *E* — 29 judeucinno] ȷudeucỹo *T*, *E*, ıudeucĩo *To* — 32 lles] leſ *To* — 33 via] uıȷa *T*, *E*, uıa *To*, *hypermetric all.* — 36 Emanuel] Hemanuel *E* — 39 quinnón] qⁱnon *T*, qⁱnnõ *To*, quĩnon *E* — 43 comunnón] comũẏõ *T*, comuẏõ *To*, Comuẏon *E* — 45 comunnón] Comũẏon *T*, comuẏon *To*, *E* — 47 entrou] etrou *T* — 54 creceu-lli] creceule *To* — 58 meteu-o] meteo *T*, *To*, *E* — 61, 68 Raquel] *The sources spell this with medial* -ch-, *but the pronunciation is without doubt as indicated. The initial is missing in T in l. 61.* —76 Misael] Mıſahel *T*, *E*, mıſael *To* — 79 assi] aſı *E* — 83 sobe-lo] ſobrelo *To* — 87 meninno] menỹo *T*, *E*, mınỹo *To*.

CANTIGA 10

SOURCES: *To*, nº 10, f. 20v–21r
T, nº 10, f. 17v
E, nº 10, f. 39v

A *cantiga* of praise.

Syllable-count (real syllables): ℜ: 10* - 11
Stanza: 10 - 10 - 10 - 11
**See Metrical Note below.*

ℜ *Rosa das rosas, e* Fror das frores,*
Dona das donas, Sennor das sennores.

Rose of [all] roses, Flower of flowers,
Lady of ladies, Liege of lieges.

I Rosa de beldad' e de parecer,
e Fror d' alegria e de prazer,
Dona en mui piadosa seer,
Sennor en toller coitas e doores. ℜ

Rose of beauty and of [fair] semblance,
and Flower of happiness and delight;
Lady, by being most compassionate;
Liege, in removing troubles and sorrows. ℜ

II Atal Sennor dev' ome muit' amar,
que de todo mal o pode guardar,
e pode-ll' os pecados perdõar
que faz no mundo per maos sabores. ℜ

Such a Liege must man greatly love,
who from every ill can guard him,
and can pardon him the sins
he commits in the world through evil desires. ℜ

III Devemo-la muit' amar e servir,
ca punna de nos guardar de falir;
des i, dos erros nos faz repentir
que nós fazemos come pecadores. ℜ

We should love and serve Her greatly,
for She strives to keep us from failing;
moreover, She makes us repent of the sins
which, as sinners, we commit. ℜ

IV Esta Dona que tenno por Sennor,
e de que quero seer trobador:
se eu per ren poss' aver seu amor,
dou ao demo os outros amores. ℜ

This Lady whom I hold as my Liege,
and whose troubadour I wish to be:
if I for aught can win Her love,
I give to the devil [all] the other loves. ℜ

*METRICAL NOTE

In a recent textual edition Parkinson (2015, p. 52) discards the conjunction *e* from *l.* 1, even though it is present in all sources, preferring to see the metre of the refrain as accentually based (four metrical accents per line) rather than dependent on syllable-count. The *e* would then be seen as an insertion intended to help balance syllable-counts, though not quite evening out the irregularity.

This is attractive both from a textual point of view — it recognises a structural parallel between the lines of the refrain — and a musical standpoint — it implies removal of the ungainly musical stress that falls on the conjunction. But the question arises as to whether the melody was devised for the text *as we have it*, and whether we would be right to adapt it to a revised text.

Musical performance without the conjunction is in practical terms possible, in theoretical terms difficult. Practically, it requires one of the remaining syllables to be spread over two notational figures. There seem two possibilities: either *Fror* is spread over a.6–7, or *das* is spread over a.7–8. Of these, the latter is æsthetically more pleasing. But the first of these options requires a syllable to be spread over two melodic components of relative duration 3+1, which it would simply not be possible to notate; the second divides the rhythmic cell equally between syllables, and so vitiates the underlying Mode III character of the rhythm. The performer will decide.

See also the solution suggested by Parkinson, mentioned in n. 23 on p. 100 above.

CSM 10: APPARATUS

Text edition based on *T/E.* Nouns relating to the Virgin have been capitalised throughout.
The beginning of the Epigraph has been abbreviated: De] [ ]ſta e de *T*, Eſta deʒẽa e de *To*, Eſta e de *E*.
1 e] *See metrical note above*; fror...frores] *sic T*, *E*, floꝛ...floꝛeς *To. Similarly in all repetitions of* ℜ *in To*. — 4 Fror] *sic T*, *E*, floꝛ *To* — 11 Devemo-la] Deuemos la *To*.

CANTIGA 15
(*To* 33, *T* 5, *E* 15)

SOURCES: *To*, nº 33, f. 43v–45v
T, nº 5, f. 10r–11r
E, nº 15, f. 42v–44r

The Emperor Julian, on his way through Cæsarea, behaves threateningly to St Basil. Seeking protection St Basil turns to the Virgin, who summons St Mercury from heaven to do earthly battle with Julian, a battle St Basil sees in a vision. It occurs that St Mercury's weapons, found to be missing, are later returned to his tomb, bloodied. The philosopher Libanios, an eyewitness of the events, arrives to recount Julian's death at the hands of a knight in white. Libanios is converted.

Syllable-count (real syllables): ℜ: 10+9 - 10+9
Stanza: 10 - 9 - 10 - 9 - 10 - 9 - 10 - 9

ℜ *Todo-los santos que son no ceo | de servir muito an gran sabor*
Santa Maria, a Virgen Madre | de Jesucristo, Nostro Sennor.

All the saints that are in heaven take much delight in faithfully serving
Holy Mary, the Virgin Mother of Jesus Christ, Our Lord.

I E de lle seeren ben mandados,
esto dereit' e razón aduz,
pois que por eles encravelados
ouve seu Fill' os ne*m*bros na cruz;
demais, per ela santos chamados
son, e de todos é lum' e luz;
por end' están sempr' aparellados
de fazer quanto ll' en prazer for. ℜ

[As to] their being fully obedient to Her,
this is conducive to right and reason,
since for their sake did her Son
have His limbs nailed on the cross;
through Her, moreover, are they called
saints, and She is the brightness and light of all;
therefore they are ever ready
to do whatever shall be to Her liking. ℜ

II Ond' en Cesaira, a de Suria,
fez un miragre a gran sazón
por san Basillo Santa Maria
sobre Juião fals' e felón,
que os crischãos matar queria;
ca o demo no seu coraçón
metera i tan grand' eregia
que per ren non podia maior. ℜ

Whereof in Caesarea, in Syria,
Holy Mary performed a timely
miracle for St Basil
against [that] false and treacherous Julian
who was seeking to kill the Christians;
for into his heart the devil
had put so enormous a heresy that
by no means could he [have put] a bigger. ℜ

III Este Juião avia guerra
con persiãos, e foi sacar
oste sobr' eles, e pela terra
de Cesaira ouve de passar;
e san Basill' a pe dũa serra
saíu a el por xe ll' omillar,
e diss' assi: «Aquel que non erra,
que Deus é, te salv', Emperador.» ℜ

This Julian was waging war
on the Persians, and he went to bring up
an army against them, and had to pass
through the land of Caesarea;
and St Basil came out to him, at the foot
of a mountain, so as to do him homage,
and he spoke thus: "May He who errs not,
— that is God —, keep you, O Emperor." ℜ

IV Juião diss' ao ome santo:
«Sabedor es, e muito me praz;
mas quer' agora que sábĩas tanto
que mui mais sei eu ca ti assaz;
e de tod' esto eu ben m' avanto
que sei o que en natura jaz.»
B*a*si*ll*o diz: «Será est' enquanto
tu connoceres teu Criador.» ℜ

Julian said to the holy man:
"You are wise, and greatly does it please me;
but now I want you to know this much,
that I know much more than you by far;
and in all of this, I take great pride
that I know what lies [hidden] in Nature."
Basil says: "This will be so [only] when
you come to know your Creator." ℜ

V O sant' ome tirou de seu sẽo
pan d' orjo, que lle foi o*fr*ecer,
dizend': «Esto nos dan do allẽo
por Deus, con que possamos viver.
Pois ta pessõa nobr' aqui vẽo,
filla-o, se te jaz en prazer.»
Juião disse: «Den-ti do fẽo,
pois me cevada dás por amor; [ℜ?]

The holy man took out from his bosom
[some] barley bread, which he offered him,
saying: "This do they give us from elsewhere,
for God['s sake], that we may live off it.
Since your noble self has come here,
take it, if it suits your pleasure."
Julian said: "Let them give you hay,
since you kindly give me barley; [ℜ?]

VI »e mais te digo que, se conqueiro
terra de Persĩa, quero vĩir
per aqui log' e teu mõesteiro
e ta cidade ti destroïr;
e fẽo comerás por fazfeiro,
ou te farei de fame fĩir;
e se t' aqueste pan non refeiro,
terei-me por d' outr' ome peior.» ℜ

and I tell you moreover that, if I conquer
the land of Persia, I intend to come
this way again and destroy
your monastery and your city;
and you shall eat hay as punishment
or else I will have you die of hunger;
and if I do not refuse this bread,
I shall consider myself the worst of men." ℜ

VII Pois san Basill' o fẽo fillado
ouve, tornando-se diss' atal:
«Juião, deste fẽo que dado
mĩ‿ás que comesse feziste mal;
e est' orgullo que mĩ‿ás mostrado,
Deus tĩo demande, que pod' e val;
e quant' eu ei ten*n*' encomendado
da Virgen, Madre do Salvador.» ℜ

When St Basil had taken
the hay, turning round he spoke thus:
"Julian, with this hay you have given me
to eat, you did wrong;
and this pride you have shown me, may God,
who has power and worth, seek answer for it;
all that I have, I hold in trust
from the Virgin Mother of the Saviour." ℜ

VIII Pois se tornou aos da cidade,
fez-los juntar, chora*n*do dos seus
ollos, contand' a deslealdade
de Juião, e disse: «Por Deus
de quen é Madre de piadade
Santa Maria, ai amigos meus,
roguemos-lle pola sa bondade
que nos guarde daquel traedor.» ℜ

When he went back to those of the city,
he had them assemble, weeping,
recounting the bad faith
of Julian; and he said: "By God
whose merciful Mother
Holy Mary is (ah, my friends!),
let us pray to Her that, by Her goodness,
She will protect us from that traitor." ℜ

IX Demais fez-lles jajũar tres dias,
e levar gran marteir' e afán,
andando per muitas romarias,
bevend' ágũa, comendo mal pan;
de noite lles fez tẽer vigias
na eigreja da do bon talán,
Santa Maria, que désse vias
per que saïssen daquel pavor. ℜ

Furthermore, he made them fast three days
and undertake great penance and devotion,
going on many pilgrimages,
drinking [only] water and eating stale bread;
by night he had them hold vigil
in the church of the Generous One,
Holy Mary, that she provide ways
for them to escape from that dread. ℜ

X Poi-lo sant' om' aquest' ouve feito,
ben ant' o altar adormeceu
da Santa Virgen, lass' e maltreito;
e ela logo ll' apareceu
con gran poder de santos afeito
que a terra toda‿*e*sclareceu,
e dizendo: «Pois que ei congeito,
vingar-m'-ei daquele malfeitor.» ℜ

Once the holy man had done this,
he fell fast asleep before the altar
of the Holy Virgin, weary and shaken.
And thereupon She appeared to him,
with a great posse of saints
that illumined the whole earth,
saying: "Since I have [it in my] power,
I shall avenge myself on that malefactor." ℜ

XI Pois esto disse, chamar mandava
san Mercuiro, e disse-ll' assi:
«Juião falso, que rezõava
mal a meu Fill' e peior a mí,
por quanto mal nos ele buscava
dá-nos dereito del ben ali
du vai ontr' os seus, en que fiava,
e sei de nós ambos vingador.» ℜ

When She said this, she had St Mercury
called [from his tomb], and told him thus:
"The false Julian, who was plotting
ill against my Son and worse against me...
[in return] for all the harm he sought for Us
[do you] give Us the right of remedy, there
where he goes among his supporters in whom
he trusted; be an avenger for Us both. ℜ

XII E mantenente, sen demorança,
san Mercuiro log' ir-se leixou
en seu cavalo branc', e sa lança
muito brandind'; e toste chegou
a Juião, e deu-lle na pança,
que en terra morto o deitou
ontr' os seus todos; e tal v*i*ngança
fillou del come bon lidador. ℜ

And straight away, without delay,
St Mercury at once set off
on his white horse, vigorously brandishing
his lance; and soon he reached
Julian, and stuck him in the paunch
and laid him down dead on the ground
amid all his followers; such vengeance
he wrought as a good warrior. ℜ

XIII Tod' aquesto que vos ora dito
ei, san Basill' en sa visó*n* viu;
e Santa Maria deu-ll' escrito
un livro, e ele o abriu;
e quant' i viu no coraçón fito
teve ben, e logo s' espidiu
dela. E pois da visón foi quito,
ficou én con med' e con tremor. ℜ

All this that I have just told
you, St Basil saw in his vision;
and Holy Mary showed him a written [copy of]
a book; and he opened it,
and whatever he saw there he fully retained
fixed in his heart; and then he took his leave
of Her. Once he was released from the vision,
he remained in fear and trembling from it. ℜ

XIV Depós aquest' un seu companneiro
[*a*] san Basi*ll*o logo chamou,
e catar foi logo de primeiro
u as sas armas ante leixou
de san Mercuiro, o cavaleiro
de Jesucrist', e non as achou;
e teve que era verdadeiro
seu sonn', e deu a Deus én loor. ℜ

After this, St Basil was summoned
by a companion of his;
and he went then in the first instance to look
where St Mercury, the knight of Jesus Christ,
previously left his arms,
but did not find them;
he concluded that his dream
was true, and gave God praise for it. ℜ

XV Essa ora logo, sen tardada,
san Basi*ll*o, com' escrit' achei,
u a gente estav' assũada
foi-lles dizer como vos direi:
«Gran v*i*ngança nos á ora dada
san Mercuiro daquel falso rei,
ca o matou dũa gran lançada,
que nunca atal deu justador; [ℜ?]

Then at once, without delay,
St Basil (as I have found it written),
when the people were assembled,
went to tell them as I shall relate:
"Great vengeance has St Mercury
now given us on that false ruler,
for he killed him with a mighty lance-thrust,
such as never did jouster ever deal; [ℜ?]

XVI »e se daquesto (pela ventura)
que digo non me creedes én,
eu fui catar a sa sepultura
e das sas armas non vi i ren.
Mas tornemos i log' a cordura,
por Deus que o mund' en poder ten,
ca este feit' é de tal natura
que dev' om' én seer sabedor.» ℜ

and if by chance you do not believe me
in this that I say,
I went to view his tomb
and I saw nothing of his weapons there.
But let us return there again with discernment
(by God who holds the world in [His] power),
for this event is of such a nature
that a man must reach understanding of it." ℜ

XVII Logo tan toste foron correndo,
e as armas todas essa vez
acharon, e a lança jazendo,
con que san Mercuir' o colbe fez,
sangoent'; e per i ente*n*dendo
foron que a Virgen mui de prez
fez fazer esto en defendendo
os seus de Juião chufador. ℜ

Then straight away they went at speed,
and this time they found
all the weapons, and the lance
with which St Mercury struck the blow
lying bloodied; and by this they gradually
understood that the Most Worthy Virgin
caused this to be done in defending
her [devotees] against Julian the trickster. ℜ

XVIII Eles assi a lança catando,
que creer podian muit' adur,
maestre Libano foi chegando,
filósofo natural de Sur,
que lles este feito foi contando
— ca se non detevera nenllur
des que leixara a ost' alçando
e Juião morto sen coor. ℜ

Whilst they were thus contemplating the lance,
[a sight] which they could hardly believe,
Master Libanios, a philosopher
native to Syria, came up,
and he told them at length of this event
– for he had stopped nowhere [in his journey]
since he had left the army retreating
and Julian pale and lifeless. ℜ

XIX E contou-lles a mui gran ferida
que ll' un cavaleiro branco deu,
per que a‿*a*lma tan toste partida
lle foi do corp'. «Aquesto vi eu,»
diss el, «por én quero santa vida
fazer vosc', e non vos seja greu,
e receber vossa lei comprida,
e serei dela preegador.» ℜ

And he recounted to them the massive wound
that a white knight gave him,
by which his soul was so quickly severed
from his body. "This did I see" he said,
"because of which I wish to lead a holy life
among you (may it not be burdensome to you)
– and to receive your faith in its fullness:
I shall be a preacher of it." ℜ

XX E log' a ágũa sobe-la testa
lle deitaron, e batismo pres;
e começaron log' i a festa
da Virgen, que durou ben un mes;
e cada dia pela gran sesta
vĩan da ost' un e dous e tres,
que lles contaron da mort' a gesta
que pres Juião a gran door. ℜ

And then they poured down water
on his head, and he accepted baptism;
and there and then they began the festival
of the Virgin, which lasted fully a month.
Each day in the afternoon heat there came
[straggling in] one, two or three from the army
who related to them the story of the death
that Julian met with much grief. ℜ

Metrical Note

The stanzas are laid out in short lines, given the presence of rhyme in each line; the Refrain, without rhyme between the ten-syllable segments, is given in long lines with cæsura.

CSM 15: Apparatus

Text edition based on *T*.

The beginning of the Epigraph has been abbreviated: Como] [ ]ſta e como *T*, Eſta xxxııȷ e como 'This 33rd [piece]...' *To*, Eſta e como *E*.

2 Jesu] ıeſo *To*, *E* — 3 lle] le *To* — 6 nembros] nebꝛos *T* — 8 todos é] *Repeated in E* — 17 eregia] er ıgıa *To*, *E* — 33 Basillo] *sic To*, Bıſılo *T*, baſılo *E* — 36 ofrecer] *sic To*, offerecer *T*, offrecer *E* — 51 Basill'] baſıl *E* — 57 tenn'] tẽ *T*, tẽn *To*, tenn *E* — 60 chorando] choꝛado *T* — 62 de] *missing in T, leaving erasure.* — 63 piadade] pıedade *To* — 64 Maria] marı *To* — 67 jajũar] ıeıũar *To*, geıũar *E* — 71 lles] leſ *To* — 77 maltreito] m̃ltreto *E* — 90 vingador] uẽgadoꝛ *To* — 97 vingança] *sic E*, uẽgãça *To*, *T*; *the form with* vin- *has been generalized (cf. ll. 82, 90, 119).* — 100 Basill'] baſıl *E*; visón] uıso *T* — 104 espidiu] eſpedıu *To*, eſpedẏu *E* — 107 companneiro] copãneıro *To* — 108 Basillo] *sic E*, baſılo *T*, baſılıo *To*. *The line is hypometric; the editorial insertion seems preferable to the adoption of the reading of To.* — 112 Jesu] ıeſo *To*, ȷeſo *E* — 113 verdadeiro] veraıẏro *E* — 116 Basillo] *sic E*, baſılıo *T*, baſılo *To* — 117 gente] gent *E*; estav' assũada] eſtaua ſũada *To* — 119 vingança] uengãça *T*. *See note to 97.* —125 fui] foı *To*; sepultura] ſepoltura *To* — 135 entendendo] entedendo *T* — 142 filósofo] phıloſopho *T* — 149 a alma] *All sources suppress one* a; *an initial vowel has been supplied, so as not to leave an acephalous* 'lma, *but it must immediately be elided. A perhaps better (if more interventionist) emendation would be* 'per que a alma toste partida'. — 156 batismo] baſtımo *To* — 157 log' i] loguẏ *To*.

CANTIGA 20

SOURCES: *To*, nº 20, f. 30r–31r
T, nº 20, f. 32r
E, nº 20, f. 46v–47r

A *cantiga* of praise.

Syllable-count (real syllables): ℜ: 5+5+7 - 5+5+7
Stanza: 6+6 - 6+6 - 5+5+7 - 5+5+7

ℜ *Virga de Jesse,*
quen te soubesse
loar como mereces,
e sén ouvesse
per que dissesse
quanto por nós padeces.

Rod of Jesse,
would that I knew how to
praise You as You deserve,
and had the wit
by which I might tell
how much You suffer on our behalf.

I Ca tu noit' e dia
sempr' estás rogando
teu Fill', ai Maria!,
por nós, que (andando
aqui pecando,
e mal obrando
que tu muit' avorreces)
non quera, quando
sever julgando,
catar nossas sandeces. ℜ

For You, night and day,
are always begging
Your Son, ah Mary!,
for us, so that (with [us] going about
sinning here
and doing wrong
which You greatly abhor)
He will not seek, when
He shall sit in judgment,
to observe our foolishness. ℜ

II E ar toda via
sempr' estás lidando
por nós a perfia,
o dem' arrancando,
que, sossacando,
nos vai tentando
con sabores rafeces;
mas tu guardando
e amparando
nos vas, poi-lo couseces. ℜ

For in every way, too,
You are always striving
on our behalf persistently,
routing the devil
who, cajolingly,
continually tempts us
with vile enticements;
but You come guarding
and sheltering
us, since You keep him under surveillance. ℜ

III Miragres fremosos
vas por nós fazendo
e maravillosos,
per quant' eu entendo,
e corregendo
muit', e sofrendo,
ca non nos escaeces,
e contendendo,
nos defendendo
do demo, qu' esterreces. ℜ

Miracles both beautiful
and wonderful
You are continually working for us,
from all I hear,
and looking after us
greatly, and being tolerant
—for You do not desert us—
and engaging in the struggle,
defending us
against the devil, whom You frighten off. ℜ

IV Aos sobervĭosos
d' alto vas decendo,
e os omildosos
en onrra crecendo,
e e*n*adendo
e provezendo
tas santas grãadeces.
Por én mĭ‿acomendo
a ti e rendo,
que os teus non faleces. ℜ

The haughty
You are ever putting down from on high,
and the humble
raising up in honour,
both providing
and incrementing
Your holy largesse.
Wherefore I commend myself
and surrender to You,
for You do not fail those who are Yours. ℜ

METRICAL NOTE: *l.* 44

Line 44, even with the marked elision, has a syllable too many, without any obvious means to correct it. In musical performance a solution might be found in moving the syllable *Por* back into the previous bar, singing it at the same pitch as the preceding syllable *–ces* from which it takes a third of the duration. The syllable *én* is thus allowed to take the musical stress at the start of the new phrase. This suggestion masks the metrical problem for performance purposes, though without removing it.

GRAMMATICAL NOTE: *ll.* 12–13

The *Dicionario da Real Academia Galega*, in the entry for 'que', states: 'Pode referirse…a unha oración enteira, indo precedida, nestes casos, dun substantivo do tipo *cousa*, *feito*, ou do artigo *o*.' If this is to be observed here, an article *o* must be found to precede the *que* at the start of *l.* 13. Mettmann's solution is '…mal obrand' — o // que…'; similarly Ferreiro & Pereiro (1996): '…mal obrand'(o // que…)'. Ferreira, meanwhile (2001, p. 202), objects to the partition of *o que* at a phrase-break on the grounds of musical structure — an observation with which I wholeheartedly agree —, but goes on to suggest '…mal obrando — [o] que…'. Neither solution is satisfactory from a musical perspective: whatever about the problem of the musical phrase-break, it is difficult to see how an apostrophe or a suppletion could be conveyed in vocal performance.

I take my own cue from Valmar (1889) and from Fidalgo (2003), both native speakers of Galego (a competence I cannot myself claim) who are content to leave the *que* to stand on its own. Their view of the text perhaps involves seeing a different syntactic function for the *que*, which, instead of referring to the whole previous clause ('doing wrong, [a thing] that you greatly abhor'), may be seen as having a more specific antecedent in the word *mal* ('doing [that] wrong which you greatly abhor'); the editorial punctuation attempts to reflect this.

CSM 20: APPARATUS

Text edition based on *T*.

The beginning of the Epigraph has been abbreviated: De] Eſta e de *T*, *E*, Eſta xx e de *To*.

5 per] poꝛ *To*; dissesse] dıſeſſe *To* — 14 quera] q̃ıra *To* — 20 arrancando] arrando *E* — 21 sossacando] ſoſacando *To* — 37 Aos] E os *E*; sobervĭosos] *The non-syllabic* ĭ *is necessary for the sake of the metre.* — 41 enadendo] *sic To*, ẽadendo *T*, *E* — 43 tas santas] *A marginal addition in To offers* cõ tuaſ, *an emendation that brings no advantage to the text.* — 44 Por én] poꝛe *E*; mĭ acomendo] mıacomendo *T*, ma comẽdo *To*, macomendo *E*. — 46 non] nõn *E*.

CANTIGA 25
(*To* 38)

SOURCES: *To*, nº 38, f. 50r–52r
T, nº 25, f. 37r–38r
E, nº 25, f. 49r–50v

A good man borrows funds from a Jew, giving statues of Holy Mary and Christ as security. When the debt becomes due, he sends the money by sea, and after some misadventures the chest containing it comes into the Jew's hands. But he hides it under the bed and pretends he is still owed the debt. The good man takes him to the church, where the statue denounces the Jew. He converts.

Syllable-count (real syllables): ℜ: 8 - 9
Stanza: 8 - 9 - 8 - 9 - 8 - 9 - 8 - 9

ℜ *Pagar ben pod' o que dever*
o que a Madre de Deus fia.

He who trusts the Mother of God
can well repay whatever he may owe.

I E desto vos quero contar
un gran miragre mui fremoso,
que fezo a Virgen sen par,
Madre do gran Rei grorioso,
por un ome que seu aver
todo ja despendud' avia
por fazer ben e mais valer
ca non ja en outra folia. ℜ

And on this [subject] I want to recount
a great and very beautiful miracle
that the Peerless Virgin,
Mother of the Great and Glorious King,
performed for a man who had spent
all his wealth
in doing good and [so] increasing his stature,
rather than on some other frippery. ℜ

II Quand' aquel bon ome o seu
aver ouv' assi despendudo,
non pod' achar, com' aprix eu,
d' estran*n*o nen de connoçudo
quen sol ll' emprestido fazer
quisess'; e pois esto viia,
a un judeu foi sen lezer
provar se ll' alg' emprestaria. ℜ

When that good man had thus
expended his fortune,
he could not find (as I learned)
either stranger or friend
who might even be willing to advance him
a loan; and when he saw this,
he went without delay to a Jew
to see if he would lend him something. ℜ

III E o judeu lle diss' entón:
«Amig', aquesto que tu queres
farei eu mui de coraçón,
sobre bon pennor, se mĭo deres.»
Disse-ll' o crischão: «Poder
d' esso fazer non averia,
mas fiador quero seer
de cho pagar ben a un dia.» ℜ

And the Jew then said to him:
"My friend, this that you wish
I shall very gladly do,
on good security, if you will give me such."
The Christian said to him: "I would not have
the power to do that;
but I want to be [my own] guarantor
of paying you it [back] on an [agreed] day. ℜ

IV O judeu lle respós assi:
«Sen pennor non será ja feito
que o per ren leves de mi.»
Diz o crischão: «Fas un preito:
ir-t-ei por fiador meter
Jesucrist' e Santa Maria.»
Respós el: «Non quer' eu creer
en eles; mas fillar-chos-ia... [ℜ?]

The Jew replied to him thus:
"Without security it shall not come about
that you borrow [the money] from me."
The Christian said: "Make a bargain:
I shall put in for you as guarantor
Jesus Christ and Holy Mary."
He replied: "I do not want to believe in them;
yet I would accept them for you… [ℜ?]

V ...porque sei que santa moller
foi ela, e el ome santo
e profeta; por én, senner,
fillar-chos quer' e dar-ch-ei quanto
quiseres, tod' a teu prazer.»
E o crischão respondia:
«Sas omágẽes, que veer
posso, dou-t' en fiadoria.» ℜ

...because I know that She was
a holy woman, and He a holy man
and a prophet; for that reason, sir,
I shall accept them, and shall give you all
you want, completely as you wish."
And the Christian replied:
"Their statues, which I [here] can
see, I give you as security. ℜ

VI Pois o judeu est' outorgou,
ambos se foron mantenente;
e as omages lle mostrou
o crischão; e ant' a gente
tangeu e fillou-s' a dizer
que por fiança llas metia,
por que ll' o seu fosse render
a seu prazo sen tricharia. ℜ

When the Jew conceded this,
they both went off at once;
and the Christian showed him
the statues; and, before the people,
he touched [them] and vouchsafed to say
that he was transferring them to him as security,
so he could pay back to him what was his
by the deadline, without fail. ℜ

VII «E vós, Jesucristo, Sennor,
e vós, sa Madre muit' onrrada,»
diss' el, «se daqui longe for
ou mĭa fazenda embargada,
non possa per prazo perder,
se eu pagar non llo podia
per mi, mas vós ide põer
a paga u mĭa eu porria; [ℜ?]

"And You, Lord Jesus Christ,
and You, His Mother most honoured,"
he said, "if I should be far from here,
or [if] my business [is] held up,
[and] cannot escape the deadline,
if I was unable to pay him it on my
own account, [then] do You step in to make
the payment, where I myself would pay it... [ℜ?]

VIII »ca eu a vós-lo pagarei;
e vós fazed' a el a paga,
por que non diga pois "Non ei
o meu", e en preito me traga,
nen mĭ‿o meu faça despender
con el andand' en preitesia;
ca se de coita a morrer
ouvesse, desta morreria.» ℜ

for I will pay it back to You;
do You make the payment to him,
so that he may not then say «I do not have
what is mine», and then bring me into litigation,
or make me expend what is mine
by getting involved with him in lawsuits;
for if I had to die
of worry, this is what I would die of." ℜ

IX Poi-lo crischão assi fis
fez o judeu, a poucos dias
con seu aver quant' ele quis
gãou en bõas merchandias;
ca ben se soub' en trameter
dest' e ben fazê-lo sabia;
mas foi-ll' o praz' escaecer
a que o el pagar devia. ℜ

After the Jew thus made the Christian
[financially] secure, within a few days
— with his funding, as much as he desired —
he profited in good trading;
for well did he realize [the need] to get involved
in this, and well was he versed in doing it.
But the time-span was getting short
by which he must pay it [*i.e.,* the loan] back. ℜ

X O crischão, que non mentir
quis daquel prazo que posera,
ant' un dia que a vĩir
ouvesse, foi en coita fera;
e por esto fez compõer
un' arca, e dentro metia
quant' el ao judeu render
ouv', e diss': «¡Ai, Deus, tu o guia!» ℜ

The Christian, who did not wish
to default on the term he had set,
one day before it was to expire
was in a desperate state.
And for this reason he had a chest
constructed, and inside he put
all he had to repay to the Jew.
And he said: "Ah!, God, do Thou guide it!" ℜ

XI Dizend est' en mar-la meteu;
e o vento moveu as ondas,
e outro dia pareceu
no porto das aguas mui fondas
de Besanç'. E pola prender
un judeu mui toste corria,
mas log' i ouv' a falecer,
que a arc' ant' ele fogia. ℜ

Saying this, he let it into the sea,
and the wind drove the waves
and the next day it appeared
in the deep-water port
of Byzantium. And a Jew
ran very hard so as to catch it,
but then in that he was to fail,
for the chest sped off before him. ℜ

XII E pois o judeu esto viu,
foi, metendo mui grandes vozes,
a seu sennor, e el saíu
e disse-lle: «Sol duas nozes
non vales, que fuste temer
o mar con mui gran covardia;
mas esto quer' eu cometer,
ben lev' a mi Deus-la daria.» ℜ

And when the Jew saw this,
he went to his master, shouting
loudly; and he came out
and said to him: "You are not even
worth two walnuts!, for you did fear
the sea, with great cowardice;
but I shall attempt this myself:
God would easily give it to me". ℜ

XIII Pois esto disse, non fez al,
mas correu alá sen demora,
e a arca en guisa tal
fez que aportou ant' el fora.
Entón foi sa mão tender
e fillou-a con alegria,
ca non se podia sofrer
de saber o que i jazia. ℜ

When he had said this, he did naught else
but ran there without delay;
and the chest behaved in such a way
that it came ashore right in front of him.
Then did he stretch out his hand
and took it with glee,
for he could not contain himself
for [want of] knowing what lay inside. ℜ

XIV Des i feze-a levar én
a sa casa, e seus din*n*eiros
achou en ela. E mui ben
se guardou de seus companneiros
que non ll' ouvessen d' entender
de como os el ascondia;
poi-los foi contar e volver,
a arca pos u el dormia. ℜ

From there he had it taken away
to his house, and in it he found
his moneys. And very carefully
he kept [it] from his friends,
that they should not find out
how he was hiding them [*i.e.*, the moneys];
and when he counted them and put them back,
he put the chest where he slept. ℜ

XV Pois ouve feito de sa prol,
o mercador alí chegava;
e o judeu, ben come fol,
mui de rijo lle demandava
que lle déss' o que ll' acreer
fora; se non, que el diria
atal cousa per que caer
en gran vergonna o faria. ℜ

When [the Jew] had [thus] sealed his advantage,
the merchant arrived;
and the Jew, foolishly,
forcefully demanded of him
that he give him back what he had
lent him; otherwise he would tell
such things by which he would cause
[the Christian] to fall into great disgrace. ℜ

XVI O crischão disse: «Fiel
bõo tenno que t' ei pagado:
a Virgen, Madre do donzel
que no altar ch' ouvi mostrado,
que te fará ben connocer
como foi, ca non mentiria;
e tu non queras contender
con ela, que mal t' én verria.» ℜ

The Christian said: "I have
a good witness that I have paid you:
the Virgin Mother of the Child
whom I showed you on the altar,
who will indeed let you know
how it was, for She would not lie;
and do not seek to dispute with Her,
for ill would come to you therefrom." ℜ

XVII Diss' o judeu: «Desso me praz;
pois vaamos aa eigreja,
e se o disser en mĭa faz
a ta omagen, feito seja.»
Entón fillaron-s' a correr,
e a gente pos eles ia,
todos con coita de saber
o que daquel preit' averria. ℜ

The Jew said: "I am contented with that;
so let us go th the church,
and if this statue of yours
tells me so to my face, so be it."
At this they took to running,
and the people went after them,
all of them anxious to know
what would come of that dispute. ℜ

XVIII Pois na eigreja foron, diz
o crischão: «Ai, Magestade
de Deus, se esta paga fiz,
rogo-te que digas verdade
per que tu faças parecer
do judeu sa aleivosia,
que contra mi cuida trager
do que lle dar non deveria.» ℜ

Once they were in the church,
the Christian said: "Ah!, Divine
Majesty, if I made this payment
I beg you to tell the truth
by which you may make patent
the treachery of the Jew,
who seeks to bring action against me
over what I am not obliged to give him." ℜ

XIX Entón diss' a Madre de Deus,
per como eu achei escrito:
«A falsidade dos judeus
é grand'; e tu, judeu maldito,
sabes que fuste receber
teu aver, que ren non falia,
e fuste a arca‿*e*sconder
so tu leito, con felonia.» ℜ

Then, according to what I found written,
the Mother of God said:
"The falseness of the Jews
is great; and you, accursed Jew,
know that you did receive
your dues, that nothing was missing,
and [that] you did hide the chest
under the bed, nefariously ℜ

XX Quand' est' o judeu entendeu,
bẽes ali logo de chão
en Santa Maria creeu
e en seu Fill', e foi crischão;
ca non vos quis escaecer
o que profetou Isaïa,
como Deus verria nacer
da Virgen por nós todavia. ℜ

When the Jew heard this,
there and then he fully
believed in Holy Mary
and in Her Son, and he became a Christian;
for I do not want what Isaiah
prophesied to pass unnoticed:
that God would yet come to be born
of the Virgin, for our sake. ℜ

CSM 25: APPARATUS

Text edition based on *T*.

The beginning of the Epigraph has been abbreviated: Como] Eſta e como *T*, *E*; Eſta xxxvııȷ e como *To*; entre] entr *To*, ontr *E*.

18 alg' emprestaria] alguempꝛeſtarıa *T*, alguen p̃ſtarıa *To*, alg enp̃ſtarıa *E* — 32 Jesu] ıeſo *E* — 41 omágẽes] omageeſ *To* — 43 Pois] Pos *E* — 45 omages] *sic T*; omagẽes *To*, *E*, *hypermetric*. — 51 Jesu] ıeſo *To*, *E* — 60 fazed' a el a paga] faʒer a el paga *E* — 104 fillou] fıllo *To* — 108 dinneiros] *sic To*; dĩeırꝯ *T*, dĩeıros *E* — 128 mentiria] metırıa *E* — 140 Magestade] maıeſtade *E* — 148 como] com *E*.

CANTIGA 38
(*To* 41)

SOURCES: *To*, nº 41, f. 54r–56v
T, nº 38, f. 56v–57r
E, nº 38, f. 61r–62r

A ruffian gambler, in mockery of a woman praying at a stone statue of the Virgin and Child, throws a stone which breaks off one of the Child's arms. The Virgin prevents it from falling, but turns an angry look towards the perpetrator whom devils promptly kill; his body is gnawed by his fellow gamblers who, driven by demons, then drown in the river — an example to all. An ensuing miracle sees a knight with a stone lodged in his jaw cured. The whole is set against a historical background.

Syllable-count (real syllables): ℜ: 9 - 10 - 9 - 10
Stanza: 11 - 14 - 11 - 14 - 9 - 10 - 9 - 10

ℜ *Pois que Deus quis da Virgen fillo*
seer por nós pecadores salvar,
por ende non me maravillo
se lle pesa de quen lle faz pesar.

Since God sought to be[come] the Son of the Virgin, to save us sinners, so then am I not surprised if He is grieved by whoever gives Him grief.

I Ca ela e seu Fillo son juntados
d'amor, que partidos per ren nunca poden seer;
e por én son mui neicios provados
os que contra ela van, non cuidand' i el tanger.
Esto fazen os malfadados
que est' amor non queren entender
com' Madr' e Fill' acordados
son en fazer ben e mal castigar. ℜ

For She and Her Son are united in love, for never by anything can They be parted; and for that reason they are proven fools, those who go against Her without regard for chafing Him thereby. This is what the unfortunates do who refuse to understand this love, [about] how Mother and Son are in accord in doing good and chastising wrong. ℜ

II Daquest' avẽo, tempos son passados
grandes, que o Conde de Peiteus quis batall' aver
con Rei de Franç'; e foron assũados
en Castro Rodolfo, per com' eu oí retraer,
— un mõesteiro d' ordĩados
monges qu' el-Conde mandou desfazer
porque os ouv' el sospeitados
que a franceses o querian dar. ℜ

On this [subject], it happened a great while ago that the Count of Poitiers [=Richard Cœur de Lion] wished to make war against the King of France; and they were confronted in Châteauroux (so I heard tell) — a monastery of ordained monks which the Count ordered [to be] dissolved, because he held them under suspicion that they wanted to hand it over to the French. ℜ

III Poi-los monges foron ende tirados,
mui maas compannas se foron tan tost' i meter,
ribaldos e jogadores de dados
e outros que lles tragian i vinno a vender.
E ontr' os ma*l*aventurados
ouv' i un que começou a perder,
per que foron del dẽostados
os santos e a Reïnna sen par. ℜ

Once the monks had been thrown out, an evil company soon went to insert itself, ruffians and dice-players, and others who brought wine there to sell to them. And among the scoundrels, there was one [gambler] who began to run up a loss, because of which the saints and the peerless Queen [of Heaven] were cursed by him. ℜ

IV Mas ũa moller, que por seus pecados
entrara na eigreja, como sol acaecer,
ben u soïan vestí-los sagrados
panos-los monges quando ian sas missas dizer,

But a woman — who (for her sins) had entered the church (as often happens) right where the monks used to vest their sacred robes when they were going to say their masses —,

porque viu i ben entallados
en pedra Deus con sa Madre seer,
os gẽollos logo ficados
ouv' ant' eles e fillou-s' a culpar. ℜ

because she saw God and His Mother there, beautifully sculpted in stone, bent her knees before them, and began to make confession [of her sins]. ℜ

V O tafur, quand' esto viu, con irados
ollos a catou, e começou-a mal a trager,
dizendo: «Vella, son muit' enganados
os que nas omágẽes de pedra queren creer;
e por que vejas com' errados
son, quer' eu ora logo cometer
aqueles ídolos pintados.»
E foi-lles log' ũa pedra lançar. ℜ

The gambler, when he saw this, looked at her with angry eyes, and began to address her harshly, saying: "Old woman, those who want to believe in stone statues are greatly deceived;
and so as you can see how mistaken they are, I intend at once to assail those painted idols." And he thereupon went and threw a stone at [the figures]. ℜ

VI E deu no Fillo, que ambos alçados
tĩia seus braços en maneira de bẽ*e*izer;
e macar non llos ouv' ambos britados,
britou-ll' end' un assi que ll' ouvera log' a caer.
Mas a Madre os seus deitados
ouve sobr' el, con que llo foi erger,
e a frol que con apertados
seus dedos tĩia foi logo deitar. ℜ

And it struck the Child, who held both His arms raised by way of blessing; and although it did not break both [arms], it broke one of them, such that it was about to fall.
But the Mother had Hers lowered over it, and so [caught it and] raised it again, and let drop the flower She held with open fingers. ℜ

VII Maiores miragres ouv' i mostrados
Deus, que sangui craro fez dessa ferida corer
do Menin*n*o, e os panos dourados
que tĩia a Madre fez ben so as tetas decer,
assi que todos desnuados
os peitos ll' ouveron de parecer;
e macar non dava braados,
o contenente parou de chorar. ℜ

Greater miracles did God perform there, for He made bright blood flow from that wound of the Child; and the golden garments that the Mother wore, He caused to slip down below her bosom,
such that her breasts appeared completely bared; and though She did not cry out, Her visage prepared to weep. ℜ

VIII E demais ouve os ollos tornados
tan bravos, que quantos a soïan ante veer
atán muit' eran dela espantados
que sol ena face no*n* ll' ousavan mentes tẽer.
E demões log' assembrados
contra o que esto fora fazer,
come monteiros ben mandados
o foron logo tan toste matar. ℜ

What is more, Her eyes were turned so fierce, that all who were previously used to seeing Her were [now] so greatly affeared of Her that they dared not even fix their attention on Her face.
And then demons, brought together against the one who had done this, went and killed him straight off, like well-ordered huntsmen. ℜ

IX Outros dous tafures demoniados
ouv i, porque foran aquel tafur mort' asconder;
por én sas carnes os endiabrados
con gran rávĩa as começaron todas de roer;
e pois no rio afogados
foron, ca o demo non lles lezer
deu, que todos escarmentados
fossen quantos dest' oïssen falar. ℜ

There were two other gamesters there possessed by devils, because they had gone to remove the dead gambler; and for that reason these diabolicals began to gnaw rabidly at his flesh.
Afterwards they drowned in the river; for the devil gave them no respite, so that all those who might hear about this [event] should be warned. ℜ

X O Conde, quand est' oíu, con armados
cavaleiros vẽo, e ant' a eigreja decer
foi. E un daqueles mais arrufados
diss' asi: «No meu coraçón non pod' esto caber:
se a pedra que me furados
os queixos ouv', e mĩa vedes trager,
e por que dinneiros pagados
ouvi muitos, se me non quer sãar?» ℜ

When he heard this, the Count came with armed knights, and dismounted in front of the church. And one of the more assured spoke thus: "This [is a matter that] cannot be confined in my heart.
If the stone that shattered my jaw — and you see me carrying it [lodged in my jawbone], on account of which I have paid a great deal of money [for a cure]..., will She not be willing to heal me?" ℜ

XI Pois esto disse, pernas e costados
e a cabeça foi log ant' a omagen merger;
e log' os ossos foron ben soldados
e a pedra ouv' ele pela boca de render.
Desto foron maravillados
todos, e el foi a pedra põer,
estand' i ómees onrados
ant' *a* omagen sobe-lo altar. ℜ

When he had said this, he inclined his knees and waist and head before the statue; and at once the bones [of his wound] knitted well, and he was able to retrieve the stone through his mouth.
At this, all were astonished; and he, with honourable men standing by, went to place the stone before the statue on the altar. ℜ

CSM 38: Apparatus

Text edition based on *T*.

The beginning of the Epigraph has been abbreviated: Como] Eſta e de como *T*, Efta xli e de como *To*, Eſta e como *E*; sangue] ſanguı *E*.

3 ende] en *E* — 6 d' amor] damos *E*, *with suprascript punctum delens.* — 17 mõesteiro] Moesteıro *E* — 18 desfazer] deffaʒ̃ *E* — 20 querian] queırıan *T* — 25 malaventurados] Marauenturados *T* — 28 Reïnna] ʀeỹna *T*, reỹa *To*, ʀeẏnna *E* — 32 panos-los] panꝯ.loſ *T*, panos.loſ *To*, p̃no.oſ *E* — 46 bẽeizer] bẽıʒer *T*, bẽeıʒer *To*, bẽeıʒ̃ *E* — 51 frol] froꝛ *E* — 52 seus] feus *E* — 55 Meninno] menỹo *T*, *E*, mınỹo *To* — 64 non ll'] noll *To* — 65 demões] demoeſ *To* — 69 demoniados] demõniados *T*, demoniados *To*, ᴅemõẏados *E*. *The metrical requirement for a word of five syllables rules out consideration of a form such as* demonnados; *even so, the possibility of two nasal vowels* (demõĩados – *articulated with perhaps a hint of velar approximation between*) *should not be overlooked.* 74 lles] les *To*, —83 dinneiros] dynneıros *T*, dĩeıros *To*, dỹeıros *E* — 84 me] mẽ *To* — 92 ant' a omagen] ant omagen *T*.

CANTIGA 41
(*To* 44)

SOURCES: *To*, nº 44, f. 58v–59r
T, nº 41, f. 59r
E, nº 41, f. 63r–v

In Soissons, Garín is so afraid of the Devil that he loses his wits, but the Holy Virgin brings him both sanity and salvation. A *cantiga* of scant narrative content. Structurally this is a *Rondel*, with the particular feature that the repeated line is sometimes integrated into the syntactic flow of the stanzas into which it is interpolated.

Syllable-count (real syllables): ℜ: 10 - 7 - 10 - 7
Stanza: 10 - *10* - 10 - *10* - 10 - 7 - 10 - 7
The repeated line incorporated into the stanza is here italicized.

ℜ *A Virgen Madre de Nostro Sennor*
ben pode dar seu siso
ao sandeu, pois ao pecador
faz aver Paraïso.

The Virgin Mother of Our Lord
can well lend Her intellect
to the dullard, since she causes the sinner
to have Paradise.

I En Seixons fez a Garín cambïador
a Virgen Madre de Nostro Sennor
que tant' ouve de o tirar sabor
a Virgen Madre de Nostro Sennor
do poder do demo, ca de pavor
del perdera o *siso*;
mas ela tolleu-ll' aquesta door
e deu-lle *Paraïso*. ℜ

The Virgin Mother of Our Lord
did [such] in Soissons for Garín, the money-changer,
the Virgin Mother of Our Lord
who had so great a desire to haul him
out of the devil's power; for through fear
of him he had lost his wits.
But She removed this misfortune from him
and gave him *Paradise*. ℜ

II Gran ben lle fez en est' e grand' amor
a Virgen Madre de Nostro Sennor,
que o livrou do dem' enganador
a Virgen Madre de Nostro Sennor,
que o fillara come traedor
e tollera-ll' o *siso*;
mas cobrou-llo ela, e por mellor
ar deu-lle *Paraïso*. ℜ

Great benefit She brought him in this, and great love,
the *Virgin Mother of Our Lord*,
who freed him from the deceitful devil
(this *Virgin Mother of Our Lord*),
[the devil] that, like a traitor, had seized him
and taken away his reason;
but She recovered it for him,
and even better, also gave him *Paradise*. ℜ

III Loada será mentr' o mundo for
a Virgen Madre de Nostro Sennor
de poder, de bondad' e de valor,
a Virgen Madre de Nostro Sennor,
porque a sa merce' é mui maior
ca o nosso mal *siso*,
e sempre a seu Fill' é rogador
que nos dé *Paraïso*. ℜ

Praised whilst the world shall last
will *the Virgin Mother of Our Lord* be,
in power, bounty and worth
(this *Virgin Mother of Our Lord*),
for Her mercy is far greater
than our poor understanding,
and She is ever a petitioner to Her Son
that He give us *Paradise*. ℜ

CSM 41: Apparatus

The text is remarkably consistent in all three sources.
The beginning of the Epigraph has been abbreviated: Como] Eſta e como *T*, Eſta xliiij e como *To*, [ ]ſta e como *E*.
25 merce'] *As it stands in all sources this line is hypermetric, with various possibilities for emendation. All sources give the form* mercee, *but in T (the only source in which this stanza is underlaid) the spacing suggests that the final two vowels correspond to the same notational figure, thus providing support for the emendation given here.*

CANTIGA 58
(*To* 73)

SOURCES: *To*, nº 73, f. 94r–95r
T, nº 58, f. 85r–v
E, nº 58, f. 78r–v

A nun who plans to elope with a knight is shown a vision of the hell that awaits her if she persists in her plan. But the Virgin pulls her from the jaws of the black pit, and she embarks on a reformed life. A *cantiga* remarkable for the vigour of the Virgin's reprimand.

Syllable-count: All lines have ten syllables.

ℜ *De muitas guisas nos guarda de mal*
Santa Maria, tan muit' é leal.

In many ways Holy Mary
keeps us from harm, so loyal is She.

I E dest' un miragre vos contarei
que Santa Maria fez, com' eu sei,
dũa monja (segund escrit' achei)
que d' amor lle mostrou mui gran sinal. ℜ

On this subject I shall recount to you a miracle
that Holy Mary performed, as I know,
concerning a nun (so did I find it written)
who showed her a great demonstration of love . ℜ

II Esta monja fremosa foi assaz,
e tĩia ben quant' en regra jaz;
e o que a Santa Maria praz,
esso fazia sempr' a comũal. ℜ

This nun was very beautiful, and held [fast]
to all that lies in the rule [of her order];
and that which is pleasing to Holy Mary,
such did she always do as a matter of course. ℜ

III Mais-lo demo, que dest' ouve pesar,
andou tanto pola fazer errar
que a troux' a que s' ouve de pagar
dun cavaleriro; e pos preit' atal... [ℜ?]

But the devil, who took umbrage at this,
took so many steps to get her to err, that he
brought her [to the point] that she took delight
in a knight; and he made a proposal such... [ℜ?]

IV ...con ele que se foss' a como quer,
e que a fillasse pois por moller
e lle déss' o que ouvesse mester;
e pos de s' ir a el a un curral... [ℜ?]

...that she should go off with him somehow,
and that he would then take her to wife
and provide her with whatever was necessary;
and she arranged to go to him in a courtyard... [ℜ?]

V ...do mõesteir'; e i a atendeu.
Mas en tant' a dona adormeceu
e viu en vijón, ond' esterreceu
con mui gran pavor que ouve mortal. ℜ

...in the convent; and there he awaited her.
But meanwhile she fell asleep
and had a vision, whereat she was struck
with mortal fear. ℜ

VI Ca se viu sobr' un poç' aquela vez,
estreit' e fond' e negro mais ca pez,
e o demo, que a trager i fez,
deitá-la quis per i no ifernal... [ℜ?]

For she saw herself at once over a pit,
narrow and deep, and blacker than pitch;
and the devil, who had had her brought there, tried
to bring her down through it into the fires... [ℜ?]

VII ...fogo, u mais de mil vozes oíu
d' omes e muitos tormentar i viu;
e con med' a poucas xe lle partiu
o coraçón; e chamou: «Sennor, val... [ℜ?]

...of hell, where she heard over a thousand voices
of men, and saw many being tormented there;
and through fear her heart came close to breaking.
And she cried: "My Liege!, help [me],... [ℜ?]

VIII ...Santa Maria, que Madr' es de Deus,
ca sempre punnei en fazê-los teus
mandamentos, e non cáte-los meus
pecados, ca o teu ben nunca fal.» ℜ

...Holy Mary, who art Mother of God,
for I always strove to carry out your
orders, and do not mark my
iniquities, for your bounty never fails." ℜ

IX Pois esto disse, foi-ll' aparecer
Santa Maria e mui mal trager,
dizendo-lle: «Venna-ch' or' acorrer
o por que me deitast', *e* non m' én cal.» ℜ

When she said this, Holy Mary did appear
to her and did chide [her] forcibly,
saying to her: "Let him for whom you left me
come to you now to help; it's not my job." ℜ

X Esto dit', un dïáboo a puxou
dentro no poç'; e ela braadou
por Santa Maria, que a sacou
del, a Reïn*n*a nobl' espirital. ℜ

This said, a demon pushed her
inside the pit; and she screamed
for Holy Mary, the noble Spiritual Queen,
who pulled her out of it. ℜ

XI E des que foi fora, disse-ll' assi:
«Des oge mais non te partas de mi
nen de meu Fillo; e se non, aqui
te tornarei, u non averá al.» ℜ

Once she was out, [Holy Mary] spoke to her
thus: "From today onwards do not depart from Me
nor from my Son; otherwise, here
will I bring you back, and no two ways about it!" ℜ

XII Pois passou esto, acordou entón
a monja, tremendo-ll' o coraçón;
e con espanto daquela vijón
que vira, foi logo a un portal... [ℜ?]

After this happened, the nun
came to, her heart racing;
and from fear of that vision
she had seen, she went at once to a gate... [ℜ?]

XIII ...u achou os que fezera vĩir
aquel*e* con que posera de s' ir;
e disse-lles: «Mal quisera falir
en leixar Deus por ome terrẽal;... [ℜ?]

...where she found those [men] sent by
the one with whom she had arranged to elope;
and she said to them: "Badly would I fail
by leaving God for an earthly man;... [ℜ?]

XIV »...mas, se Deus quiser, esto non será,
nen fora daqui non me veerá
ja mais null' ome; e ide-vos ja,
ca non quer' os panos nen o brial;... [ℜ?]

...but, God willing, this will not be [so],
nor never will no man see me
outside this place; go ye now, for I have no wish
for the [fine] clothes nor the tunic;... [ℜ?]

XV »...nen mentre viva, nunca amador
averei, nen non quer' eu outr' amor
senón da Madre de Nostro Sennor,
a Santa Reïnna celestial. ℜ

...and as long as I live, never shall I take
a lover, nor do I wish for any other love
but [that of] the Mother of Our Lord,
the Holy Queen of Heaven." ℜ

CSM 58: APPARATUS

Text edition based on *T*.

The beginning of the Epigraph has been abbreviated: Como] [ ]ſta e como *T*, Eſta LXIII e de como *To*, Como *E*; a monja] aa monıa *E*.

8 tĩia] tĩja *T*; tıĩa *To*, *perhaps yielding* tiinna; tỹna *E*, *hypometric*; regra] regla *To*, *E* — 10 comũal] *sic T*, comunal *To*, *E* — 11 Mais] Mas *To*, *with visible erasure of* -ı-, Mas *E* — 16 fillasse] filaſſe *E*; pois] depoıs *E*, *hypermetric* — 17 e lle déss' o] ele ⁊ deſſo *E*; o] e *To* — 18 pos] poıs *E* — 19 mõesteir'] moeſteır *T* — 24 negro mais] maıſ neg° *E* — 26 infernal] ınfernal *E* — 28 omes] omeeſ *T*, *hypermetric*; omeſ *To*, omes *E* — 31 Santa] Sancta *E* — 33 cáte-los] cates los *E* — 38 e non] a non *T*, a nõ *To*, e nõ *E* — 42 Reïnna] ʀeỹa *T*, *To*, reyña *E*; nobl'] nobꝛ *E* — 43 E des que foi] Deſ q̃a poꝛ *To*, Des q̃a pos *E* — 51 u achou] U v achou *E* — 52 aquele] aqueles *T*, aquele *followed by erasure To*; aquele *E* — 54 terrẽal] terreal *T*, tʳrẽal *To*, terrẽal *E* — 55 mas] Maıs *E* — 62 Santa] Sancta *E*; Reïnna] ʀeẏnna *T*, reỹa *To*, reẏna *E*.

CANTIGA 76

SOURCES: *T*, nº 76, f. 112v
E, nº 76, f. 94r–v

The mother whose felonious son is hanged gives the Virgin a hard time. Following what we might be tempted to see in modern terms as kidnap combined with blackmail, the Virgin intervenes to restore the life of the woman's son. A *cantiga* that illustrates the interpenetration of the spiritual world and the physical world, with a statue as the point of concurrence.

Syllable-count (real syllables): ℜ: 11 - 11
Stanza: 13 (12) - 13 - 11 (10) - 11
For questions of metrical instability, see Metrical Note below.

ℜ *Quen as sas figuras da Virgen partir*
quer das de seu Fillo, fol é sen mentir.

Whoever seeks to separate figures of the Virgin from those of Her Son is foolish indeed.

I Por end' un miragre vos quer' eu ora contar
mui maravilloso, que quis a Virgen mostrar
por ũa moller que muito fiar
sempr' en ela fora, segú*n* fui oïr. ℜ

For that reason I now want to relate to you a miracle most wonderful that The Virgin saw fit to perform for a woman who had always trusted greatly in Her, according [to what] I did hear. ℜ

II Esta moller bõa ou*v*' un fillo malfeitor
e ladrón mui fort', e tafur e pelejador;
e tanto ll' andou o dem' arredor
que o fez nas mãos do joïz vĩir. ℜ

This good woman had a miscreant son, a recalcitrant thief, a gambler and a hoodlum; and the devil ran such rings around him that it caused him to come into the hands of the justice. ℜ

III E poi-l*o* achou con furto que fora fazer,
mandou-o tan toste en ũa forca põer;
mas sa madr' ouvera por el a perder
o sen, e con coita fillou-s' a carpir. ℜ

And when he found him in possession of goods he had stolen, he ordered him straight away to be put on the gallows; but his mother had lost her mind over him, and in her affliction started to cry out. ℜ

IV E como moller que era fora de sen,
a ũa eigreja foi da Madre do que ten
o mund' en poder, e disse-lle: «Ren
non pode*s*, se meu fillo non resurgir.» ℜ

And as a woman who was out of her mind, she went to a church of the Mother of Him who holds the world in His power. And she said to Her: "If my son does not revive, You have no power." ℜ

V Pois est' ouve dito, tan gran sanna lle creceu
que aa omagen foi e ll' o Fillo tolleu
per força dos braços e desaprendeu,
dizend': «Este terrei eu trões que vir...[ℜ?]

When she had said this, such a great anger rose in her that she went to the statue and took the Son by force from [His Mother's] arms and detatched [Him], saying: "I shall hold [on to] this until I see... [ℜ?]

VI ...o meu san' e vivo vĩir sen lijón nen mal.»
Quand' est' ouve dito, log' a Madr' Esperital
resurgiu o dela, que vẽo sen al
dizendo: «Sandia, mal fuste falir,...[ℜ?]

...mine coming, alive and well, without hurt or harm." When she had said this, the Spiritual Mother revived [the woman's] son, who came at once saying: "Foolish woman, gravely did you sin,... [ℜ?]

VII ...madre, porque fuste fillar seu Fillo dos seus
braços da omagen da Virgen Madre de Deus;
por én m' enviou que entr' ontr' os teus,
per que tu ben possas comigo goïr.» ℜ

...mother, because you took the Son from the arms of the statue of the Virgin Mother of God; for all that, She sent me to come between your [arms], so you may indeed be able to rejoice over me. ℜ

VIII Quand' a moller viu o gran miragre que fez
a Virgen Maria, que é Sennor de gran prez,
tornou-lle seu Fillo; e log' essa vez
meteu-s' en orden pola mellor servir. ℜ

When the woman saw the great miracle the Virgin Mary — who is Liege of great worth — had performed, she gave back to Her Her Son; and thereupon joined an order, the better to serve Her.

Metrical Note

The text of this piece suffers from a degree of metrical instability which affects accommodation of the text to the melody in two respects.

First, the third line of the stanza, which might be expected to have 11 syllables in imitation of the opening line of the Refrain, has only ten syllables in stanzas I, II (as edited here), IV and VII; the melody is notated to fit this. The remaining stanzas, with eleven syllables in this line, thus require some form of adaptation; in performance the additional syllable can be accommodated by splitting the figure at e.5 to match that at a.5–6.

Second, the opening line of the stanza normally has 13 syllables, and is notated to match. In two cases, however — stanzas IV and VIII — the first line is a syllable short. This is harder to resolve, since the sources give no assistance. The best suggestion that can be offered (due weight having been given to the effect on the placement of textually stressed syllables later in the line) is to take figures c.5–6 together, and spread a single syllable over them in the verses in question.

It may further be noted that a number of other points of disagreement between the sources also embody a difference in syllable-count, as will be clear from the variants given below. Some of the editorial choices (*e.g.*, adoption of the reading of *E* in *l.* 11, rejection of Mettmann's emendation *entr[e]* in *l.* 29) have been made with a view to averting unfortunate stressing of unaccented syllables.

CSM 76: Apparatus

Text edition based on *T*.

The Epigraph has been abbreviated: Como] Eſta e como *T*; fillara] fılara *E*. *The version in E adds a final comment:* ꝛ começa aſſı 'and it begins like this'.

1 *as sas*] aſas *E*; *figuras*] feguras *T*, *but* fıguras *in two later partial repetitions of* ℜ. — 6 sempr'] ſempꝛe *E*; según] ſegund *T*, ſegundo *E* — 7 ouv' un] ouun *T*, *E* — 9 arredor] en derredoꝛ *E*, *hypermetric* — 10 joïz] ıuẏȝ *E* — 11 poilo achou] Poılachou *T*, poılo achou *E* — 12 mandou-o] mãdoo *E* — 13 mas] maıs *E*; — 14 fillou-s'] fılouſ *E* — 15 E] *Missing in E* — 16 eigreja] egreıa *E* — 18 podes] podeſſ *T* — 19 sanna] ſana *E* — 23 san'] são *E* — 25 resurgiu] reſurgıo *E* — 29 entr' ontr' os] entroutros *E* — 30 comigo] cõmıgo *E*.

CANTIGA 87
(*To* 21)

SOURCES: *To*, nº 21, f. 31r–v
T, nº 87, f. 127v
E, nº 87, f. 101r–102r

A cleric of Pavia who is a faithful servant of the Virgin — from the Epigraph we learn that his devotion consists in always saying her Office — is rewarded for his constancy: Holy Mary appears and ensures his election as the next bishop. A cantiga with unusual structural features (*see below*).

Syllable-count (real syllables): ℜ: 8 - 7
Stanza: 8 - 8 - 8 - 7
The text of the Refrain varies, and is given here in full after each stanza.

Muito punna d' os seus onrar *sempre Santa Maria.*	*Greatly does Holy Mary strive* *ever to honour those who are Her own.*
I E desto vos quero contar un gran miragre, que mostrar quis a Virgen que non á par na cidad' de Pavia. *Muito punna d' os seus onrar* *sempre Santa Maria.*	And on this subject I will recount to you a great miracle, that the peerless Virgin sought to perform in the city of Pavia. *Greatly does Holy Mary strive* *ever to honour those who are Her own.*
II Un crérig' ouv' i, sabedor de todo ben, e servidor desta groriosa Sennor quant' ele máis podia. *D' onrar os seus* á gran sabor *sempre Santa Maria.*	There was a priest there, well-versed in every good thing, and servant as much as he could be of this glorious Liege-Lady. *Holy Mary ever has great desire* *to honour those who are Her own.*
III Ond' avẽo que conteceu, poi-lo bispo dali morreu, a un sant' om' apareceu a Virgen que nos guia. A*os seus onr*ou e ergeu *sempre Santa Maria.*	Whereof it came to pass, when the bishop of the place died, that the Virgin who guides us appeared to a holy man. *Holy Mary ever honoured* *and raised up those who are Her own.*
IV E pois lle foi aparecer, começou-ll' assi a dizer: «Vai, di que façan esleer cras en aquele dia... *Os seus* faz *onra*dos seer *sempre Santa Maria.*	And when She had appeared to him, She began to speak to him thus: "Go, tell [them] to be sure to elect tomorrow on the appointed day... *Holy Mary ever causes* *those who are Her own to be honoured.*
V »...por bisp' un que Gerónim' á nome, ca tanto sei del ja que me serve, e servid' á ben com' a mí prazia.» *Os seus onr*ou e *onrará* *sempre Santa Maria.*	...as bishop one who has the name Jerome, for so much do I already know of him who serves me, and has served [me] quite as was pleasing to me." *Holy Mary ever honoured* *and will honour those who are Her own.*

VI Poi-lo sant' ome s' espertou,
ao cabídoo contou
o que ll' a Virgen nomeou
que por bispo queria.
*D' os seus onrar muito punn*ou
sempre Santa Maria.

When the holy man woke up,
he told the chapter
the one the Virgin had named to him
that She wanted as bishop.
Holy Mary ever greatly strove
to honour those who are Her own.

VII Acordados dun coraçón,
fezeron del sa esleiçón;
e foi bisp' a pouca sazón,
ca ben o merecia.
*Os seus onr*ou con gran razón
sempre Santa Maria.

United [and] of one mind,
they made him their choice;
and he shortly became bishop,
for well did he deserve it.
With good reason did Holy Mary
ever honour those who are Her own.

STRUCTURAL NOTE

As presented above, this *cantiga*, unusually, has a refrain that is variable, and integrated into each stanza by means of its first rhyme. This is not, however, how this piece is presented in the sources. In both *To* and *T* the variable refrain after each stanza is further followed by a repetition of the refrain in its original form; in *E* this is taken a step further, and the original invariable refrain is repeated both *before* and *after* the variable refrain.

A good case can be made for seeing these extended versions as errors arising from a misunderstanding of the nature of the variable refrain, which is, after all, not a common feature. If this is so, then the text as given above provides the basis for performance that is complete and cogent. The option remains, however, for performers to adhere more closely to the sources by including repetitions of the *fixed* refrain (*ll.* 1–2) after each complete stanza-plus-variable-refrain (*i.e.*, after *ll.* 8, 14, 20 *etc.*), or, more extremely (following *E*), both before and after each variable refrain (*i.e.*, after *ll.* 6, 8, 12, 14, 18 *etc.*).

See also the opening paragraphs on this *cantiga* in Section IV above, and corresponding footnotes.

CSM 87: APPARATUS

Text edition based on *To*/*T*, with due attention to suppression of textual material so as to respect the piece's form.

The Epigraph has been abbreviated: Como] Eſta e como *T*, Eſta xxı e como *To*, [ ]omo *E*, *with missing initial*; fezessen] *sic T*, *E*, fızeſſen *To*; dizia sas] dııʒıa ſempre ſas *E*; *at the end of the epigraph E adds*: ꝛ começa aſſı 'and it goes like this'.

Repetitions of initial refrain (not included above): *In E the repetitions included after stanzas II*, *III*, *give* puna *for* punna.

23 façan] façam *E* — 24 aquele] aquel *E*, *later emended* — 27 Gerónim'] ıeronım *E* —29 serve] ſeru *E* — 33 s' espertou] ſe eſpertou *E* — 37 *D' os seus*] Os ſeus *E*; *punnou*] punou *E* — 39 dun] dum *E* — 41 bisp'] bıſpo *E*.

CANTIGA 97
(*To* App. VIII)

SOURCES: *To* Appendix nº VIII, f. 153r–154r
T nº 97, f. 140v-141v
E nº 97, f. 108v–109v

A retainer, falsely accused in a grave matter, appeals to the Virgin and is exonerated after careful investigation. A *cantiga* that presents King Alfonso as a thoughtful dispenser of justice.

Syllable-count (real syllables): ℜ: 7 - 3 - 7 - 3
Stanza: 9 - 9 - 9 - 9 - 3 - 10

ℜ *A Virgen sempr' acorrer,*
acorrer
vai o coitad', e valer,
e valer.

The Virgin always goes
to aid
the wretched, and
to assist.

I Dest' un miragre vos contarei
que en Ca*n*ete, per com' achei,
a Virgen por un ome dun rei
fez, que mezcraran, com' aprés ei;
e ben sei
que o cuidaran a fazer morrer. ℜ

On this subject I shall recount to you a miracle
which the Virgin performed in Cañete
(as I have discovered), for the king's man
whom they had got into trouble [with the king]
(as I have learned), and I well know
that they had a mind to get him killed.

II De tal guisa o foron mezcrar,
que o mandou log' el-rei chamar
ante sí. Mas el, con gran pesar
e con coita, fillou-s' a chorar
e rogar
a Virgen quanto máis podo fazer. ℜ

They implicated him in such a way
that the king at once ordered him to be called
before him. But he, with much grief
and tribulation, began to weep,
and to pray to
the Virgin as fervently as he was able to do.

III Demais, un rico pano i deu
na eigreja; e fezo-se seu
ome da Virgen, com' aprix eu.
E est' avia nome Mateu;
e ben leu
podê-l-án en cas del-rei connocer. ℜ

In addition, he donated a a rich fabric there
in Her church; and dedicated himself as
the Virgin's devotee (as I learned).
And he had the name Matthew;
and quite easily
can he be recognised in the king's household.

IV E pois na eigreja pos seu don
e fez chorando sa oraçón,
meteu-se ao camin*n*' entón,
con mui gran med' en seu coraçón
de lijón,
onde morte por tal mezcra prender. ℜ

And when he had placed his gift in the church
and tearfully made his prayer,
he then set off on his way,
with great fear in his heart
of [coming to] harm,
thereby meeting his death because of such slander.

V E quand' u era el-rei chegou,
seus ómẽes por el log' enviou;
mas aa Virgen se comendou
muit' el; des i ant' el-rei entrou,
e parou-
-s' e pois começou-ll' assí a dizer:...

And when he came to where the king was,
the latter at once sent his men for him;
but he commended himself fervently
to the Virgin; and then he entered the king's
presence, composed
himself, and then began to speak to him thus:...

VI ...«Sennor, vós enviastes por mí,

...'My Lord, you sent for me,

e tanto que vossa carta vi,
vin quanto pud', e aque-m' aqui.»
E el-rei logo respós-ll' assi,
com' oí:
«Ũa ren querria de vós saber:...

and as soon as I saw your letter,
I came the quickest I could, and here I am.'
And the king then replied to him thus
(as I heard [tell]):
'One thing I would like to know from you:...

VII ...se é verdade que tanto mal
fezestes, e tan descomunal,
como mi dizen.» Respós el: «Qual?»
El-rei contou-lle: «Tal e atal.»
Diss' el: «Val-
-me, Santa Maria, con teu poder!...

...whether it is true that you committed
wrongdoing as great and as grievous
as they tell me.' He replied: 'Such as?'
And the king told him: 'Such-and-such.'
And he said: 'Holy Mary,
help me with your power!...

VIII ...esto que vos disseron, Sennor,
mentira foi, non vistes mayor.
E se a vossa mercee for,
meted' i un voss' enqueredor,
e mellor
podedes per i o feit' entender.» ℜ

...this which they told you, my Lord,
was a lie — a greater one you never came across.
And if it were your pleasure,
[pray] send in an investigator,
and you will better
be able to understand the facts thereby.'

IX Respós el-rei: «Daquesto me praz,
e tenno que comprides assaz
e fazê-lo quer', u al non jaz.»
E meteu i un ome de paz
que viaz
fosse daquest' a verda*d*' enquerer. ℜ

The king replied: 'With this I am contented;
and I consider that you are quite fulfilling your duties,
and I [too] wish to do so, [in a case] where
no other [consideration] is to be found.'
And he put in a neutral party, who at once
should go and seek out the truth of this [matter].

X Est' ome punnou toste de s' ir,
e fez gente da terra vĩir,
que foron o feito descobrir
da verdad', e de quanto mentir
e falir
foran al-rei. E fez-lo escrever...

This man strove right away to get going,
and he made people from the [same] area come;
and they did reveal the facts
of what really happened, and of the extent to which
[people] had been going to the king
to lie and falsify. And he had it written up...

XI ...e enviou-llo. E pois abriu
el-rei aquel escrito, e viu
que ll' end' a verdade descobriu,
log' entón todo mui ben sentiu
e cousiu
que falsidade foran apõer...

...and sent him it. And when the king
opened the document, and saw
that it uncovered the truth thereof to him,
he at once appreciated everything keenly,
and he concluded
what falsehood they had laid...

XII ...a aquel om'. E logo porén
lle perdõou, e fez-lle gran ben;
e os mezcradores en desdén
tev', e nunca por eles deu ren;
e des én,
non os ar quis de tal feito creer. ℜ

...upon that man. And therefore he at once
exonerated him, and showed him great favour;
and he held the calumniators in disdain,
and never gave any [consideration] for them;
and from that point [on],
he refused to believe them in [any] such matter.

CSM 97: Apparatus

Text edition based on *To*.

The beginning of the Epigraph has been abbreviated: Como] Eſta oıtaua e como 'This eighth [piece] is [about] how' *To*; Eſta e como *T*; [ ]omo *with missing initial E*.

6 Canete] cãnete *To*; Canete *T*, *E* — 20 Mateu] Matheu *T* — 21 leu] lleu *T*, *E* — 25 caminn'] camĩ *To*; camẏn *T*; camỹ *E* — 28 onde] *sic To*, *T*, *E*; *Mettmann (taking a diffident suggestion of Valmar's) emends to* ou de, *but this is unnecessary: the construction, though elliptic, is comprehensible if we take the infinitive* prender *in a consecutive sense.*

— 30 ómẽes] omees *To*; omẽes *T*, *E* — 58 daquest' a] *sic To*, *E*; aqueſta *T*; verdad'] uerdat *To* — 66 aquel] *sic To*, *E*; aqueſt *T* — 70 foran apõer] foꝛa apõer *T*, foꝛa põer *E* — 71 a aquel] E aquel *T*, *E*.

CANTIGA 162
(*To* App. VI)

SOURCES: *To*, Appendix, nº VI, f. 152r–v
T, nº 162, f. 217v
E, nº 162, f. 156r–v

A statue of the Virgin is removed from the high altar on the bishop's instruction, and located elsewhere, but when the chaplain opens the church he discovers the statue has returned to its original place overnight.

Syllable-count (real syllables): ℜ: 8 - 8
Stanza: 8 - 10 - 8 - 10 - 8 - 8*
**For the change in metre from Stanza III on, see Metrical Note below.*

ℜ *A̱s sas figuras muit' onrar*
devemos da Virgen sen par.

We ought greatly to honour images
of the peerless Virgin.

I Ca en onrá-las dereit' é
e en lles avermos gran devoçón,
non ja por elas, a la fe,
mas pola figura da en que son;
e sol non devemos provar
de as trager mal nen viltar. ℜ

For there is a fitness in honouring them,
and in our having great devotion to them,
not for themselves, i' faith,
but for the One of whom they are a likeness;
and especially we must not attempt
to mistreat or vilify them. ℜ

II E daquesto vos contarei
ora un mui gran miragre que fez
en Canete (per com' achei
en verdad') esta Sennor de gran prez
dũa omagen, que comprar
foi un cavaleir' e i dar... [ℜ?]

And on this subject I shall now recount
to you a very great miracle
that this Liege-Lady of great worth performed
in Cañete (as I truly discovered),
about a statue, that a knight
did buy and donate there... [ℜ?]

III ...na sa eigreja que está
fora da vila cabo do portal,
en que grandes vertudes á
que faz esta Sennor espirital.
Por end' os gẽollos ficar
foi, e pose-a no maior altar,... [ℜ?]

to Her church, which stands
outside the town near the gate,
[a statue] in which there are great spiritual powers
which this spiritual Liege exercises.
And so he went [down] on bended knees,
and placed it on the high altar... [ℜ?]

IV ...u esteve gran temp' assi,
e Deus por ela miragres mostrou,
ta que un bispo vẽo i
de Conca, que a toller én mandou
e põê-l' en outro logar,
porque a non viu de bon semellar. ℜ

...where it thus stood a great while,
and through it God worked miracles,
until a bishop came there from Cuenca
and he ordered [them] to take it from there
and to put it somewhere else,
because he did not see it as pleasant-looking . ℜ

V Ao crérigo capelán
mandou o bispo aquesto fazer,
e ele logo manamán
foi a omagen do altar toller;

The bishop ordered the cleric [who was]
chaplain to do this,
and he then straight away
went and took the statue from the altar;

mas en outro dia achar-	but the next day he found
-a foi u x' ante soïa estar. ℜ	it where previously it had usually stood. ℜ
VI Quando o crérig' esto viu,	When the priest saw this,
cuidou a pran que o fezer' alguén,	he fully imagined someone had done it,
e por aquesto comediu	and so he thought
que a omagen tornasse por én	he should put back the statue therefore
u ll' o bispo fora mandar	where the bishop had ordered him to,
e a eigreja fosse ben serrar. ℜ	and should lock the church securely. ℜ
VII E ar fez come sabedor	[But] he also acted shrewdly,
e levou a chave; e pela luz	and went off with the key; and as dawn
tornou i, quando o alvor	was appearing, by its light
parecia, e achou ant' a cruz	he went back and found the statue
a omagen, e amostrar-	in front of the cross; and he pointed it out
-a foi a quantos s' i foran juntar... [ℜ?]	to all who had gathered there... [ℜ?]
VIII ...entón polas missas oïr.	...at that hour to hear mass.
E todos deron loor end' a Deus	And they all gave praise for it to God
e a ela, que sen falir	and to Her, for She unfailingly
mostra ali grandes miragres seus,	performs great miracles of Her own there,
por que a vẽen aorar	because of which many people come to venerate Her
muitas gentes e do seu ofertar. ℜ	and make offerings of what they possess. ℜ

Metrical Note

As was mentioned in the paragraphs relating to this piece in Section IV above, a change of metrical pattern affecting the last line of the stanza occurs from Stanza III onwards. For the first two stanzas the line in question has eight (real) syllables; thereafter the syllable-count rises to ten. No solution seems available to the problem of how to accommodate the later stanzas to the melody without some form of radical intervention to allow the last phrase of the melody to carry the extra syllables.

What might be proposed is the break-up of the ligature at h.4 into *three*, applying the same dotted rhythm as occurs in the previous bar. In this way the metrical problem may be masked in performance in a way that maintains the rhythmic character of the piece.

CSM 162: Apparatus

Text edition based on *T*/*E*.

The beginning of the Epigraph has been abbreviated: Como] [ ]ſta e , Eſta vı e como *To*, Como *E*; fez que a sua] feȝ a sa *E*; tornass'] toꝛ toꝛnaſſ *E*.

1 As sas] *The opening refrain in all sources, and all repetitions in E, have* A sas; *from the repetition after Stanza IV onwards, both To (in all stanzas) and T (for two stanzas) have* As sas, *surely the correct version.* — 11 Canete] Cãnete *T*, cannete *To*, Canete *E*; *cf CSM* 97, *l.* 6. — 12 verdad'] ũdat *To* — 16 do] dũ *To* — 19 gẽollos] gẽolos *To* — 20 pose-a] pusea *To* — 25 logar] lugar *To* — 31 mas] maıs *To* — 49 vẽen] ueen *To*.

CANTIGA 255
(*To* 74)

SOURCES: *To*, nº 74, f. 95r–96r
E, nº 255, f. 231v–232v

A woman wrongly rumoured to be guilty of incest takes desperate action which leads to a sentence of death by burning. Following her appeal to the Virgin, repeated attempts to execute her fail, and she emerges unscathed from the flames. A case in which mercy prevails over justice.

Syllable-count (real syllables): ℜ: 5+5 - 5+6
Stanza: 10 - 10 - 10 - 10 - 5+5 - 5+6
For the question of divided lines and internal rhyme, see Metrical Note below.

ℜ *Na malandança, | noss' amparança*
e esperança | é Santa Maria.

In misfortune, our protection
and hope is Holy Mary.

I Dest' un miragre vos direi ora
que a Virgen quis mui grande mostrar,
Santa Maria, a que sempr' ora
polos pecadores de mal guardar,
dũa burguesa | nobr' e cortesa,
que fora presa | per sa gran folia. ℜ

On this subject I shall now tell you a very great
miracle which the Virgin Holy Mary
sought to perform, — She who ever prays
to keep sinners from evil —,
concerning a townswoman, noble and urbane, who
had been arrested through her [own] great folly. ℜ

II Esta foi rica e ben casada
e mui fremosa e de bõo sen,
e en León do Rodán morada
ouve mui bõa, per quant' aprix én;
e ouve bela | filla donzela,
de que mazela | ll' avẽo un dia. ℜ

This woman was rich and well married,
beautiful and of good sense,
and had a very good dwelling
in Lyon, on the Rhone, by all I learned of it;
and she had a beautiful young daughter,
on whose account adversity came upon her one day. ℜ

III Ela e seu sennor ambos deron
sa filla a marid' a seu prazer,
e morada de sũu fezeron
por se per i mais viçosos tẽer.
Mais mal empeço | foi no começo,
ca mao preço | a sogra avia… [ℜ?]

She and her lord together gave
their daughter to a husband of her liking,
and these made house on their own,
the better to luxuriate thereby.
But a bad start came at the outset.
for the mother-in-law got a bad reputation
[over having an affair]… [ℜ?]

IV …con seu genro; pero a gran torto,
ca non fezeran eles feit' atal
com' este. Mais ela per que morto
fez foi o genro, e non ouv' i al;
ca mantenente | deu muit' argente
a maa gente | que o matar-ia. ℜ

…with her son-in-law, but quite wrongly,
for they had not committed such a deed
as [was rumoured]. But she contrived such that
her son-in-law died, and no two ways about it;
for out of the blue she gave lots of cash
to unscrupulous people who would kill him. ℜ

V E esse dia, pós missa dita,
assentaron-s' a jantar, e mandou
chamar seu genr' a sogra maldita;
e sa moller, que por el foi, achou
mort' o marid ' e escoorido,
e apelido | mui grande metia. ℜ

And that day, after Mass being said,
they sat down to breakfast, and the accursèd
mother-in-law sent to call her son-in-law;
and [the latter's] wife, who went for him, found
her husband dead and drained of colour;
and she let out a massive shriek. ℜ

VI Aqueste feito toste sabudo
foi pela vila, e vẽo log' i
o meirin*n*o dela, mui sannudo,
e preguntou como morrer' assi.
E tant' andando | foi, trastornando
e preguntando, | que achou a via… [ℜ?]

This fact was soon known
around the town, and at once there arrived
the local magistrate, very angry,
and asked how he had died like that.
He went around so much, turning things inside out
and asking questions, that he found the means… [ℜ?]

VII …per que soub' a verdade do preito;
e mantenente recadar mandou
os que fezeran aquele feito.
Mais a sogra entón mãefestou
de com' ouvera | coita tan fera,
per que fezer' aquela diabria. ℜ

…by which he discovered the truth of the case,
and at once he ordered the arrest of
those who had committed the said act.
But the mother-in-law then gave evidence
of how she had [suffered] so vexed a dilemma,
because of which she had done that devilish deed. ℜ

VIII O meirin*n*o, que foi fort' e bravo,
mandou fillar log' aquela moller,
e por queimá-la non deu un cravo,
ca muito fazia ben seu mester.
Nen fez en jogo | nen fillou rogo,
mas ao fog' a levou que ardia. ℜ

The magistrate, who was strong and assertive,
then ordered that woman to be taken,
and he cared not a whit about having her burned,
for he did his duty very well.
He did not do [it] lightly nor did he suffer pleas,
but to the fire that burned he brought her. ℜ

IX E u a levavan pela rua
ant' a igreja da Madre de Deus,
se non da camisa, toda nua,
diss' aos sergentes: «Amigos meus,
por piedad', ant' a Magestade
vós me parade, | e rogá-la–ia.» ℜ

And as they were bringing her through the street
before the church of the Mother of God —
quite naked, but for her shift —,
she said to the guards: "My friends,
for pity's sake in front of Her Majesty
[do you] stop me, [for] I would beseech Her. ℜ

X Eles fezeron-ll' o que rogava,
e ela log' en terra se tendeu
ant' a omagen; muito chorava,
dizendo: «Madre daquel que morreu
por nós, agin*n*a, | Virgen Reïn*n*a,
acorr' a mesquin*n*a que en ti fia.» ℜ

They did for her what she requested,
and she at once fell prostrate on the ground
before the statue; she was weeping sorely,
saying: "Mother of Him who died
for us, quickly, O Virgin Queen,
help the wretch who trusts in You." ℜ

XI E logo tan toste o meirin*n*o
disse «Varões, levade-a ja
fora da vila cab' o camin*n*o
u ũa casa mui vella está;
i a metede | dentr' e odede,
des i põede-ll' o fog' a perfia.» ℜ

Then at once the magistrate
said: "Take her, men, straight away
out of the town beside the road
where a very old house stands;
put her inside and bind her,
then, nothing loth, set fire to it. ℜ

XII Esto foi feito tost' e correndo;
e a casa dentro e en redor
chẽa de lenna foi, com aprendo,
e de fogo, dond' ouv' ela pavor;
ca viu a chama | queimá-la rama,
de que a Ama | de Deus defendia. ℜ

This was done, swiftly and soon;
and the house, inside and out,
was piled with wood (as I learn),
and [then filled] with fire, of which she had a dread;
for she saw the flames consuming the branches,
from [all of] which the Mother of God shielded her.

XIII Peró a casa toda queimada
foi, e a lenna se tornou carvón,
a moller desto non sentiu nada;
ca a Virgen, a que fez oraçón,
lle deu saüde | per sa vertude,
e a mẽud' o fogo lli tollia. ℜ

Although the whole house was burnt
down, and the wood turned to charcoal,
the woman felt nothing of this;
for the Virgin, to whom she made her prayer,
gave her immunity by Her power,
and repeatedly drove the fire from her. ℜ

XIV A casa foi per duas vegadas
acenduda; mais vede-lo que fez
Santa Maria, que as coitadas
acorre sempre: non quis nulla vez
que s' i perdesse | nen que ardesse
nen que morresse | a que ben queria. ℜ

The house was twice
torched; but see what
Holy Mary (who always helps
afflicted women) did: at no stage did She allow
that the one She loved [so] well should be lost there,
or should burn, nor that she should die. ℜ

XV Quand' est' o meirin*n*o e as gentes
viron, fillaron-s' end' a repentir,
e mandaron log' aos sergentes
que a fezessen do fogo saïr;
des i con cantos | ela foi tantos
levada, quantos | mui de dur diria. ℜ

When the magistrate and the people saw
this, they came to repent of [their actions],
and at once they ordered the officers
to have her brought out of the fire;
thereupon she was led off, with so many [joyful]
songs I would with difficulty say how many. ℜ

XVI E pois que ela foi na igreja,
os crérigos se pararon en az;
e loaron a que sempre seja
bẽeita polos miragres que faz
maravillosos | e piadosos,
e saborosos | d' oïr todavia. ℜ

And after she went into the church,
the clerics stood in formation;
and the One whom they praised — may She
ever be blest for the miracles She performs,
so marvellous and merciful
and always delightful to hear. ℜ

METRICAL NOTE

The Refrain is presented here in long lines with internal rhyme, and the last section of the stanza is treated likewise. This is done because the overriding need to keep the syllable-count regular leads in some cases to an elision, present in the sources, which causes the internal rhyme to be eclipsed. The phenomenon is most easily dealt with if the layout, as here, keeps the elision within the confines of a single line; if the lines in which elision occurs were to be split into two lines at the mid-point, editorial intervention to restore 'missing' vowels would become a dangerous temptation. For specific cases, *see below* the notes on *ll.* 31, 44, 50, 55, 62 and 80. So great in some instances is the interpenetration (whether phonetic or syntactic) between the two halves of the line that it becomes difficult to mark a cæsura.

CSM 255: APPARATUS

Text edition based on *To*.

The beginning of the Epigraph has been abbreviated: Como] Eſta Lxxiiij e como *To*.

4 grande mostrar] grand amoſtrar *E* — 8 per] poꝛ *E* — 9 casada] Caſſada *E* — 13 bela] bella *E*; donzela] Donȝella *E* — 14 mazela] manȝella *E* — 17 sũu] ſoũu *E* — 18 per i] poꝛ ẏ *E* — 27 pós] pois *E* — 28 assentaron] aſentaron *E* — 31 marid'] *The internal rhyme implied by* marido *is eclipsed by the elision.* — 33–36 *A perplexing choice faces the editor, since three versions of these lines are presented in the two sources, differing in the even-numbered lines. First is the main text of* To, *edited above. Second is a 'revision' (?) given in cursive script in the lower margin of* To, *problematic because its second line (corresponding to 54) is hypermetric. Third is the version appearing in* E:

...per que soub' a verdade do preito;
e fez recadar de mui mal talán
os que fezeran aquele feito.
Mais a sogra mãefestou a pran *&c.*

...by which he discovered the truth of the case;
and he had arrested — very angrily —
those who had committed that deed.
But the mother-in-law flatly declared *&c*

Both versions are narratively cogent, and it is not clear why a 'revision' was contemplated. Adoption of the marginal version from To *would require emendation, effectively bringing it into line with* E; *the version from the main text of* To *has been preferred, but interesting questions are raised about the relationship between the sources.* — 44 *The internal rhyme is spread across a word-boundary.* —50 fog'] fog *To*, *E*, *eclipsing the internal rhyme implied by the full form* fogo. — 55 piedad'] piedad *To*, *eclipsing the internal rhyme;* piadade *E*, *requiring explicit elision.* — 61 aginna] agĩa *To*, agỹa *E*; reïnna] reỹa *To*, *E* — 62 mesquinna] meſquĩa *To*, *E*; *the internal rhyme is a syllable late in this line.* — 63 meirinno] meirĩo *To*, meirẏ̃nno *E* — 65 caminno] camĩo *To*, *E* — 80 a mẽud'] amẽud *To*, ameud *E*, *with internal rhyme eclipsed.* — 91 des i] *written over erasure in To*; log. ꝛ *E* — 97 'maravillosos e piadosos' *is a quotation from the opening of Cantiga 139.*

CANTIGA [407]
(*To* App. XII *bis*)

SOURCE: *To*, Appendix, nº XII *bis*, f. 158v–159r

Having stubbed his foot on a stone a man denies God, but having then gone over to the Devil he is afflicted with paralysis and blindness. Because he suffers his misfortune with patience, the Virgin appears to him and brings about his cure.

Syllable-count (real syllables): ℜ: 8+5 - 8+5
Stanza: 11 - 11 - 11 - 7

ℜ *Como o demo confonder,*
nos quer acorrer
Santa Maria, e valer,
e del defender.

Just as the devil [seeks to] confound [us]
[so too] does Holy Mary
seek to come to our aid and help us
and protect us from him.

I Dest' un miragre vos contarei que vi
escrit' en livro, e dizia assi
com' oïredes adeante per mi,
que foi a Virgen fazer… [ℜ?]

On this subject I shall recount to you a miracle
— [one] that I saw written in a book, and it told just
as you will hear shortly from me —,
that the Virgin did perform… [ℜ?]

II …*en* un cativo d' ome que foi errar
porque do pee en ũa pedra dar
foi, e doeu-se; [e] por én braadar
começou, e descreer: [ℜ?]

…on a wretch of a man who [had] sinned
because he stubbed his foot on a stone
and hurt himself; whereat he began
to wail, and to utter profanities: [ℜ?]

III «Aquesta pedra o demo a ficou
aqui por mi que mi meu pee britou;
e pois que pode tan muit', a el mi dou
e non quer' en Deus creer.» ℜ

"This stone the devil put here
[just] for me, [the one] that broke me my foot;
and since he can [achieve] so much, to him do I give
myself, and refuse to believe in God. ℜ

IV Aquesto disse con gran sanna mortal,
e log' ali o prendeu un tan gran mal
que come tolleito se parou, atal
que cuidou log' a morrer. ℜ

This did he say with mortal[ly] great anger;
[but] at once so great an affliction took him
that he was left as if paralyzed, such that
he expected soon to die. ℜ

V E demais-la vista dos ollos perdeu,
e o poder do corpo si ll' ar tolleu;
e con mui gran coita en terra caeu
que se non pod' end' erger. ℜ

And moreover he lost the sight of his eyes,
and it took from him too the strength of his body;
and in very great distress he fell on the ground,
for he was unable to raise himself therefrom. ℜ

VI Mas seus parentes o fillaron d' ali
e o levaron a sa casa, e i
o deitaron en un leito; e assi
leixaron-o i jazer. ℜ

But his family took him from there
and brought him to their house, and there
they left him in a bed; and thus
did they leave him to lie there. ℜ

VII E pidindo por Deus jouv' i gran sazón,
chorand' e rogando-lle de coraçón
que dos seus erros podess' aver perdón
e que lle foss' en prazer. ℜ

And he lay there a great while, beseeching God,
weeping, and begging Him heartily
that he might have pardon for his wrongdoings
and that [such] might be in [God's] pleasure. ℜ

VIII Mas pois, na festa en que Deus resurgiu,
dos madodin*n*os a campãa oíu
e ũa dona cabo si estar viu,
e começou-ll' a dizer: [℟?]

But then, on the festival on which God rose [from the dead], he heard the bell for matins;
and he saw a lady standing beside him,
and She began to say to him:

IX «Porque sofriste teu mal e ta door
en paz, por ende praz a Nostro Sennor
que cedo sães, e recebas sabor
per que possas ben viver; ℟

"Since you suffered your pain and misfortune
so meekly, it pleases Our Lord therefore
that you recover quickly, and [so] gain a desire
to live righteously;

X »e creï ora esto que ti dig' eu:
fas que te leven tost' ant' o altar meu;
e pois i fores, saüd' o corpo teu
logo poderá aver.» ℟

and now believe this that I say to you:
get them to carry you at once before my altar;
and once you go there, your body
can at once have healing."

XI Respós el: «Esto farei logo de pran.»
E feze-s' entón levar i manamán;
e tornou são pela do bon talán,
a de que Deus quis nacer. ℟

He replied: "This will I do forthwith."
And he had himself taken there at once;
and he was healed by the One of Good Will,
She from whom God deigned to be born.

CSM [407]: Apparatus

Text edition based on *To* (unique source).

The beginning of the Epigraph has been abbreviated: Como] Eſta xıȷ e como *To*.

9 en un] Eun *To* — 11 e] *Missing in To, leaving the line hypometric. Mettmann's emendation has been adopted.* — 34 madodinnos] madodỹos *To* — 41 creï] *Two syllables are necessary for the metre.*

CANTIGA [415]

SOURCES: *To*, *FSM* nº II, f. 139r–v
E, *FSM* nº V, f. 6r–v

A meditation on the greeting brought by the (Arch)angel Gabriel to the Virgin announcing that She was to be the mother of the Saviour, in celebration of the Feast of the Annunciation (25th March). There are frequent textual allusions to the *Ave, Maria*.

Syllable-count: All lines have ten syllables.

ℜ *Tan bẽeita foi a saüdaçón* *per que nós vẽemos a salvaçón.*	*So blessed was the greeting* *by means of which we come to salvation.*
I Esta troux' o angeo Gabriel a Santa Maria come fiel mandadeiro, por que Emanuel foi logo Deus e pres encarnaçón. ℜ	This [greeting] did the Angel Gabriel bring to Holy Mary, as a faithful messenger; through it God at once became Emmanuel and took flesh. ℜ
II Ca ben ali u lle diss' el «Ave» foi logo Deus ome feit', a la fe; e macar el atan poderos' é, ena Virgen foi enserrad' entón. ℜ	For just at that point where he said "Hail" to Her, then was God made man, i' faith; and although He is so powerful, He thereupon became confined in the Virgin. ℜ
III E u «Gracia plena» lle dizer foi o angeo, nos fez connocer a Deus, que non podiamos veer ante; mas pois vimos ben sa faiçón. ℜ	And when the angel did say "Full of grace" to Her, he brought us to know God, whom we were previously unable to see; but later we indeed saw His face. ℜ
IV E u lle disse «Contigo é Deus», enton foi prenne do que polos seus salvar quis morte prender per judeus, por nos tirar da ifernal prijón. ℜ	And when he said to Her "God is with Thee", She then became pregnant with Him who, to save His [people], was willing to accept death at the hands of the Jews, to bring us out of the prison of hell. ℜ
V E u lle disse «Bẽeita es tu entr' as molleres», logo de Jesu- Cristo foi prenne, que naceu pois u tres reis lle deron cada un seu don. ℜ	And when he said to Her "Blessèd art Thou amongst women", then did she conceive Jesus Christ, who was then born, whereupon three Kings gave Him each one his gift. ℜ
VI E u lle disse «Bẽeito será aquel fruto que de ti nacerá», ali nos deu carreira por que ja ouvessemos sempre de Deus perdón. ℜ	And when he said to Her "Blessed will be the fruit that will be born of Thee", thereby he provided the way for us always to have God's pardon. ℜ

CSM [415]: APPARATUS
Text edition based on *To*.
The beginning of the Epigraph has been abbreviated: Como] Eſta ſegunda e de como *To*, Eſta quĩta e de como *E*; Gabriel] gubꝛiel *E*; festa é no mes] feſta no mes *E*. *At the end To adds* e começa aſſı 'and it goes like this'.
3 troux'] trox *E* — 3, 12 angeo] *The musical setting leaves little doubt that this word is stressed on the middle syllable when* ángeo *might have been expected*. — 12 connocer] coñoſçer *E* — 14 mas] maıs *E* — 15 contigo] contıg *E* — 18 ifernal] ınfernal *E*.

CANTIGA [419]

SOURCES: *To, FSM* n° V, f. 141r–145r
E, FSM n° IX, f. 8v–10v

A compendium of non-scriptural episodes relating the illness, death, burial and bodily assumption into heaven of the Virgin Mary, in celebration of the Feast of the Assumption (15th August). Of particular interest is the prominent rôle assigned to St Thomas who, being a doubter as presented in biblical accounts, is here shown seeking tangible proof of the Assumption.

Syllable-count (real syllables): All lines have 13 syllables
divisible at a strongly-marked cæsura into 7 + 6.

ℜ *Des quando Deus sa Madre | aos ceos levou,*
de nos levar consigo | carreira nos mostrou.

Ca pois levou aquela | que nos deu por Sennor
e el fillou por madre, | mostrou-nos que amor
mui grande nos avia, | non podia maior,
ca pera o seu reino | logo nos convidou. ℜ

II Mas como passou ela | deste mundo contar
vos quer’, *e* en qual guisa | a vẽo Deus levar
consigo ao ceo, | u a foi corõar
por Reïn*n*a dos santos, | tan muito a onrou. ℜ

III Assi foi que o dia | que Deus morte prendeu,
a sa bẽeita Madre | viu quanto pedeceu
na cruz por nós; e logo | tal pesar recebeu
que a fillou quartãa | que nunca én sãou. ℜ

IV E depois morou sempre | dentr’ en Jerussalém,
e non *vinna* a ela | enfermo que log’ én
são se non partisse; | mas a ela *per* ren
non leixou a quartãa | atẽes que fïou. ℜ

V Mas no templo estava | a comprida de fe;
un ángeo lle disse: | «Madre de Deus, ave!
O teu Fillo te manda | dizer que ja temp’ é
que leixes este mundo | mao u t’ el leixou.» ℜ

VI E u*n* ramo de palma | lle deu log’ en sinal
que dend’ a te*r*cer dia | non averia al
que verria por ela | o Rei espirital,
seu Fillo Jesucristo, | que en ela‿encarnou. ℜ

VII Disso-ll’ a Santa Virgen: | «Sennor, e qual nom’ ás?»
O ángeo lle respós: | «Esto non saberás,
ca meu nom’ é mui grande; | mais cedo veerás
os apóstolos tigo, | que Deus vĩir mandou…[ℜ?]

VIII …por onrar-t’ en ta morte.» | E foi-se log’ entón
o ángeo. E ela | foi fazer oraçón
ben a Mont’ Olivete, | u aquela sazón
morava, e tan toste | en seu banno entrou…[ℜ?]

From the time God took His Mother into heaven, He showed us the way He will take us with Him.

For since He took [up] Her whom he gave us as Liege and whom He took as mother, He showed us He had for us a very great love, that could not be greater, for then he invited us into His kingdom.

But I wish to tell you how She passed from this world, and in what manner God came to take Her with Him to heaven, where He crowned Her Queen of Saints, so greatly did He honour Her.

So it was that the day God accepted death, His Blessed Mother saw how He suffered on the cross for us. She suffered such grief that a quartan fever seized Her, and She never recovered from it.

Afterwards She still lived in Jerusalem, and no sick person ever came to Her but went away cured by it; but the quartan fever did not leave Her at all, even until She died.

She of full faith was in the temple; an angel said to Her: "Mother of God, hail! Your Son sends to tell You that it is now time for You to leave this evil world where He left You.

And he then gave Her a palm branch as a sign that on the third day from then — it would not be otherwise — the Spiritual King would come for Her, Her Son Jesus Christ who in Her took flesh.

The Holy Virgin said to him: "My Lord, what name have you?" The angel replied to Her: "This You shall not know, for my name is very great; but soon You will see the Apostles with You, whom God has commanded to come…

…to honour You at Your death. And the angel then departed. And She went to say prayers at the Mount of Olives, where She dwelt at that time, and straight away She entered her boudoir…

IX …e vestiu os mellores | panos que pud' aver;
e San Joán fez logo | chamar, e a dizer
lle começou seu feito | de como a veer
o ángeo vẽera | que lle Deus enviou. ℜ

…and put on the best clothes there could be, and then had St John called and began to tell him Her news of how the angel God had sent to Her had come to see Her.

X E disse-lle chorando: | «Nembre-te, San Joán,
de com' en ta comenda | o do mui bon talán
me leixou, o meu Fillo; | por én guardar de pran
me deves en mĭa morte, | pois te mĭ‿acomendou. ℜ

And weeping, She said to him: "Be mindful, John, how my Son, He of great favour, left Me in your care; and so you must fully watch over me at my death, for He commended me to you.

XI »E com' eu ei oïdo, | estes maos judeus,
que mataron meu Fillo | como falsos encreus,
meaçan de queimaren | a carn' e estes meus
ossos, pois for passada; | un deles mĭo contou.» ℜ

And (as I have heard), those evil Jews who as false unbelievers put My Son to death are threatening to burn my flesh and these bones of mine once I have passed away; one of them told me so."

XII Enquant' eles en esto | falavan entre sí,
ũas nuves mui craras | adusseron log' i
os Apóstolos onze; | e non vẽo ali
Santo Tomás con eles, | ca chegar non uvĭou. ℜ

While they were speaking of this between them, bright clouds at once brought the eleven Apostles there; [but] St Thomas did not come with them, for he missed the arrival.

XIII E logo que chegaron, | com' a‿*E*scritura diz,
os recebeu mui leda | a Santa‿*E*mperadriz;
e disso-lles: «Amigos, | este dia fiiz
foi que Deus vos adusse | aqui e vos juntou. ℜ

And once they arrived, as Scripture says, the Holy Empress received them most happily, and said to them: "My friends, a happy day was this when God brought you here and assembled you.

XIV E pois juntados sodes, | esto vos rogarei:
que vigiedes migo, | ca eu de certo sei
que cras en aquel dia | deste mundo m' irei,
ca un ángeo de Deus | comig' esto falou.» ℜ

And since you are together, I shall beg this of you: that you keep vigil with Me, for I know for certain that on the morrow's day I shall depart this world, for an angel from God spoke this to Me."

XV Eles quand' est' oïron | choraron log' assaz;
pois disseron: «Faremos, | Sennor, o que vos praz.»
E rezaron seus salmos | com' ena lee jaz,
e ela en seu leito | ant' eles se deitou. ℜ

When they heard this they wept sorely, then said: "We shall do, O Lady, what is pleasing to You." And they recited their Psalms, as stands in the Law, and She laid herself down on her bed before them.

XVI Outro dia San Pedro | a voz de Deus oíu
que lles diss': «Aqui *sõo* | vosc'.» E logo sentiu
tod' aquela companna | mui bo*n* odor, e viu
claridade que todo | o mund' enlumeou. ℜ

The next day St Peter heard the voice of God saying to them: "I am here with you." And then that whole company breathed a most sweet smell, and saw a light that lightened the whole earth.

XVII Mas a ora de sesta, | dire-vo-lo que fez
Deus, que foi Padr' e Fillo | desta Virgen de prez:
vẽo levar-ll' a alma, | que el ja outra vez
lle metera no corpo | u a santivigou. ℜ

But at the sixth hour, I shall tell you what God did, He who was the Father and the Son of this worthy Virgin: He came to take her soul, which once again He put into Her body where He sanctified it.

XVIII E disso a San Pedro: | «Direi-ch' o que farás:
pois mĭa Madr' é fĭada, | non esperes a cras,
mas enterra seu corpo | no Val de Josefás,
en atal sepultura | com' ela t' ensinou. ℜ

And [God] said to St Peter: "I shall tell you what you will do: after My Mother has died, do not wait for tomorrow, but bury Her body in the Valley of Jehosafat, in such a tomb as She showed you.

XIX Esto foi en agosto, | en meiante do mes,
que Jesucrist' a alma | de sua Madre pres;
e o corpo San Pedro | fillou con set' e tres
Apóstolos e en Jo- | -sefás-lo enterrou. ℜ

This happened in August, in the middle of the month, that Jesus Christ took the soul of His Mother; St Peter took the body with [ten] Apostles, and buried it in Jehosaphat.

XX E pois-la enterraron | en sepulcro mui bel,
foron-s' aa cidade; | mas logo San Miguel
levou o corpo dela | con outro gran tropel
d' ángeos que vẽeron, | e cada un cantou. ℜ

And when they [had] buried Her in a most fair tomb, they went [back] to the city; but then St Michael took away Her body with another host of angels who came, and each of them sang.

XXI Eles indo cantando, | Santo Tomás subir
os viu, que Deus fezera | ena nuve vĩir;
e viu Santa Maria | entr' eles todos ir,
e por saber quen era, | logo lles preguntou. ℜ

XXII E ela respondeu-lle: | «Tomás, amigo meu,
a mĩa alma meu Fillo | levou, ben ti dig' eu,
e meu corp' ora levan | pera o reino seu
estes ángeos santos, | e con eles me vou.» ℜ

XXIII E San Tomás lle disse: | «Sennor, mui m' é mester,
por que creüdo seja | desto, se vos prouguer,
que algún sinal aja, | que quando o disser
que eu amostrar possa.» | E ela lle llançou… [ℜ?]

XXIV …a cinta que cengia, | que vos non foi don vil;
ant' era mui ben feita | e d' obra mui sotil.
E el deu end' a ela | por én loores mil,
e sa cinta na mão, | aa vila chegou. ℜ

XXV Os onze, poi-lo viron, | disseron: «Tol-t' alá;
e que te Deus non ama | gran mostra ch' én feit' á,
que non viste sa Madre | morrer, nen fust' acá
u a nós soteramos; | tanto te despreçou. ℜ

XXVI Santo Tomás, chorando, | respondeu-lles adur:
«Dized' u a metestes; | mas sei eu que nenllur
achar non a podedes | quant' o Bretón Artur,
ca eu a vi na nuve | subir, e me chamou. ℜ

XXVII »E por que me creades | esta cinta me quis
dar, e que de seu feito | sejades todos fis:
que eu vi o seu corpo | mui mais branco ca lis
ir subind' aos ceos, | e mui pouc' i tardou.» ℜ

XXVIII Entón disse San Pedro: | «Tenno que sera prol
d' irmos provar aquesto | que nos diz este fol;
e se non for verdade, | ũa folla de col
non demos mais por ele, | ca sempr' este dultou.» ℜ

XXIX Entón foron dizendo: «Mentira nos aduz.»
E cataron na fossa | daquela que na cruz
viu morrer o seu Fillo; | mas peró, se non luz,
nulla ren non acharon. | E muito se sinou…[ℜ?]

XXX …San Pedro, e os outros | todos a ũa voz
en terra se deitaron, | pedindo por Aioz
a Santo Tomás perdón; | e diss' el: «ũa noz
non daria por esto, | pois con verdad' estou.» ℜ

With them singing as they went, St Thomas (whom God had caused to come, on a cloud) saw them rise up; and he Saw Holy Mary go amid them all; and so as to know who it was, he at once asked them.

She replied to him: "Thomas, my friend, My Son took my soul, indeed do I tell you, and these holy angels now carry my body to His kingdom; with them I go.

And St Thomas said to Her: "My Liege, greatly is it to my need — so I may be believed in this [matter] — if it please You, that I should have some sign, so that when I tell it, I may be able to give demonstration." And She threw to him…

…the girdle she wore, which was no mean gift; rather was it well made and delicately worked. And he gave Her a thousand praises in return. Her girdle in his hand, he arrived [back] at the city.

The eleven, when they saw him, said: "Take yourself away; that God loves you not, He has made a clear show of it to you, for you did not see His Mother die, nor were you here when we buried Her; so much did He despise you.

St Thomas, in tears, replied to them with difficulty: "Tell where you put Her; but I know that no-where can you find Her, [any more than] Arthur of Britain, for I saw Her rise on the cloud , and She called to me.

And so that you may believe me, She saw fit to give me this girdle, and [wanted] you all to be certain of Her deed; for I saw Her body, whiter than a lily, rising up to heaven; She did not tarry in doing so.

Then St Peter said: "I consider it would be beneficial for us to go and test what this fool is telling us; and if it be not true, let us give no more than a cabbage-leaf for him, for he always doubted.

And they went on saying: "He is bringing us a lie!" And they looked into the grave of Her who had seen Her Son die on the cross; but yet they found nothing, unless it was [a beam of] light. And St Peter…

…crossed himself vigorously, and all the others in concert prostrated themselves on the ground, asking pardon of St Thomas by God's Holy Name. And he said: "I would not give a walnut for this, because I stand in the right."

CSM [419]: Apparatus

Text edition based on *To*.

The beginning of the Epigraph (version from *To*) has been abbreviated: Como] Eſta q^{t}ta e como 'This fifth [piece] is [about] how…' *To*; [ ]ſta IX e da uıgılıa de ſc̃a Marıa dagoſto como ela paſſao [*sic*]

deſte mundo e foı leuada ao çeo 'This ninth [piece] is from the vigil of Holy Mary['s feast] in August, how She passed from this world and was taken to heaven' *E*.
1 *Madre*] madr *To*, *here and in all subsequent repetitions; the melody as given in To lacks a note for the missing syllable.* — 6 reino] regno *E* — 7 Mas] Maıs *E* — 8 e en] eu en *To*, e en *E* — 10 Reïnna] reỹa *To*, Reyna *E* — 15 Jerussalém] ıeruſalem *E* — 16 vinna] uĩja *To*, uınna *E*; *the metre requires a disyllable.* — 17 mas] maıs *E*; per] *missing in To* — 18 fĩou] fınou *E* — 19 templo] templ u *E* — 22 t' el] te *E* — 23 un] ũu *To* — 24 tercer] tecer *To* — 28 *The final syllable of the first hemistich is accented; Mettmann inverts*: respos-lle. *Cf. l. 121.* — 29 mais] mas *E* — 35 pud'] pod *E* — 48 ũas] huũas *E* — 50 non uvĩou] nõo uıou *E* — 51 com a Escritura] coma ſcrıtura *To*, com a eſcᶦtura *E* — 52 Santa Emperadriz] ſantan peradrız *To*, ſantan peradꝛız *E* — 58 de Deus] ſanto *E*; de deꝰ *To*, *partially erased.* — 61 salmos] pſalmoſ *E* — 64 sõo] ſoõ *To*, ſõo *E* — 65 bon] boõ *To*, bon *E* — 66 mund'] log *E* — 67 Mas] Maıs *E*; de] da *E* — 72 fĩada] fınada *E* — 73 Josefás] ıoſaphas *E* — 76 -crist' a alma] xp̃o aalma *E* — 77 set' e tres] ſete e tres *E* — 78 Josefás] ıoſafas *E* — 79 sepulcro] ſepulcre *E* — 80 cidade] ciddade *E*; mas] maıs *E* — 83 subir] ſobir *E* — 84 vĩir] uıjr *E* — 86 quen] quem *E* — 89 reino] regno *E* — 95 cengia] cıngıa *E* — 104 mas] maıs *E* — 106 subir] ſobır *E* — 110 subind'] ſobınd *E* — 117 mas] maıs *E* —119 Pedro] pedꝛ *E* — 120 por] per *E* — 121 *The final syllable of the first hemistich is accented (cf. l. 28); Mettmann inverts*: perdon a Santo Tomas, *but without resolving the problem.*

BIBLIOGRAPHY

Sources

Sigla:

To The 'Toledo ms'.
Madrid, Biblioteca Nacional, ms 10069 (previously held in the archive of Toledo Cathedral).
Facsimile: *Afonso X o Sabio, Cantigas de Santa María. Edición facsímile do códice de Toledo* (Santiago de Compostela: Consello da Cultura Galega, 2003).
This now supersedes the engraved reproduction in Ribera 1922.

T (= E_2 , E2, e, R, Re, CRe), known as the 'códice rico'.
Escorial ms T.I.1 (= T.J.1, T.j.1).
Facsimile: *Alfonso X El Sabio 1221–1284, Las Cantigas de Santa María, Códice Rico, Ms T-I-1, Real Biblioteca del Monasterio de San Lorenzo de El Escorial. El Códice Rico de las Cantigas de Santa Maria*, coord. Laura Fernández Fernández & Juan Carlos Ruiz Sousa (Madrid: Testimonio, 2011). [*See also CP*-11 *below.*]
This now supersedes the earlier facsimile edition, *Alfonso X el Sabio, Las Cantigas de Santa María. Edición facsímil. El Códice Rico del Escorial (Manuscrito escurialense Tj1)*, 2 vols (Madrid: Edilán, 1979).

F (= f, Rf, CRf), the (incomplete) continuation of the 'códice rico'.
Florence, National Library, Banco Rari 20.
Facsimile: *Alfonso X el Sabio, Cantigas de Santa María. Edición facsímil del códice B. R. 20 de la Biblioteca Nazionale Centrale de Florencia. Siglo XIII*, 2 vols (Madrid: Edilán, 1989–91).

E (= E_1 , E1), sometimes referred to as the 'códice de los músicos'.
Escorial ms b.I.2 (= B.j.2, j.b.2).
Photographic reproduction in Vol. I of Anglés 1943–64.

Editions

Music: Complete editions: *see* Anglés 1943; Pla 2001; Elmes 2004–14.

Partial editions: *see* Ribera 1922 (edition of *To*);
Cunningham 2000 (edition of *Loores*, melodies and full texts);
López Elum 2005 (edition of *To*).

Other transcriptions of pieces edited in the present volume are referred to in the relevant sections.

Texts: Complete editions*: see* Valmar 1889; Mettmann 1959–72; Mettmann 1986–89.

Partial editions: *see in particular* Fidalgo 2003 (edition of *Loores*);
Schaffer 2010 (edition of *To*);
Parkinson 2015 (in anticipation of a new full edition).

Translations: *see* Kulp-Hill 2000 (*into English*).
See also the translations into Modern Castilian in Filgueira Valverde 1985.

Internet Resources

<csm.mml.ox.ac.uk> (Oxford *Cantigas de Santa Maria* Database: information on sources, bibliography, with critical editions of some texts, *etc.*)

<www.cantigasdesantamaria.com> (*Cantigas de Santa Maria* for singers, including fully syllabified texts following Mettmann's edition, guide to pronunciation, *etc.*)

<www.medieval.org/emfaq/composers/cantigas.html> (Extensive discography.)

CP
Collective Publications • Conference Proceedings Collected Papers

CP-87a *Studies on the 'CSM'. Art, Music, and Poetry. Proceedings of the International Symposium on the CSM of Alfonso X, el Sabio [1221–1284] in Commemoration of its* [*sic*] *700th Anniversary Year, 1981* [New York, November 1981], ed. I. J. Katz *et al.* (Madison, Wisconsin: Hispanic Seminary of Medieval Studies, 1987).

CP-87b *Alfonso X el Sabio y la música* (Madrid: Sociedad Española de Musicología, 1987).

CP-98 *Ondas do Mar de Vigo. Actas do Simposio Internacional sobre a Lírica Medieval Galego-portuguesa*, coord. D. W. Flitter & P. Odber de Baubeta (Birmingham: Seminario de Estudios Galegos, Department of Hispanic Studies, 1998).

CP-99 *El scriptorium alfonsí: de los libros de astrología a las 'CSM'*, coord. J. Montoya Martínez & A. Domínguez Rodríguez (Madrid: Universidad Complutense, 1999).

CP-00 *Cobras e Son. Papers on the Text, Music and Manuscripts of the CSM*, ed. S. Parkinson (Oxford: Legenda, 2000).

CP-01 *Literatura y cristiandad. Homenaje al profesor Jesús Montoya Martínez* (Granada: Universidad, 2001).

CP-09-FERR FERREIRA, Manuel Pedro, *Aspectos da Música Medieval no Ocidente Peninsular*, 2 vols (Lisbon: Imprensa Nacional/Fundação Gulbenkian, 2009), esp. vol. I: *Música palaciana.*

CP-09b *Poets and Singers on Latin and Vernacular Monophonic Song*, coord. E. Aubrey (Burlington, Vermont: Ashgate, 2009).

CP-10a *Estudos de edición crítica e lírica galego-portuguesa*, coord. M. Arbor Aldea *et al.* Published as Anexo 67 of *Verba, Anuario Galego de Filoloxía* (Santiago de Compostela: Universidade, 2010)

CP-10b *'De ninguna cosa es alegre posesión sin compañía.' Estudios celestinescos y medievales en honor del profesor Joseph T. Snow*, coord. D Paolini. 2 vols (New York: Hispanic Seminary of Medieval Studies, 2010), esp. vol. II.

CP-11 *Alfonso X El Sabio, Las CSM. Códice Rico, Ms T-I-1, Real Biblioteca del Monasterio de San Lorenzo de El Escorial* [Estudios], coord. L Fernández Fernández & J. C. Ruiz Sousa. 2 vols (Madrid: Testimonio, 2011).

CP-13 *Analizar, interpretar, hacer música: de las CSM a la organología. Escritos in memoriam Gerardo V. Huseby*, ed M. Plesch (Buenos Aires: Gourmet Musical Editions, 2013).

Books and Articles

Note: The abbreviation BCSM is used for the «[Bulletin of the] Cantigueiros [de Santa Maria]»

ANGLÉS, Higinio, 1943–64: *La música de las CSM del Rey Alfonso el Sabio* (Barcelona: Biblioteca Central), 3 vols in 4: I (1964) *Facsímil del Códice j. b. 2 de El Escorial;*
II (1943) *Transcripción musical;*
III-i (1958) *Estudio crítico;*
III-ii (1958) *Las melodías hispanas y la monodía lírica europea de los siglos XII–XIII.*

APEL, Willi, 1942: *The Notation of Polyphonic Music, 900–1600* (Cambridge, Massachusetts: The Mediaeval Academy of America; 5th ed., 1961).

— 1943: Review of Anglés 1943 in *Speculum* 22 (1947), 458–60. Reprinted in Apel, *Medieval Music* (Stuttgart, 1986), 185–7.

— 1944: *Harvard Dictionary of Music* (Medieval Society of America: Cambridge, Massachusetts; fifth edition, 1961).

AUBREY, Elizabeth, 1996: *The Music of the Troubadours* (Bloomington and Indianapolis: Indiana University Press).

— 2006: 'La langue musicale de dévotion: les *cantigas de loor* et les chansons de Guiraut Riquier', in *L'espace lyrique méditerranéen au Moyen Âge*, ed. Dominique Billy *et al.* (Toulouse: Presses Universitaires du Mirail), 219–29.

AUBRY, Pierre, 1907: 'Les *CSM* de don Alfonso el Sabio', *Sammelbände der Internationalen Musik-Gesellschaft* 9.1, 32–50.

CAMPBELL, Alison D., 2011: 'Words and music in the *CSM*: The *Cantigas* as song', Thesis for the Degree of M.Litt, University of Glasgow. Accessible at <http://theses.gla.ac.uk/2809/>.

COLANTUONO, Maria Incoronata, 2007: 'El bon son en las *CSM*', in *Actas do VII Congreso Internacional de Estudos Galegos. Mulleres en Galicia. Galicia e os outros pobos da Península* [May, 2003], ed. H. González Fernández & M. X. Lama López (A Coruña: Edicións do Castro/Asociación Internacional de Estudos Galegos), 1129–32.

— 2013: 'Le strutture melodiche di Alfonso X *el Sabio* nelle *CSM*', in *Vox Antiqua* 1, 71–91.

COLLET, Henri, & Luis VILLALBA, 1911: 'Contribution à l'étude des *Cantigas* d'Alphonse le Savant d'après les codices de l'Escurial', *Bulletin Hispanique* 13, 270–90.

CUETO, Leopoldo de — *see under* VALMAR.

CUNNINGHAM, Martin G. (ed.), 2000: *Alfonso X el Sabio: Cantigas de Loor* (Dublin: University College Dublin Press).

ELMES, Chris (ed.), 2004–14: *'CSM' of Alfonso X el Sabio: A Performing Edition*, 4 vols (Edinburgh: Gaïta Medieval Music; Vol. I, 2004, re-edited 2014; Vol. II, 2008, re-edited 2014; Vol. III, 2010; Vol. IV, 2013. *Unless otherwise stated, reference is to the later editions, the revisions being substantial.*)

FERNANDES LOPES — *see under* LOPES.

FERNÁNDEZ de la CUESTA, Ismael, 1983: *Historia de la música española*, 1: *Desde los orígenes hasta el "ars nova"* (Madrid: Alianza), 295–304.

— 1984: 'Los elementos melódicos en las *Cantigas de Santa María*', *Revista de Musicología* 7.1, 1–44.

— 1985: 'Las *CSM* et la musique traditionnelle Hispanique', *Studia Musicologica Academiae Scientiarum Hungaricae* 27, 203–7.

— 1985 *bis*: 'Alfonso X el Sabio y la música de las Cantigas', in *Estudios alfonsíes: lexicografía, lírica, estética y política de Alfonso el Sabio*, ed. J. Mondéjar & J. Montoya (Granada: Universidad de Granada), 119–25.

— 1987 'Las *CSM*. Replanteamiento musicológico de la cuestión', *Revista de Musicología* 10.1, 15–37. Repeated in *CP*-87b, 15–37.

— 1987 *bis*: 'La interpretación melódica de las *CSM*', in *CP*-87a, 155–88.

— 1987 *ter*: 'Les traits d'acuité et de longueur dans le traitement musical de l'accent rythmique des *Cantigas de Santa María*', *Revue de Musicologie* 73.1 (1987[a]), 83–98.

— 2001: 'Clave de retórica musical para la interpretación y transcripción del ritmo de las *CSM*', in *CP*-01, 685–718.

— 2011: 'Las *CSM*, precedente del Villancico Hispano: música de un trovador para la liturgia sacra', *Alcanate* 7, 163–77.

FERNÁNDEZ FERNÁNDEZ, Laura, 2009: '*CSM*: fortuna de sus manuscritos', *Alcanate* 6, 323–48.

— 2011: ' "Este livro, com' achei, fez á onr' e á loor da Virgen Santa Maria." El proyecto de las *CSM* en el marco del escritorio regio. estado de la cuestión y nuevas reflexiones', in *CP*-11, II: 43–78.

FERREIRA, Manuel Pedro. *Note: for those who have access, the contributions of this author may generally be found on the website* <academia.edu>.

— 1986: *O Som de Martin Codax. Sobre a dimensão musical da lírica galego-portuguesa (séculos XII–XIV)* (Lisbon: Imprensa Nacional–Casa da Moeda).

— 1987: 'Spania *versus* Spain in the *CSM*', in *Actas del CIEMO [Congreso Internacional 'España en la música de Occidente']* (Madrid: Ministerio de Cultura–INAEM), I: 109–11. Slightly amplified in Portuguese translation in *CP*-09-FERR, I: 175–79.

— 1987 *bis*: 'Some remarks on the *Cantigas*', *Revista de Musicología* 10.1, 115–16. Also available in *CP*-87b, 115–16.

— 1993: 'Bases para la transcripción: el canto gregoriano y la notación de las *CSM*', in *Los instrumentos del Pórtico de la Gloria: Su reconstrucción y la música de su tiempo*, coord. J. López-Calo. 2 vols (La Coruña: Fundación Pedro Barrié de la Maza; 2nd ed., 2002), II: 573–94, with English translation pp. 595–621. The section dealing with the *CSM* now in Portuguese translation in *CP*-09-FERR, I: 180–95.

— 1993 *bis*: '*CSM*: Música', in *Dicionário da literatura medieval galega e portuguesa*, coord. G. Lanciani & G. Tavani (Lisbon: Caminho), 146a–147b.

— 1994: 'The Stemma of the Marian Cantigas: Philological and Musical Evidence', *BCSM* 6, 58–98. Now in Portuguese translation with additional material in *CP*-09-FERR, I; 196–229.

— 1995: *Cantus Coronatus: Sete Cantigas d'Amor d'El-Rei Dom Dinis* (Kassel: Reichenberger)

— 1997: 'A música das cantigas galego-portuguesas: balanço de duas décadas de investigação (1977–1997), in *Congresso O Mar das Cantigas* (Santiago de Compostela: Xunta de Galicia), 235–50. Reprinted in *CP*-98, 58–71. Now also available in *CP*-09-FERR, I: 35–48.

— 1998: 'The Layout of the *CSM*: A Musicological Overview', *Galician Review* 2, 47–61. Now in

Portuguese translation in *CP*-09-FERR, I: 49–70.
— 1998 *bis*: 'Codax revisitado', *Anuario de Estudios Literarios Galegos* 1998, 157–68. Now also available in *CP*-09-FERR, I: 88–100.
— 2000: 'Andalusian Music and the *CSM*', in *CP*-00, 7–19. Republished in *CP*-09b, 253–65. Now in Portuguese translation, re-titled 'A música andaluza, o ritmo segundo al-Farabi e as «CSM»' in *CP*-09-FERR, I: 246–57
— 2000 *bis*: 'The Influence of Chant on the *CSM*', *BCSM* 11–12, 29–40. Now in Portuguese translation in *CP*-09-FERR, I: 258–67.
— 2000 *ter*: 'Iberian Monophony', in *A Performer's Guide to Medieval Music*, ed. R. W. Duffin (Bloomington: Indiana University Press), 144–57.
— 2001: 'Afinidades musicais: as *Cantigas de loor* e a lírica profana galego-portuguesa', in *Memória dos afectos: Homenagem da Cultura Portuguesa a Giuseppe Tavani* (Lisbon: Colibri), 187–205. Republished in *CP*-09-FERR, I: 71–87.
— 2004: 'Rondeau and virelai: the music of Andalus and the *CSM*', *Plainsong and Medieval Music* 13.2, 127–40. Republished in *CP*-09b, 253–65. In Portuguese translation in *CP*-09-FERR, I: 230–45.
— 2007: 'Alfonso X, compositor', *Alcanate* 5, 117–37. Also available in *CP*-09-FERR, I: 282–302.
— 2007 *bis*: 'A propósito de una nueva lectura de la música de las *CSM*' [Review of López Elum 2005], *Alcanate* 5, 307–15. Now available in Portuguese, incorporated into 'A propósito de duas edições musicais de *CSM*', in *CP*-09-FERR, I: 268–81.
— 2010: 'Ambigüidade, repetição, interpretação: o caso das *CSM* 162 e 267', in *CP*-10a, 287–98.
— 2011: 'A música no *Códice Rico*: formas e notação', in *CP*-11, II: 187–204.
— 2011 *bis*: 'Medieval Music in Portugal Within its Interdisciplinary Context (1940–2010)', in *The Historiography of Medieval Portugal (c. 1950–2010)*, ed. José Mattoso (Lisbon: Instituto de Estudos Medievais), 111–29. Available in Portuguese translation at <academia.edu>.
— 2013: 'Understanding the *Cantigas*: Preliminary Steps', in *CP*-13, 127–52.
— 2013 *bis*: 'Jograis, *contrafacta*, formas musicais: cultura urbana nas *CSM*', *Alcanate* 8, 43–53.
— 2014: 'Editing the *CSM*: Notational decisions', *Revista Portuguesa de Musicologia*, New Series, 1/1, 33–52.
— 2014 *bis*: 'Paródia e *contrafactum*: em torno das cantigas de Afonso X, o Sábio', in *Cantigas Trovadorescas: da Idade Média aos nossos dias*, ed. Graça Videira Lopes & Manuele Massini (Lisbon: Instituto de Estudos Medievais), 19–43.
— 2015: 'Rhythmic paradigms in the *CSM*: French versus Arabic precedent', *Plainsong and Medieval Music* 24.1, 1–24.
— 2015 *bis*: 'The Periphery Effaced: The Musicological Fate of the *Cantigas*', in *'Estes Sons, esta Linguagem'. Essays on Music, Meaning and Society in Honour of Mário Vieira de Carvalho*, ed. G. Stöck, P. Ferreira de Castro & K. Stöck (Leipzig: CESEM/Gudrun Schröder Verlag), 23–39.
— 2015 *ter*: 'Notas sibilinas: Alfonso X, Braga y María', in *La Sibila: Sonido, Imagen, Liturgia, Escena*, ed. M. Gómez Muntané & E. Carrero Santamaría (Madrid: Alpuerto), 87–104.
— 2016: 'The Medieval Fate of the *CSM*: Iberian Politics Meets Song', *Journal of the American Musicological Society* 69.2, 295–353.
FERREIRO, Manuel, C. P. MARTÍNEZ PEREIRO & L. TATO FONTAÍÑA, 2007: *Normas de edición para a poesía trobadoresca galego-portuguesa medieval* (A Coruña: Universidade da Coruña).
FIDALGO, Elvira (ed.), 2003: *As Cantigas de Loor de Santa María* (Xunta de Galicia).
— (ed.), 2011: *Códice Rico, Ms. T-I-1, Real Biblioteca del Monasterio de San Lorenzo de El escorial. Edición crítica*, in *CP*-11, vol. I.
FILGUEIRA VALVERDE, José, 1985: *Alfonso X el Sabio. CSM. Códice Rico de El escorial. Introducción, versión castellana y comentarios.* Colección Odres Nuevos (Madrid: Castalia).
FRANCO OF COLOGNE — *see under* REANEY.
HUSEBY, Gerardo V., 1983: 'The *CSM* and the Medieval Theory of Mode', unpublished doctoral dissertation, Stanford University [UMI: 83-07167].
— 1983 *bis*: 'Musical Analysis and Poetic Structure in the *CSM*', in *Florilegium Hispanicum. Medieval and Golden Age Studies presented to Dorothy C. Clarke*, ed. J. S. Geary *et al.* (Madison, Wisconsin: Hispanic Seminary of Medieval Studies), 81–101.
— 1987: 'The Common Melodic Background of "Ondas do mar de Vigo" and *Cantiga* 73', in *CP*-87a, 189–202.
— 1988: 'La conmixtura modal en las *CSM*', *Revista del Instituto de Investigación Musicológica Carlos Vega* 9, 65–78.
— 1988 *bis*: 'Durum y molle. Bemol, becuadro y transposición modal en la monodía del Siglo XIII', in *Actas de las Terceras Jornadas Argentinas de Musicología* [Buenos Aires, septiembre de 1986] (Buenos Aires: Instituto Nacional de Musicología «Carlos Vega»), 27–34.
— 1995: 'La delimitación del texto y el contexto: el caso de las *CSM*', in *Actas de las VIII Jornadas*

Argentinas de Musicología y VII Conferencia Anual de la Asociación Argentina de Musicología {Buenos Aires, agosto de 1993], ed. I. Ruiz & M. A. García (Buenos Aires: Instituto Nacional de Musicología Carlos Vega), 103–10.

— 1999: 'El parámetro melódico en las *CSM*: Sistemas, estructuras, fórmulas y técnicas compositivas', in *CP*-99, 215–70.

KATZ, Israel J., 1987: 'The study and performance of the *Cantigas de Santa Maria*: A Glance at Recent Musicological Literature', *BCSM* 1.1, 51–60.

— 1990: 'Melodic Survivals? Kurt Schindler and the tune of Alfonso's cantiga "Rosa das rosas" in oral tradition', in *Emperor of Culture. Alfonso X the Learned and his Thirteenth-Century Renaissance*, ed. Robert I. Burns (Philadelphia: Pennsylvania University Press), 159–81 & 251–7.

— 1990 *bis*: 'Higinio Anglés and the melodic origins of the *Cantigas de Santa María*: a critical view', in *Alfonso X of Castile, the Learned King (1221-1284). An International Symposium* [Harvard, November 1984], ed. F. Márquez Villanueva & C. A. Vega (Cambridge, Massachusetts: Harvard University Press), 46–75.

KULP-HILL, Kathleen, 2000: *Songs of Holy Mary of Alfonso X, the Wise. A Translation of the CSM.* Medieval and Renaissance Texts and Studies 173 (Tempe, Arizona: Arizona Center for Medieval and Renaissance Studies).

LLORENS CISTERÓ, José María, 1986: 'El ritmo musical de las *Cantigas*: estado presente de la cuestión', *Anuario Musical* 41, 47–61. Repeated in *CP*-87a, 203–22.

— 1987: 'El Rey Sabio y su obra personal en la confección de las *Cantigas*', *Nassarre* 3, 129–52.

LOPES, Francisco Fernandes, 1945: 'A música das *CSM* e o problema da sua decifração', *Brotéria* 40, 49–70.

LÓPEZ ELUM, Pedro (ed.), 2005: *Interpretando la música medieval del siglo XIII: Las CSM* (Valencia: PUV).

METTMANN, Walter (ed.), 1959–72: *Cantigas de Santa Maria*, 4 vols (Coimbra: Acta Universitatis Conimbrigensis; reimpression in 2 vols, Vigo: Edicións Xerais, 1982).

— (ed.), 1986–89: *Cantigas de Santa María*, 3 vols (Madrid: Castalia).

PALACIO, Dionisio, 1993: 'Variantes musicales existentes en las diferentes estrofas de las *CSM*, según el códice de El Escorial T.I.1', *Revista de Musicología* 16, 2390–4.

PARKINSON, Stephen, 1987: 'False Refrains in the *CSM*', *Portuguese Studies* 3, 21–55.

— 1988: 'The First Re-Organization of the *CSM*', *BCSM* 1.2, 91–7.

— 1992: 'Migrares [*sic*] de maldizer? Dysphemism in the *CSM*', *BCSM* 4, 44–57.

— 1993: 'Final Nasals in the Galician-Portuguese Cancioneiros', in *Hispanic Linguistic Studies in honour of F. W. Hodcroft*, ed. D. Mackenzie & I. Michael (Tredwr: Dolphin), 51–62.

— 1997: 'Editions for Consumers: Five Versions of a *CSM*', in *IV Congreso de Estudios Galegos* [setembro 1994], ed. B. Fernández Salgado (Oxford: Oxford Centre for Galician Studies), 57–75.

— 1998: 'As *CSM*: estado das cuestións textuais', *Anuario de Estudos Literarios Galegos*, 179–205.

1999: 'Meestria métrica: Metrical Virtuosity in the *CSM*', *La corónica* 27.2, 21–35.

— 1999 *bis*: 'Meestria', *La corónica* 28.1, 220–25.

— 2000: 'Layout and Structure of the Toledo Manuscript of the *CSM*', in *CP*-00, 133–53.

— 2000 *bis*: 'Layout in the *códices ricos* of the *CSM*', *Hispanic Research Journal* 1.3, 243–74.

— 2000 *ter*: 'Phonology and Metrics: aspects of Rhyme in the *CSM*', in *Proceedings of the Tenth Colloquium of the Medieval Hispanic Research Seminar*, ed. A. D. Deyermond. Papers of the Medieval Hispanic Research Seminar 30 (London: Department of Hispanic Studies, Queen Mary and Westfield College), 131–44.

— 2006: 'Rules of Elision and Hiatus in the Galician-Portuguese Lyric: The View from the *CSM*', *La corónica* 34.2, 113–33.

— 2006 *bis*: 'Concurrent Patterns of Verse Design in the Galician-Portuguese Lyric', in *Proceedings of the Thirteenth Colloquium*, ed. J. Whetnall & A. D. Deyermond. Papers of the Medieval Hispanic Research Seminar 51 (London: Department of Hispanic Studies, Queen Mary and Westfield College), 19–38.

— 2010: 'Questões de estrutura estrófica nas *CSM*: estruturas múltiplas, asimetrías e continuações inconsistentes', in *CP*-10a, 315–36.

— 2011: 'Alfonso X, Miracle Collector', in *CP*-11, II: 79–105.

— 2015: *Alfonso X, the Learned: CSM. An Anthology*. MHRA Critical Texts 40 ([Cambridge]: Modern Humanities Research Association).

PARKINSON, Stephen, & David BARNETT, 2013: 'Linguística, codicologia e crítica textual: interpretação editorial da variação interna nas *CSM*', in *Ao sabor do texto: Estudos dedicados a Ivo Castro*, ed. R. Álvarez *et al.* (Santiago de Compostela: Instituto da Lingua Galega/Universidade de Santiago de Compostela), 467–80.

PARKINSON, Stephen, & Rip COHEN, 2009: 'The *CSM*', in *A Companion to Portuguese Literature*,

ed. S. Parkinson *et al.* (Woodbridge: Tamesis), 40–43.
PARRISH, Carl (1957): *The Notation of Medieval Music* (New York: Norton).
PLA SALES, Roberto (ed.), 2001: *CSM. Alfonso X el Sabio. Nueva transcripción integral de su música según la métrica latina* (Madrid: Música Didáctica).
RANDEL, Don M, 1987: 'La teoría musical en la época de Alfonso X el Sabio', *Revista de Musicología* 10, 39-51. Repeated in *CP*-87b, 39–51.
RASTALL, Richard, 1998: *The Notation of Western Music: An Introduction*, 2nd ed. (Leeds: Leeds University Press).
REANEY, Gilbert, & André GILLES (eds), 1974: *Franconis de Colonia Ars Cantus Mensurabilis*. Corpus Scriptorum de Musica 18 (American Institute of Musicology).
RIBERA y TARRAGÓ, Julián, 1922: *La música de las Cantigas. Estudio sobre su origen y naturaleza con reproducciones fotográficas del texto y transcripción moderna* (Madrid: Real Academia Española; Reprinted Madrid: Real Academia Española/Caja de Madrid, 1989). Published in an adapted translation, with fewer transcriptions, under the title *Music in Ancient Arabia and Spain* (Stanford: University Press, 1929. Reprinted New York: Da Capo Press, 1970).
ROSSELL, Antoni, 1985: 'Algunos aspectos musicales de las *CSM* a partir de las transcripciones manuscritas de Higinio Anglés', in *La lengua y la literatura en tiempos de Alfonso X*, Actas del Congreso Internacional [Murcia 1984] ed. F. Carmona & F. J. Flores (Murcia: Universidad de Murcia), 519–30.
— 1996: 'A música da lírica galego-portuguesa medieval: un labor de reconstrucción arqueolóxica e intertextual a partir das relacións entre o texto e a música', *Anuario de Estudios Literarios Galegos*, 41–76.
— 2001: 'Las *CSM* y sus modelos musicales litúrgicos, una imitación intertextual e intermelódica', in *CP*-01, 403–12.
SCHAFFER, Martha E., 1995: 'Marginal Notes in the Toledo Manuscript of Alfonso el Sabio's *CSM*: Observations on Composition, Correction, Compilation and Performance', *BCSM* 7, 65–84.
— 1999: 'Los códices de las *CSM*: su problemática', in *CP*-99, 127–48.
— 2000: 'The "Evolution" of the *CSM*. The Relationships betweed MSS T, F and E', in *CP*-00, 186–213.
— (ed.), 2010: *Afonso X o Sábio. CSM. Códice de Toledo: Transcripción* (Santiago de Compostela: Consello da Cultura Gallega).
SNOW, Joseph T., 2012: *The Poetry of Alfonso X: An Annotated Critical Bibliography (1278–2010)*, Research Bibliographies and Checklists: New Series, 10 (Woodbridge: Tamesis).
STEVENS, John, 1990: 'Medieval Song', Ch. ix of *The New Oxford History of Music*, vol. II (new edition): *The Early Middle Ages to 1300*, ed. Richard Crocker & David Hiley (Oxford & New York: Oxford University Press), 519–30.
SWITTEN, Margaret, 1999: 'Music and versification', Ch. 9 of *The Troubadours: An Introduction*, ed. S. Gaunt & S. Kay (Cambridge: Cambridge University Press), 141–63.
TINNELL, Roger D., 1980: *An Annotated Discography of Music in Spain before 1650* (Madison, Wisconsin: Hispanic Seminary of Medieval Studies).
VALMAR, Leopoldo Augusto de CUETO, Marqués de (ed.), 1889: *Las 'CSM' de Alfonso el Sabio*, 2 vols (Madrid: Real Academia Española; reprinted Madrid: Caja de Ahorros, 1989).
VAN DER WERF, Hendrik, 1987: 'Accentuation and Duration in the Music of the *CSM*', in *CP*-87a, 223–34.
WULSTAN, David, 1982: 'The Muwa*shshah* and Za*j*al Revisited', *Journal of the American Oriental Society* 102.2, 247–64.
— 1994: ' "Pero cantigas"...', *BCSM* 6, 12–29.
— 1996: 'Decadal Songs in the *CSM*', *BCSM* 8, 35–58.
— 1998: 'Contrafaction and Centonization in the *CSM*', *BCSM* 10, 85–109.
— 2000: 'The Rhythmic Organization of the *CSM*', in *CP*-00, 31–65.
— 2000 *bis*: 'The Compilation of the *Cantigas* of Alfonso el Sabio', in *CP*-00, 154–85.
— 2001: *The Emperor's Old Clothes: The Rhythm of Medieval Song* (Ottawa: Institute of Medieval Music).
— 2005: 'Bring on the Dancing-Girls! (*a Gadibus usque auroram*)', *Al-Masaq* 17.2, 221–49.
— 2009: 'A Pretty Paella: The Alfonsine *CSM* and their Connexions with Other Repertories', *Al-Masaq* 21.2, 191–227.
— 2010: 'Keep to the Lesbian Feet', in *The Secular Latin Motet in the Renaissance*, ed. R. Rastall (Lewiston, New York: Edwin Mellon Press), 33–94.
— 2013: 'Bookish Theoricke and the *CSM* of Alfonso el Sabio', in *CP*-13, 171–86.

TABULA EXCURSUUM

INDEX OF CANTIGAS EDITED